Dolce Vita

DITCH THE BOOZE
AND STEP INTO
THE GOOD LIFE

BY PAUL CHURCHILL

Dolce Vita: Ditch the Booze and Step Into the Good Life
Copyright © 2026 by Paul Churchill.

Disclaimer
This book contains data, facts and methods about alcohol addiction and treatment that the reader may implement into their life. The author voices that he has no formal training or background and it is highly recommended a reader consult with a medically trained doctor or physician if you decide to quit drinking. Therefore, the author should not be held responsible for any outcomes that may result from implementing strategies mentioned in this book. All facts and sources have been double checked before the publication of this book, but the author cannot guarantee full accuracy within its first publication.

Most names have been changed to ensure privacy

Edited by Danielle Marr and Katya Poltorak
Published by: Goat Block Publishing © 2026

For Information on how to reach the author and Recovery Elevator go to https://www.recoveryelevator.com or email info@recoveryelevator.com.

First Edition
ISBN: 979-8-9934294-0-3

Cover design by: Klassic Designs

Thank you for reading.
I'm honored to walk this journey with you.

DEDICATED TO:

To those who are seeking truth or a better way.
To my family, wife, son and dog Ben

Dolce Vita

Table of Contents

Introduction

At one point in my life, I found myself drinking multiple beers and a box of wine before 6:15 AM.

This went on for longer than I'd like to admit. I told myself it wasn't a problem, that I had it under control. I didn't see it as anything to worry about—definitely not a drinking problem, and certainly not something as serious as being an alcoholic. But of course, that's exactly what it was. Not long after, I crashed and burned HARD with alcohol. Looking back, it's like I never really stood a chance.

I've met with psychologists, therapists, psychiatrists, doctors, naturopaths, shamans, acupuncturists, astrologers, chiropractors, energy workers, a blood analyst with no front teeth, and a wellness coach whose office was located above a donut shop to figure out what the hell happened. Where did things derail, and how did it happen so fast? When my friends began to drink less, get married, have kids, and begin their professional lives, I found myself alone with one nightly goal: To drink myself into oblivion. Towards the end, it could be said it was a slow suicide.

Today, or at least as I write this, I'm alcohol-free. It's been over ten years since my last drink, and I know without a doubt that if I hadn't quit, I wouldn't be here. My relationship with substances has shifted over time, and I'll be honest about that in the pages ahead, but removing alcohol specifically is what saved my life. I was lucky. I was able to quit. I got my life back. And while it's not perfect, it's a life I no longer want to escape from…most of the time :)

Looking back now, what once felt like the greatest curse of my life has also been one of my greatest gifts. Breaking free from alcohol forced me to face myself, to question the way I was living, and to discover something deeper, more real, and far more fulfilling than I could have ever imagined. In a way, the very thing that nearly destroyed me became the doorway to the life I was meant to live.

This book isn't just my story, though. It's an invitation to stop fighting your addiction and start listening to it. What if the thing you've been calling a problem—your addiction—is actually a messenger? A painful, persistent signal that something in your life is out of alignment. Not a moral failing, but a turning point. An invitation to slow down, listen, and begin again. I didn't know it at the time, but my drinking wasn't just trying to destroy a part of me that wasn't working. It was trying to get my attention.

The details of my story are my own; the pain underneath it—the confusion, the numbing, the slow drift away from self—is, unfortunately, not unique or uncommon in the slightest.

It's a weight that so many carry, often quietly. Maybe that's why, while I was sobering up, the universe seemed to recognize I needed additional support and accountability. I decided to launch a podcast called Recovery Elevator in February 2015 (about five months into my alcohol-free journey) with the hope that it would help me stay sober.

It was a risky move to launch a sobriety podcast when I knew very little about quitting drinking, and I was still relatively raw in my sobriety. The statistics say I should have crashed and burned in front of a public audience, but somehow, I didn't. I am here today, sober, and I am whole.

I interviewed guests to learn, I listened, I took notes, and I replayed their interviews when I was feeling shaky and wanted to drink. I'm so thankful for the over 500 guests who shared their stories on the podcast with the single goal of helping others quit drinking. It helped me immensely, and I've identified some trends that contribute to successful quitting, which I will share with you.

Today, the podcast has been downloaded over 10 million times, in all 50 states and over 155 countries. There are over 4 million podcasts in existence, and Recovery Elevator is in the 96th percentile of all of them. I'd like to think the success is because I'm a wonderful storyteller, an attentive interviewer, and my jokes are hilarious. This may partly be true, but in reality, SO MANY people struggle with alcohol addiction (more than the populations of Michigan, Georgia, Ohio, and Illinois combined), and they are tuning in to find out how to quit drinking in a drunken world, where it is expected and celebrated to drink a nefarious molecule.

The scale of this podcast's reach only confirmed what I already sensed: that struggling with alcohol addiction is not a fringe issue—it's everywhere. And beneath the pain and confusion, there's a deeper pull happening. People aren't just looking to quit drinking; they're being invited to change, to step into a different way of living, to grow into who they really are.

Since I have landed in the "recovery" or "quit drinking" space, a significant amount of real estate in this book is dedicated to sharing what I have learned about alcohol, alcohol addiction, and addiction in general. To summarize, it could easily be said that the chemical alcohol is the most dangerous drug on the planet, and there is no shortage of data to back that up. Thank goodness, the antiquated paradigm that alcohol is good for you is being replaced by more accurate information that alcohol, in any amount, is harmful to your health.

Think about it: After just one drink, the processing power of your prefrontal cortex begins to slow. If you drink two to three more, you are legally unfit to drive a vehicle. If you consume enough alcohol in one sitting, you will die.

This book is also part memoir. I decided to share this story for a couple of reasons. First, storytelling is how we pass on knowledge and wisdom. It has held the fabric of our species together for roughly 10,000 human generations. If you are reading this book with hopes of your own sobriety goals, I will do my absolute best to tell you how to quit drinking, but I've realized, the best way for me to do this is to show you how I quit drinking: by telling the story. And it's a rollercoaster ride of a story.

At the age of 13, I discovered an elixir that solved my loneliness and allowed me to feel comfortable in my own skin for the first time. I built a profound relationship with this socially accepted chemical, but soon the alliance shifted, and I barely escaped with my life. I was then faced with a mission of deep exploration—to recover all the scattered parts of myself and figure out how to put them back together.

Writing this book is part of my healing process, and I hope that it can be a valuable tool on your healing journey as well. I find writing to be therapeutic since it slows down the thinking mind, takes what's inside, and releases it to the universe: here you go, take it. It turns out I like to write, and I had to remove alcohol from my life to discover this.

If you are reading this book to self-diagnose if you have a drinking problem, well, good news on this one, as it's easy: You reading a quit lit book answers the question. People without drinking problems don't read 'how to quit drinking' books. Sorry if that was abrupt. But hey, now, stick with me. There can be something pretty wonderful waiting for you beyond all the pain and suffering that comes with addiction. Addiction serves as an important evolutionary purpose in human development. Think of it as nature's way of forcing us to evolve. When our current coping mechanisms stop working (when alcohol stops numbing the pain and starts creating the pain), we're thrust into a crisis that demands growth. This biological imperative pushes us to shed what's no longer serving us and step into a more balanced, authentic, harmonious, and joyful way of living—the Dolce Vita—or the 'Good Life' in Italian.

It's not a punishment. It's a metamorphosis. The caterpillar has no choice in becoming a butterfly; the process is built into its biology. Similarly, addiction can be the cocoon that forces our metamorphosis if we choose life. Today, my life is "lit" 💧 as the kids say, and I have my drinking problem to thank for that.

If you're reading this book so you can learn how to better support a loved one, husband, wife, family member, or friend, then YES, YES, and YES. I am so happy to have you. The ultimate healing frequency is non-judgmental love, which I hope you can apply towards the problematic drinker in your life, and yourself, since you most likely have experienced heaps of pain and suffering on account of the addict in your life. I hope to bridge the gap between the normal and problematic drinker. To take the alcoholic out of the church basement, bring both sides of the aisle together for healing (as we are not separate), and both parties need healing.

This story is about what it's like to be human.

We enter the world with nothing, leave the same way, and somehow we are supposed to make peace with this irrefutable fact. We ALL get kicked in the groin while on planet earth, whether you struggle with an addiction or not. I have learned that even when we find ourselves waist-deep in the shit storms of life, we are still on the right path, and something magnificent is always taking place behind the scenes. Through loss, despair, and intense suffering, we become bold enough to peek through the veil of illusion we call separation. When we embrace this suffering, eventually it tilts us into living life from a place of gratitude. And what if an addiction, which we have labelled as a "tragic mistake," is the evolutionary mechanism that propels us into an unimaginable life? That is, of course, only if we quit drinking and turn our gaze inward.

Many of us use alcohol to bend the world into a more acceptable and satisfactory version, and it works wonders…until it doesn't. Alcohol escorted my existential loneliness to the back door, followed by a warm embrace, until it didn't. When alcohol stops working, we find ourselves in a mighty predicament, one that you may be trying to solve with this book. Keep reading.

The overall point of this book is to help.

We—Homo sapiens—are getting our asses kicked like no other time in history. Despite impressive medical and scientific discoveries, we are currently in a period of de-evolution, and the life expectancy in America, especially for men, is now in decline. Cancers, autoimmune disorders, diabetes, depression, anxiety, obesity, chronic inflammation, and chronic pain are all on the rise, and it could be said these are diseases of unease, unrest, or messengers that we are living wildly out of balance. Pediatricians, who used to see children for rashes, coughs, and colds, are now treating anxiety and depression with more and more frequency. It could have something to do with the fact that we are treating planet Earth like our children's futures don't matter. Unfortunately, I think the modern phenomenon of addiction is just lacing up its ass-kicking boots, and the greatest addiction humanity will face is looming. Hint: it's not a substance.

While this book focuses on alcohol, the problem isn't just about what we put in our bodies. Things such as screens, social media, and technology in general wreak havoc on our modern society. At some point, we'll be forced to reckon with these addictions that are already upon us at large and much further along than we think.

Humans are currently struggling in such a profound way that our unrest is now affecting everything under the sun: animals, marine life, nature, and, of course, Mother Earth. I feel called to help, and this is one of the ways I hope to do so. But this isn't about despair. It's about what we can choose to do next, together.

As we are reminded on every commercial airliner before takeoff, we must first put on our own oxygen mask before assisting those around us. Said another way, you must first get your shit together before you can help others, and ditching the booze is a great place to start. The good news is, we don't have to colonize Mars to begin the healing process. It's the opposite, actually. We have to return to our roots, connect on a deeper level with our fellow humans, animals, food, and the land. No, I am not suggesting you hurl your smartphone off a cliff or move to a high-altitude mountain yurt with no internet, but we absolutely have to take an honest look at the way we are living.

Now I want to make it clear, this book is not all doom and gloom, not even close. There is so much beauty and GOOD in the world. However, we do have to bring awareness to what is out of balance before healing can begin. I hope this book carries an overall positive and uplifting tone as I work to honor my goal of assisting you in becoming a more whole, grounded version of yourself. We've all heard that laughter is the best medicine, and I hope you laugh on occasion while reading.

There is a better way of living, and there have already been some rare flowers in humanity that have pointed the way: The Buddha, Jesus Ben Joseph, Laozi, and many feminine voices as well. The answer is there, but we must first recognize the root of all dysfunction: the human ego, which lives in a constant state of lack and has an unquenchable thirst for more, more, and more.

Throughout this book, I'll refer to the ego—the part of us always whispering that we're not good enough, that we need more, that we should just have one more drink—as the "Bruno Voice." Inspired by the Disney character from *Encanto*, it's the inner saboteur we pretend not to hear. But it's always there, steering the ship unless we learn how to name it and take back the wheel. It's the fearful, limiting thoughts in our heads that keep us trapped in addictive patterns. Learning to **recognize this voice** and quiet it is essential to breaking free from addiction and stepping into authentic living.

Before we begin, I request that at no moment while reading this book, we take ourselves too seriously. Yes, you may be reading in search of answers for BIG questions, but let's not forget to enjoy ourselves along the way. It's only the journey that matters, and there's a high likelihood, there is no destination. There's a good chance you'll find that what you've been seeking has been there all along. Yes, we can make changes in our lives, and quitting drinking is a move that will positively impact every aspect of your life, and for generations to come, but I want to reinforce my belief that you are not fractured, and there is nothing fundamentally wrong with your circuitry. A drinking problem is simply your DIY attempt at installing temporary sanity in an insane world. It's an almost expected adaptation to living in a world that loses a few more marbles daily.

As you read or listen, you may hear a familiar voice. The inner child has been patiently waiting for you to return. By universal design, we split from this inner kiddo in adolescence, then lose ourselves in the world of "things" before being called home again. I hope this book fans oxygen on a dormant spark of remembrance deep within you. I have learned that those who struggle with addiction are on what is called the "Hero's journey," and we are primed to embody the only thing that matters in life: love. To overcome an addiction, one must unequivocally love the self. Not just the parts you like and admire, but the whole package. Another component of this self-love is when. Are you going to wait till the end of this book to love yourself? Until you have a certain number of days away from your last drink? As Einstein discovered, time is an illusion, and the only moment that has ever existed to love yourself is right now. Again, you need to love the part of you that looks good in front of the mirror and also the part that perhaps had two bottles of wine last night and a large bowl of Lucky Charms.

Verbiage and Things to Keep in Mind While Reading

The word alcoholic is heavy…I've broken up with the word several times, even though, yes, that's exactly what I was, and with traditional 12-step thinking, that's what I still am. I'm also a lot of other things: a father, husband, author, podcaster, goat herder, reptile enthusiast, and a mediocre drummer. I've learned that the word alcoholic can be a barrier to entry and can delay the healing process. For example, someone might think they have to be living under a bridge before they consider themselves to have a drinking problem.

A big part of this comes from the bias built into the word itself. For decades—both in society at large and even in the medical community—"alcoholism" was seen primarily as a moral failing, a weakness of willpower or character, rather than what we now know it to be: a physiological condition with roots in biology, psychology, and environment. That stigma has done real damage, keeping people from getting help sooner. In this book, you will hear words like drinking problem, problematic drinker, alcohol use disorder (AUD), a drunk, addict, binge drinker, sober curious, raging alcoholic, and perhaps more. And on the flip side, you'll see sober, alcohol-free, recovered, and a person in recovery. We are all searching for the appropriate box or label to put ourselves in, but at the end of the day, it's all basically the same, and it doesn't really matter. I encourage you to be open and use the verbiage that works for you.

I do remember the surprising feeling of liberation when I called myself an alcoholic out loud, in front of other people for the first time. I was like, "fucking finally," let the healing journey begin. And while we grapple with finding the 'right' words, the addiction continues tightening its noose around the soul. At the end of the day, the word you use doesn't matter. If something walks with a shell on its back, loves fresh lettuce, and can remain submerged under water for a long time, then it's probably a turtle.

A classic trait of an addiction is that it separates. As you read, the addiction will interject to highlight the differences and probably has already done so in the previous 2,800 words. My advice is to FOCUS ON THE SIMILARITIES and not the differences. I'm guessing your name isn't Paul, and you may not play the ukulele. But maybe you have found it difficult to stop drinking once you've started. Or perhaps you've promised yourself you'll take a few nights off, only to find yourself filling up your glass for a third time later that same evening. Maybe you find part of yourself is desperately wanting to quit drinking, yet at the same time, another voice says NOPE. These are the things I want you to focus on, and be vigilant of the Bruno Voice that tries to distance you from the content of this book.

I encourage you to name or personify the drinking problem or addiction. In this book, I use the name "Bruno Voice." If it helps, come up with your own version of the "Bruno Voice." Or use mine. Whatever works. Native cultures recognized that healing can only take place when we have named the issue we are trying to heal. This is especially pertinent with alcohol, as many cultures, including ours, view alcohol as an actual spirit or entity. You've seen the neon storefront sign: Beer, Wine, and Spirits. In Arabic, the name for alcohol is *al-kuhl,* which translates to "mind-and body-eating spirit."

The Fish I Caught Was 'This Big'

All stats, data, and information in this book are accurate to the best of my ability. I will never fabricate a story or statistic to better illustrate a point, and all information in this book comes from reputable sources, which can be researched or fact-checked with some inquiry. I do not include a 'sources' section at the end of this book since most of the information is in my head, and usually the source is listed after the statement. I have an almost Rainman-like memory where I can remember numbers, stats, percentages, etc. from books I read years ago, but don't necessarily remember the exact book title. All facts have been double-checked for accuracy, and when possible, I do include the book title, authors, and publication when possible. In today's age, truth has been sidelined for falsities aimed at grabbing your attention, but I won't be playing that game. I don't need to. Proving that alcohol is harmful in any quantity is the easy part. What I ask you to stay open to is on the other side of the bottle, when it comes to the healing journey, and that alcohol is the driver that wakes you up to the true nature of your life. That awakening, for me, is what I call the *Dolce Vita*—the good life. Funny enough, it's also the name of the bar I once owned in Spain, where my drinking story hit some of its darkest notes. Back then, *Dolce Vita* was just a name on a neon sign. Today, it's a way of living.

Chapter 1
Welcome to the Infinite

I was lying in a hammock in the jungle of Costa Rica, gazing at the stars on a moonless, cloudless night. Through a break in the canopy, thousands of stars glimmered overhead. Accompanied by Venus, Orion's Belt, the grounding soundtrack of crickets, and a light breeze rocking me gently, I felt peace, serenity, and my heartbeat seemed to match the resting pulse of planet Earth.

While swaying back and forth in the hammock, I realized my mind had been void of thoughts for the past hour or so, which was rare for me. Shortly after this realization, the book *The Power of Now* by spiritual teacher Eckhart Tolle came into my consciousness.

I tried to nudge the mind back to its thoughtless state, but I kept hearing a voice inside my head on repeat saying, "the present moment." I remember being slightly annoyed—just moments before I was experiencing deep peace with Mother Nature, and now I had Eckhart Tolle's voice in my ear. At the same time, I recalled a phrase from another teacher: "If the conditions are right."

Again, I tried unsuccessfully to shake these looping thoughts from my mind, but I then realized that perhaps they were trying to tell me something. "The present moment"—"If the conditions are right"—"Focus on the present moment." So that's exactly what I did, and I pulled all my mental energies into the present moment.

Since the night was panther black and I couldn't see much past my hammock, I narrowed in with my ears. At first, there was nothing but the cacophony of the crickets, but as I continued to see with my ears, I noticed a pocket of crickets about 20 feet behind me suddenly stop. When they resumed their chorus, another group of crickets stopped chirping, yet this group was roughly 15 feet away from me. When those crickets began singing again, I heard another gap in the chorus, about 10 feet away. The voice "the present moment" rang louder in my mind. "If the conditions are right."

The hairs on my forearms lifted like antennae picking up a signal, and my pulse quickened. Something was moving through the tall grass, close enough to silence the crickets in a widening ripple. The hush was moving closer, closer, until it was five feet behind me—then suddenly, it stopped, directly to my left. Every cell in my body felt electric, certain that something powerful was just an arm's length away, hidden behind the thin veil of grass.

Earlier that day at the retreat I was attending, a speaker gave a presentation about the wildlife that calls the jungle home. I don't know why, but of all the animals that flashed on the screen, I pulled out my phone and took a photo of a 250-pound jaguar and didn't think much of it. The image suddenly flashed into my mind, and I unequivocally knew what was directly to my left. A second later, to confirm this realization, I heard a whhuuuuuuuuffffffffff, a long, soft, deep purr that ended in a whisper. I remember saying to myself, "ohhhh shit," yet despite my accelerated heart rate, for some reason, I wasn't afraid, and I sensed the big cat wasn't there to eat me. However, I thought distance from the animal wouldn't be a bad idea, so I slowly stepped out of the hammock and, while facing the jungle's edge, I tiptoed backward towards the safety of the structure nearby.

About 45 seconds later, I sat on the steps thinking about what had just happened. Was I dreaming? Did I really just have an encounter with the jungle's apex predator? And at that same moment, in the distance, a chachalaca, a bird that notifies the jungle's inhabitants when a predator is nearby, gave a rare nighttime call to warn the jungle's sleeping creatures that a jaguar was passing below. A flood of emotions poured through me, followed by tears, and if I could summarize them all with one word, it would be gratitude. Yes, perhaps I had just survived a potential near-death experience, but the gratitude was tied to the immensity of the journey we call a human life. Life was being lived in that moment. I later came to learn that a visit by a jaguar in that capacity is incredibly rare. I've spoken with locals who have lived their entire lives in the jungles and have never seen a jaguar, as they are built for stealth and secrecy—if they don't want to be seen or heard, they won't be.

I lead off with the jaguar story with you for a couple of reasons. First, because now you have also been visited by the jaguar, which represents power, intuition, transformation, and rebirth. It takes strength and courage to read a book about ditching the booze when it "seems" the rest of the world is throwin' 'em down like Betty Ford. You have listened to your inner guidance or intuition and have sensed that a change is needed. Your transformation and rebirth are already underway, and you have everything needed to keep moving forward. Jaguar spirit and I are with you every step of the way.

Second, this story represents the infinite possibilities that await us when we quit drinking. I picked the story of the jaguar, but I could have also shared about the time I danced salsa with my soon-to-be wife while traveling in Colombia or when the sun's initial beams of light spilled over the iconic Jim Bridger mountain range and into the hospital room at 5:56 AM, on June 1st, 2024, at the exact moment my son was born. I could have led off with skydiving on New Year's Day in New Zealand. All life experiences that were only possible after ditching the booze.

If a problematic drinker continues drinking, they will most likely find themselves with only two options: institutions or death. Just four years prior, the Costa Rican hammock was an old couch, and the glistening stars were cheap vodka sloshing in a clear 1.75 L plastic bottle as I drank alone on a moonless night. My life was shrinking, the possibilities ahead of me were dwindling, and the spirit alcohol straight up had me by the balls.

When we put down the bottle, life begins to expand again.

Another way to say this is that living an alcohol-free life is the OPPORTUNITY OF A LIFETIME, and that's the fuel source I want you to eventually tap into. Later in this book, I'll share the tools, mindset shifts, and community-based pathways that helped me step into this opportunity so you can discover what might work for you.

However, at first, you might be exploring ditching the booze out of fear of where you feel your life is headed. You may be beyond sick and tired of being sick and tired. Perhaps a physician has recently notified you that your liver is giving out distress signals. It could be the existential hangxiety we feel in the morning after a night of drinking. Fear is a powerful motivator, especially at first, and let's definitely let that work to our advantage.

We face a double fear: not only do we dread what lies ahead if we keep drinking, but we're equally terrified of what awaits us on the other side when we put the bottle down—the vast unknown of sobriety. For many of us, we have been drinking for so long that it's hard to imagine a life without alcohol, and when we do, it causes anxiety to spike. The fear of the unknown often keeps us waist-deep in the muddy waters of inner warfare, because that's what we're used to. The unconscious mind/body thrives in consistency and would prefer a predictable future over the unknown, even if it consists of hangovers, puffy eyes, bloating, shame, regret, and serious traffic violations.

I wanted to include this chapter early in the book to show you the magic awaiting you on the other side of alcohol. When drinking takes over, our lives contract, resulting in a closing of the aperture of life possibilities. Usually, this withdrawal from life happens at such a slow pace that we aren't aware it's even taking place. That's one of the most dangerous characteristics of alcohol—how slowly it kills us. Unlike crack, meth, cocaine, or fentanyl, which can derail your life hard and fast, the slow suicide from alcohol can be drawn out for decades.

Within a year of taking my last drink on September 6th, 2014, a feeling from childhood returned, which was that I could do anything that I put my mind to. Do I want to be president? Let's go for it. Buy a house in a Blue Zone on the Gold Coast in Central America? I don't see why not (I'm currently writing this section of the book from my house in Guanacaste, Costa Rica). A childlike state has returned to my life, where I find myself constantly curious about how the natural world works. A well-known thought leader who lived 2,000 years ago said one must be like children to enter the kingdom, and this playful, explorative state has returned to my life, and it appears it's here to stay.

I aim to keep this book real. I still have days when I push back against life, but I no longer need an artificial dopamine hit to make life more tolerable. As I put more distance between myself and my last drink, the understanding of my circuitry builds, and I identify more and more as an artist. Like many artists, I slip into occasional bouts of depression, trying to console and reconcile the parts of a troubled soul. But within a few days, I always emerge from these states with more inspiration, clarity, and creativity than before. With alcohol in my life, these depressions lasted weeks, months, and years, but now they pass within a couple of days.

Removing alcohol from your life will take work. There will be pain, suffering, and you may try to backtrack on a path that no longer exists. However, the only thing harder than quitting drinking will be NOT quitting drinking and continuing down the path of self-destruction. But trust me, this is the most important journey one can embark upon in a human life if you are to even begin exploring the big hitter questions like, "What is my purpose?" "Why am I here?" "What's the point of life?" And "Why does chocolate milk taste so good?"

Today I have a life. Ten years ago, I woke up in a suicide-proof jail cell wearing a giant padded moo-moo after getting a DUI while driving to work. Now I'm an active participant in the world of the infinite, where anything is possible, and I can nudge my sails in the direction the winds of life desire to take me. I do still have days where I try to power my watercraft against the current of life, but I'm learning more and more—and I have my alcohol addiction to thank for this—that rowing my boat gently down the stream always yields a better result.

I wish this book contained a set, concrete pathway away from alcohol, or a sequential set of steps that would zap your drinking problem with 100% efficacy. I wish I could tell you how to control or moderate your drinking. I wish I could share with you a pill, a diet, or an Amazonian brew that did all the work for you, but I can't. These don't exist, and that's a good thing. As Miracle Max from the Princess Bride says, "If you rush a miracle, you get rotten miracles." You didn't walk into the woods in a day, and the journey out of the dense, blackened forest—back into your heart—is going to take time.

Recovering the person you were fully meant to be is going to take more than a hot minute, and it won't happen day one, or even day one hundred. Sure, there will be significant breakthroughs, and I'm confident you'll experience them while reading this book, but it's the thousands of small realizations that create the overall miracle.

I share in this book how I quit drinking and provide countless pathways for you to explore. There is no right or wrong way to live life, since it's always the "mistakes" that provide us with the biggest growth opportunities. Similarly, there is no right or wrong way to quit drinking. AA works for some, but not for everyone, and our alcohol-free community Café RE has worked for many, but not for all.

In the chapters ahead, I'll share what I've learned about alcohol and addiction, blending the personal stories that shaped me with the practical insights that can support you. This is your invitation to step into your own *Dolce Vita*—the good life that waits on the other side of alcohol.

Chapter 2
Your Blueprint for REcovery

I have wonderful news for you about the healing process. This isn't about adding more layers of complexity to your already complicated and complex lives. Sure, we can always learn more, and that's never a bad idea. But healing from alcohol addiction is less about adding new knowledge and more about REstoring the original circuitry we arrived on the planet with.

If there is anything I want you to get out of this book, it is this: You already have everything you need to quit drinking.

First, know this: there is nothing fundamentally wrong with you—nothing whatsoever. You are not permanently broken or damaged. Your authentic self has always been there, waiting beneath the noise of addiction.

Second, you already possess the tools you need—mental, emotional, spiritual, and an able body—to live in alignment with that authentic self once you stop denying it. You don't have to go out and "get fixed." You don't have to earn your wholeness. It's already here.

We simply need to remove the layers of muck, grime, false stories, and outdated paradigms that have accumulated over the decades from trying to live in a strange society that rewards dysfunction. Developing a drinking problem is almost inevitable when you're trying to survive in a world that calls itself normal but is completely absurd. I'll expand on this later in the book.

This journey into wholeness is anchored to a bunch of words that start with RE. It's about REturning home, to a state where we no longer pollute our inner world, nor the external environment.

It's about REbuilding a sturdier foundation after an intense storm.

It's REplenishing the 120 trillion cells in your body and letting them heal now that a toxin has been removed from your diet.

This is about REorganizing your thought systems, placing a higher emphasis on community and deeper, authentic connections with other human beings.

This is about REkindling the spark for life and embracing the greatest miracle of all time: you being here.

This journey is all about REinforcing what matters most to you—setting healthy boundaries, letting everything else go, and REaffirming your decision to accept life as it comes.

It's REarranging the furniture on a ship that is no longer sinking. It's REcharging your internal batteries that imperialism, colonialism, capitalism, and Meta have nearly fully depleted.

It's REplacing friendships built around ethanol with more altruistic relationships.

It's REpurposing past experiences for a better future, and more importantly, so you're better equipped to assist someone on their journey of healing.

This is about REimagining the possibilities in your life. You're REplacing alcohol with nourishing vitamins, minerals, nutrients, amino acids, and smiles.

This is about REjuvenating your body, mind, and spirit with deep, dreamy REM sleep, leaving you REfreshed when you awake in the morning.

You are REtracing steps, so we no longer have to walk the way of the scorched earth. In short, you are part of a REvival, one that now carries a torch that shines the way towards a better pathway for you and those who choose to follow.

Now, let's not make this entirely about ourselves. You have a duty to pass along how you REcovered—how you crossed to the other side—to your fellow human brothers and sisters.

We are ALL in need of healing, as it appears the world is on fire both metaphorically and literally. As you clean up your inner mess, you're laying the foundation for others to begin their healing. When you heal, it cues the healing of others nearby—a phenomenon known as entrainment theory in biology. We don't need to solve the world's most complex problems or build shinier technology. We need to meet at the campfire, share our stories, bring awareness to injustices, find what we have in common, and discover a path forward that doesn't destroy our bodies or the planet. You REmoving alcohol from your life can save the world, and I fully believe this.

Chapter 3
Alcohol - What It Is

That awkward moment when alcohol is the 3rd leading preventable cause of death in the US, but you still get asked why you don't drink…

Alcohol has many beneficial uses. It kills bacteria, it's a powerful disinfectant and antiseptic, it's the main ingredient in hand sanitizer, it's a solvent, it works well to remove stains, it's used as a fuel additive, an antifreeze, an ingredient in pesticides, and most mouthwash companies would be out of business without alcohol (ethanol).

However, nothing good comes from drinking alcohol, and you already know this. I don't need to tell you it's a class 1 carcinogen—a label that includes asbestos, radiation, tobacco, and welding fumes—because after a night of heavy drinking, you've probably experienced the following:

Dawn breaks with the percussion section of your own personal headache orchestra, but there seems to be no agreed-upon rhythm, the conductor being the last shot of tequila you don't even remember drinking. Your mouth has transformed into the Serengeti Desert—bone dry and seemingly home to several small deceased creatures. Your tongue feels as if it has doubled in size and been wrapped in sandpaper. Your stomach performs acrobatics that would impress Olympic judges, oscillating between nausea and hunger with remarkable agility, demanding a coat of grease one moment and wanting to dramatically empty itself the next. The force of gravity seems to have tripled overnight, pinning you to the mattress or tile floor like a Division 1 wrestler. When you do make an effort to move, the world spins like a vindictive merry-go-round operated by a deaf and mute possum. Your body temperature regulation system malfunctions spectacularly—somehow, you are sweating and shivering at the same time. Light becomes your arch nemesis—the soft glow of your smartphone feels like you're staring directly into the sun. The innocent ticking of a clock in the next room has transformed into a major jackhammer operation. You find yourself in a vacuum where time itself stretches like licorice-flavored taffy. Minutes crawl by with excruciating slowness, each hour an eternity of self-inflicted suffering, with the persistent question echoing in your mind: "Why did I do this to myself?"

Alcohol and the Individual

You already know what alcohol is. You've logged enough 'field research' with it to know that, at least the way you drink, nothing good comes from it. Perhaps some can seemingly drink alcohol with impunity, but if you're reading this book, you've likely connected enough data points to recognize it's not what it's advertised to be. On the surface, while it seems to enhance the lives of others, it keeps creating a chasm of emptiness in yours.

Alcohol gives you wings, then takes away the sky. It promises joy yet delivers misery. It's call of sophistication quickly morphs into slurred words. It robs you of restorative, dreamy REM sleep, gifting you morning anxiety upon awakening with heavy eyes instead. Alcohol mutes the harmonious melodies of songbirds and ocean waves, leaving you with a constant hum of sadness that seems to accompany you at all times. We drink to relax, but end up with crippling anxiety instead. We drink to reach a heavenly state, but the word that best describes where it takes us is hell.

For the remainder of this chapter, I'll cover what your inner child, your prefrontal cortex, and the lining of your small intestine already know—that ethanol is quite insidious. Maybe you've read my first book, titled "Alcohol is SH!T," and perhaps you've forgotten how rotten alcohol is and need a refresher. No problem, I've got you covered. But keep in mind, these facts alone aren't enough to keep you on the sobriety path. Doctors tell patients all the time that if they keep drinking, their liver will fail and they'll die—yet they continue drinking. Yes, knowledge about what alcohol really is will help you reinforce the idea that it's time to say goodbye, but knowledge alone isn't enough to keep you sober.

Alcohol and Depression

Alcohol is a depressant that wreaks havoc on brain chemistry, particularly neurotransmitters involved with mood regulation, such as serotonin and norepinephrine. When alcohol is always in the picture, the brain begins to stop its own natural secretion of chemicals like dopamine and GABA (which calms the nervous system) since it's expecting alcohol to do the heavy lifting.

Dopamine is often called the "feel-good chemical," but it's really the brain's motivation and learning signal—the neurological "gold star" that reinforces habits. Most drugs affect this circuitry, but alcohol is unique because it directly stimulates dopamine and, over time, alters the dorsal striatum, the brain's habit center. This makes drinking patterns especially sticky.

Wow, was I depressed when drinking alcohol, like, for a decade. To be fair, I still get visits from the black dog of depression, but not the three-hundred-pound weighted blanket variety, and it always lifts in a day or two. While drinking, the depression was so heavy that I tried to end my life once.

In 1988, Marc Schuckit, an experimental psychologist at San Diego State University, observed a group of depressed men who went to the hospital for four weeks and received no treatment for depression apart from stopping their alcohol consumption. After one month of not drinking, 80% of the men no longer met the criteria for clinical depression. Brown University researchers (2018) found that abstinence from alcohol for just three to four weeks led to improved mood and decreased depression scores in moderate to heavy drinkers.

When I was drinking, if I wasn't depressed, I was anxious. After a night of heavy drinking on the job at my bar in Spain, and then a dozen more drinks at a club till 7:00 AM, I woke around 3:00 PM with the sensation that my heart had signed up for a marathon. For two hours, I tried to relax my breathing, but then, scared shitless, I jumped into a taxi cab and said, "HOSPITAL—I'm having a heart attack." When the taxi stopped at a red light, I yelled to keep moving, since I indeed thought I was having a heart attack. Upon arrival at the hospital, I was treated for an acute panic attack caused by alcohol withdrawal.

Research from the University of Colorado (2020) showed that four to six weeks of abstinence led to significant reductions in anxiety symptoms among former heavy drinkers. The "Sober Curious" study (2021) followed moderate drinkers who quit for 100 days and found that approximately 71% of them reported reduced anxiety levels.

Hangxiety—the existential anxiety the morning after heavy drinking or binges—is something I wouldn't wish on anyone. The nervous system is acting like it's about to lose a real-life game of Battleship. Alcohol says, "Thanks for the fun, but I've completely rearranged your neurotransmitters, drained your hydration bank account, and left your glutamate system WIDE AWAKE." Glutamate, by the way, is the balancing act to GABA— the neurotransmitter that calms the nervous system—so when alcohol leaves the scene, the brain's balance tips hard toward overstimulation. My hangxiety was so bad at times that it felt like my soul was trying to break the emergency glass inside me, trying to warn me that I was headed down a perilous, destructive pathway toward death.

The relationship between anxiety and alcohol creates one of the most insidious cycles in the world of addiction. It's a perfect storm of biological and psychological factors that trap people in an increasingly harmful loop. Drink to suppress anxiety, but then it comes back worse— drink a little more, get temporary relief, then it comes back even worse. The person is now managing not only their original anxiety, but also withdrawal-induced anxiety, shame-based anxiety about their drinking, anticipatory anxiety about the eruption of anxiety in the very near future, the actual physical symptoms of anxiety, and the anxiety of knowing their life is derailing with you somehow in the driver's seat. This was the worst phase of my addiction—knowing temporary relief was a drink away, yet that drink only added to the mountain of anxiety on the other side of the bottle. It's soul-crushing, and I didn't think I'd make it out alive.

When I quit drinking, 85% of my anxiety went away within six months. Most interviewees on the Recovery Elevator podcast report a similar experience. Without alcohol in my life, I still do experience anxiety—I have anxious mornings or days—but it's manageable and not cheese-grinder-to-the-solar-plexus level anxiety like it was before. When I am feeling anxious or depressed, I use my mind to place my energies on the sensations in my body to try to understand what these emotional states are trying to tell me.

We often drink alcohol to place ourselves in the sweet spot of the present moment, which works temporarily, only to then send us reeling further into either the past (depression) or future (anxiety).

Alcohol and Stress

Alcohol alters the relationship between the hypothalamus, the pituitary gland, and the adrenals—the HPA Axis. The hypothalamus, which is about the size of a gumball and sits above the roof of the mouth, provides a specific set of signals for the pituitary gland, which then releases hormones into the bloodstream that communicate to your adrenals, which sit above your kidneys in your lower back. The adrenals then release a chemical called epinephrine and cortisol, which are involved in the longer-term stress response. The hypothalamus, the pituitary gland, and the adrenals maintain the overall physiological balance of what you perceive as stressful. When this system is functioning properly, the stress response is actually important—this activation isn't necessarily bad. It's just our body's way of getting the "go time!" signal when action is needed. The problem begins when we experience unnecessary activation or when the parasympathetic system doesn't complete its job of helping us recover from stress.

All drinkers—light and chronic drinkers—experience changes between the hypothalamus, the pituitary gland, and the adrenals, which result in more cortisol being released at baseline… and here's the punch in the groin: just one drink can send this entire system into an imbalance, and imagine what 30-40 drinks a week does to this. People who drink alcohol in general feel more stress, even if their last drink was several days ago, and most medical professionals agree that stress is the number one contributor to disease or dis-ease.

When we consume alcohol, the body recognizes it as a level-10 toxin that needs immediate attention, and all other functions are halted until the alcohol has been expelled. The liver, as your primary detoxification organ, can only handle one standard drink per hour. During this time, the liver diverts resources away from its other vital functions, such as processing other toxins, managing glucose levels, metabolizing fats, and producing essential proteins. This prioritization creates a metabolic bottleneck. While your liver is busy processing alcohol, other substances must "wait their turn," which can lead to impaired blood sugar regulation, accumulation of fats in the liver (potentially leading to fatty liver disease and weight gain), and slower processing of other toxins. Essentially, your sophisticated biochemical processing plant goes into single-task mode, with all workers focused on showing ethanol the exit door while everything else gets a "back after lunch" sign.

Alcohol places your prefrontal cortex (PFC) in a headlock, and the more alcohol that passes through your PFC, the more likely you are to think you can have a conversation with a tortoise. It's well known in the medical world that long-term alcohol use rewires the brain circuits, loosening impulse control when drinking and also when not. Studies show chronic alcohol use can reduce PFC volume by up to 11%, with gray matter particularly affected – the brain shrinks. Alcohol radically disrupts the neurotransmitters in the PFC, basically telling the brain's executive supervisor it's break time. As a result, the limbic system (i.e. "lizard brain") is calling the shots, which is why we end up acting like toddlers when we're drunk.

Alcohol and Gut Health

As I mentioned at the beginning of this chapter, alcohol is quite effective at killing bacteria, but the problem is that when we drink it, it kills the good bacteria in the gut as well, which can lead to leaky gut syndrome and a disruption of your happy chemical serotonin, 90% of which is created in your gut. Alcohol loosens the tight junctions in your intestinal wall faster than a toddler unravels toilet paper.

Because of the chemical structure of alcohol, it is both water-soluble and fat-soluble, meaning it can pass into all the cells and tissues of your body. Other substances and drugs can only attach to the surface of cells, but alcohol has its own mechanism to enter directly into the cells and tissues of your body—think trillions of them.

Alcohol delivers no nutritional value, even if your happy hour cocktail costs $14. Unlike calories from whole foods, alcohol provides seven calories per gram without any essential nutrients—no vitamins, minerals, protein, fibre, or healthy fats. It's essentially something your body must reject, as it lacks the building blocks necessary for a healthy body. Alcohol is considered empty calories because it's metabolically costly—it's a massive strain on the system to process without delivering any helpful amino or fatty acids. Straight-up sugar cane water is a better source of fuel than alcohol.

Now, for the sake of simplicity, we mention alcohol as the blanket villain, but to be accurate, the liver uses an enzyme called alcohol dehydrogenase to transform alcohol into the master poison, acetaldehyde. Acetaldehyde is far more toxic than the original alcohol. It's a reactive compound that can damage proteins and DNA in the human body, and is also one of the main causes of the unpleasant hangover symptoms. Most people don't realize that the sensation of being drunk is a poison-induced disruption in the way that your neural circuits work, caused by acetaldehyde and not alcohol. Interestingly, the medication disulfiram (Antabuse), used to treat alcohol dependence, works by blocking the enzyme that breaks down acetaldehyde, causing it to build up and produce immediate, unpleasant symptoms like fierce, intense projectile vomiting shortly after drinking.

Alcohol's impact on body chemistry has always baffled me in two ways:

1) Why did it eventually become so hard to stop drinking after I started

2) Why do I seem to pick up right where I left off, even after months or years since the last drink?

For example, I went 2.5 years without alcohol from 2010 to mid-2012, and my first night back, I found myself next to my computer at 2:30 AM, after gas stations could no longer sell alcohol, Googling if I could drink rubbing alcohol or hydrogen peroxide to keep the party going. This was after 25+ drinks, including my roommate's bottle of champagne he saved from his wedding day (my bad). Thankfully, Google convinced me to put the caps back on the bottles that were bookending my computer, and two years later, I was back on the sobriety train.

From what I've researched, there are clear reasons why it's so hard to stop drinking once we start—and why we pick up right where we left off even after significant time away. When we binge drink, it causes an excessive buildup of acetaldehyde in the brain. This acetaldehyde then converts into tetrahydroisoquinolines (THIQs), which permanently reside in the brain. Due to the brain's incredible ability to heal itself with neuroplasticity, nearly all damage to the brain can be reversed with abstinence, except the deposit of THIQs in the brain. This buildup of THIQs in the brain does two things: it makes it nearly impossible to stop drinking after the first drink, and it acts as a memory foam of sorts, prompting us to return to how we used to drink nearly immediately, even if it's the first time drinking in weeks, months, or years. Another factor involves dopamine circuits, which can also undergo long-lasting changes. In 2020, researcher Esther Visser's "footprint" study found that alcohol leaves behind a kind of "memory trace" in the brain—neural pathways that lie dormant until alcohol reenters the system. When it does, they reignite like a late-summer lightning storm, which helps explain why even after decades of sobriety, one drink can send someone right back into old patterns. This is why an alcoholic with 20 years of sobriety will quickly find themselves in a nosedive shortly after taking the first drink.

It's not the 10th drink that gets us into trouble; it's always the first. So if you're saying to yourself, "It's been months or years since my last drink, it will be different this time," this is me telling you it won't. Yes, some can keep a fence around their drinking for a month or two, but soon they're right where they left off.

For me, this permanent accumulation of THIQs in the brain is a blessing. I know with 100% accuracy what will happen if I take a drink—a tailspin.

Memory is a damn good thing. Our ancestors memorized terrain for hundreds of miles, knowing the exact locations of watering holes, where grizzlies roamed, and where wild blueberries grew. We probably wouldn't be here if our ancestors drank alcohol like we do today. Alcohol particularly affects your hippocampus, the brain's region responsible for forming new memories. When blood alcohol levels rise to a certain threshold, the hippocampus essentially gets overwhelmed and then goes offline, resulting in brownouts or blackouts. While you can still process information during a blackout—which is why you can still talk and attempt the moonwalk—alcohol prevents the transfer of experiences from short-term to long-term memory storage. This is why people often wake up with no recollection of how they got home or what they did, despite seemingly functioning at the time. It is worth noting that meditation has the exact opposite effect—it strengthens the hippocampus instead of shutting it down, helping you stay present enough to actually *REmember* your life as it happens.

Alcohol Tolerance: The Hidden Inflation

Think of your first-ever drinking experience: two beers, and suddenly you're about to breakdance on a piece of cardboard in the street. Fast forward a few years of regular drinking, and those same two beers barely get your feet tapping. Increased tolerance to alcohol (meaning more drinks are required to get the same feelings of euphoria), is a clear sign that the body and mind have adapted to repeated alcohol use. The liver says, "I didn't sign up for this shit," but then adapts to the constant barrage of alcohol by creating alcohol-processing enzymes like it's getting paid by the molecule. In our initial escapades with alcohol, GABA, dopamine, and serotonin flood the scene, but after repeated and prolonged use, most of them opt for the bleachers instead of the dance floor, causing us to drink more and chase the initial highs that alcohol produced when we first started drinking. Another tragedy of tolerance is the financial impact. Remember when $20 could fund your entire night out? Now you're dropping $60 before you even feel a buzz, making tolerance the hidden inflation no economist warns you about. In the end, tolerance is just your body's passive-aggressive way of saying, "I'm adapting to your poor decisions, but I'm keeping receipts, and we WILL be discussing this later."

Alcohol's Strain on the Healthcare System

The healthcare system is bombarded 24/7 by alcohol. There is a healthcare stat that says anywhere from 40 to 70% of occupied American hospital beds have underpinnings related to alcohol, which would make sense when Americans, on average, drink 2.85 gallons of a class 1 carcinogen each year. When I've asked hospital doctors or nurses if they feel this stat checks out, without much hesitation, their answer is always yes. The two leading causes of death in America, heart disease and cancer, are almost always linked with alcohol. Studies have repeatedly shown that any amount of alcohol raises blood pressure, damages the heart muscle (cardiomyopathy), produces abnormal heart rhythms (arrhythmias), skyrockets your chances of stroke, and primes the heart for failure. According to the World Health Organization (WHO), alcohol is known to cause at least seven types of cancers, and thankfully, their website now states there are no studies that would demonstrate light and moderate drinking as beneficial to your health.

Alcohol is truly shit. If anyone wants to reach their full potential in life, alcohol can't be part of the equation.

During the 2024 Paris Summer Olympics, I watched an interview on NBC with the American men's rowing team, who had just won a gold medal. The host poured the four chiseled rowers a glass of champagne and then one for herself. She congratulated the rowers with a toast, and they all took a drink—or it looked like they took a drink.

Noticing the rowers weren't drinking the champagne, the host said, "You all don't have to drink the champagne if you don't want to."

Without hesitation, each rower quickly passed the drinks back to the table, as if the contents of the glass contained poison. I'm guessing the elite athletes made a pact as a team long ago that alcohol wasn't part of the plan.

The Olympic committee took a similar stance that year, declaring the Paris Games booze-free after concluding the costs—public drunkenness, fights, trash, and excess littering—outweighed the benefits. When the games ended, watching medalists raise water bottles instead of champagne said more about how culture is shifting than any statistic could. And with 49,000 alcohol-related deaths each year in France, it's clear why change is overdue.

The true mindfuck of alcohol is that it can kill you when you drink it and also when you abruptly stop drinking it. Drink, you're sick. Don't drink, you're sick. It becomes a blurred line between medicine and poison.

Alcohol is the most dangerous drug in the world to detox from—ask Amy Winehouse fans—and it can take the body anywhere from 3 to 21 days to fully rid itself of the toxic chemical. So, before we move on, I want to pause here and say: If you're a chronic or daily drinker and you're thinking about quitting, please, please seek medical attention. You absolutely should not try to do it on your own.

The Ripple Effect:
Alcohol's Impact on Families and Relationships

Alcohol's destructive power extends far beyond the individual drinker, creating seismic waves through entire family systems. Studies from the *American Journal of Public Health* estimate that for every person with an Alcohol Use Disorder, between four to six people in their immediate circle are directly affected. These aren't just statistics—they represent partners who become hypervigilant, frightened caregivers; children who develop anxiety disorders at three times the normal rate; and friendships that slowly dissolve under the weight of unpredictability and broken promises.

The family adapts to accommodate the drinking, often without realizing it. Research from the University of Michigan found that family members typically spend two to three years in "adjustment mode" before acknowledging there's a problem—crafting elaborate systems of excuses, developing emotional calluses, and creating unspoken rules (like never confronting Dad before dinner or only inviting Mom to morning events). Children in these households often develop what therapists call "emotional whiplash"—never knowing which version of their parents will walk through the door. Long-term studies from Harvard Medical School show that these children are four times more likely to develop substance problems themselves, not because of genetics, but because of the coping mechanisms they've learned by watching their parents. What's particularly heartbreaking is how alcohol erodes trust across generations. A 2022 study in the *Journal of Family Psychology* found that even after a person achieves sobriety, family trust takes an average of 14 months to begin rebuilding, and some relationship damage never fully heals. This explains why recovery isn't just an individual journey but a family one. As one recovery specialist aptly stated, "When someone gets sober, the whole family needs rehabilitation from the habits they developed while living with someone in active addiction."

The Collective Hangover:
How Alcohol Impacts Work and Society

The societal costs of alcohol use represent one of the most significant preventable economic burdens we collectively bear. According to CDC data, alcohol costs the U.S. economy approximately $249 billion annually—an average of $807 per person, regardless of whether they drink or not. These costs add up fast—in lost workdays, hospital visits, run-ins with the law, and busted property.

In the workplace alone, the impact is staggering. The average employee with an alcohol problem misses 34% more workdays than their peers and operates at approximately 67% capacity when present, according to research from the National Institute on Alcohol Abuse and Alcoholism. Even moderate drinkers who occasionally overindulge contribute significantly to this burden—a Stanford University study found that hangover-related productivity loss accounts for an estimated $77 billion annually across the U.S. workforce. Companies often don't recognize this slow leak in their productivity until it becomes a flood.

What makes alcohol unique is how its costs are spread across society, yet its burdens weigh heaviest on those with the fewest resources. While alcohol addiction affects people across all socioeconomic levels, the consequences often hit the most vulnerable the hardest. Communities with limited resources experience higher rates of alcohol-related violence and have fewer treatment options available. Meanwhile, research from the University of Chicago found that alcohol advertising is 33% more concentrated in lower-income neighborhoods, creating a perfect storm of increased exposure and reduced support for those already facing greater vulnerabilities.

The collective tolerance for these societal costs mirrors the individual tolerance for self-destruction you may have experienced while drinking—extraordinary damage becomes normalized simply because it develops incrementally. Just as you may have needed more alcohol over time to feel normal, society keeps absorbing more alcohol-related costs, treating them as "just the way things are." Both scenarios demand the same first step: acknowledging the full scope of the problem rather than continuing to accommodate it. We are reaching a breaking point where this can no longer be postponed. Quitting drinking is challenging, but continuing to poison yourself is far more painful. The same principle applies to society—addressing this massive problem may be difficult, but continuing to ignore alcohol's widespread carnage is ultimately more costly and destructive.

Wait a Second—What About Red Wine? Isn't That Good for You?

No. If you want the health benefits of polyphenols or resveratrol (particularly popular with the anti-aging crowd), then just eat grapes or drink grape juice. The alcohol in the wine always offsets the health benefits the grapes deliver. And the amount of red wine one would have to drink to potentially notice the health benefits of these polyphenols would land you in a coma first. So the next time Sir Charles Rioja Tannins III starts talking about earthy notes, a crisp blackberry finish, and whispers of oak in his 2018 bottle of Bordeaux, know that he's built an expansive vernacular to mask the fact that he just likes to drink wine and get drunk.

Here, let me help you decipher sommelier talk:

- "An assertive wine with bold structure" = "This will get me drunk faster."
- "A playful vintage with a lingering finish" = "I can drink this all night without passing out."
- "Notes of leather and tobacco" = "Tastes terrible but has high alcohol content."

Note: This 2018 Global Burden of Disease study analyzed 694 data sources and 592 studies to assess alcohol's health impacts across 195 countries from 1990-2016. Their key finding: Alcohol was the seventh leading risk factor for death and disability globally, and among people aged 15-49, it was the **leading** *risk factor. Most significantly, they found that the level of alcohol consumption that minimizes health harm is* **zero drinks per week**—*not the moderate amounts previously thought protective. The risk of death and cancer rises with any level of consumption. Translation: That glass of red wine isn't doing your heart any favors—no matter what your wine-loving aunt insists.*

And The Most Lethal Trait of Alcohol...

It gives you a taste of the present moment, and then steals it forever.

Chapter 4
Hello World

Is there ever a clear line between where one story ends and another begins? So much has unfolded for us to be here, and none of it stands apart. Maybe our story began 13.8 billion years ago, when a single point of infinite heat exploded into everything that ever was. Or 4.5 billion years ago, when a small blue planet found its orbit around a burning ball of hydrogen and helium we call the sun.

Maybe it started when single-celled organisms filled the sea, later becoming the fossil fuels that drive our modern world, or 400 million years ago, when life crawled from the ocean and took its first trembling steps on land. Perhaps it began 6 million years ago, when we split from our chimpanzee relatives and left the trees, or 2.5 million years ago, when *Homo erectus* and Neanderthals—whose DNA still hums in us—ventured out of Africa. Or maybe it began just 300,000 years ago, when *Homo sapiens* appeared on the scene, carrying the same spark that burns in us now.

Or does my existence hinge on a single moment in June 1944, when a German officer ordered the gunner to swivel the panzer tank barrel directly at the third-story apartment balcony where my 17-year-old French grandma was standing, but then had a sudden change of heart and gave the order not to fire? Perhaps we start the following day, when my grandpa, with the 10th Mountain Division, liberated a small French village where he told my grandma that if he survived the war, he'd come back to France and marry her. He then left for Belgium, the Netherlands, Germany, and then the high mountain slopes of Italy, before returning to France, and then America with my grandma to start a family.

Again, the chain of events that led to this very moment is staggering. The chances are unbelievably slim. Just us being here, reading and listening together, is an absolute miracle—one we should never forget.

I entered the world a day before Easter Sunday, on April 10th, 1982, at 7:07 PM, just south of Salt Lake City, Utah. I had a good childhood. Everyone did their best with what they had. My parents are amazing people, and they did everything they could to raise a happy and healthy baby. My father left home early in the morning for work, six days a week, wearing a suit and tie. He worked at a ski resort in the Little Cottonwood Canyon of the Wasatch Mountain Range, where he started as a ski instructor and worked his way up to vice president of the entire organization. Despite working 50 to 60+ hours per week, he never missed a Pop Warner football game, taught me how to alpine ski by the age of two, and took me and my older brother fishing more times than I can remember. My father took us on camping trips to the deserts of the American Southwest dozens of times, where I would catch as many frogs and lizards as I could. He showed me how to find Orion's belt, built me skateboard ramps, and every time I came to him with a wild idea that probably made no sense at all, he'd look at me and say, "Wow, go for it, Paul." Now that I think about it, I've never seen my father and Superman in the same room.

I have wonderful memories of my mother from childhood. She was a dance instructor, and she took me to the studio often, where I was exposed to expression through movement, music, and creativity. Her parents divorced when she was 13, which was extremely painful for her, and she made it a life goal to start a family and keep it together, which she did—and I'm so thankful for that. My mom was and still is my #1 cheerleader. She created the conditions in my childhood that allowed me to bloom. I was encouraged to dance, sing out loud, wear crowns of Play-Doh on my head, and race remote control cars throughout the house. If I found myself in a breakdance battle, a bar fight, or any type of altercation, I'd pick her to be by my side. She's the ultimate warrior. In 2016, she was diagnosed with stage 4 lung cancer and given months to live. She is still kicking ass today, and we are all so thankful for that.

My older brother didn't want much to do with me, and I can't blame him. I was way too sensitive (still am), loaded with energy, and I think I was just plain annoying to be around. But we loved to wrestle and fight, which made me tough, and the skill of how to defend myself would later turn out to be vital and save my life on one particular occasion. I always looked forward to Christmas Eve because we would stay up all night playing *Mario Bros* on Nintendo. Our relationship drastically improved once he left for college, and he would later become a rock in my corner while I battled with alcohol. My brother has been a solid role model for me, and I thank the universe for all the wonderful memories we've had together.

Now you might be saying to yourself, "Damn, you hit the jackpot, Paul. What a delightful youth." To that, I say you are mostly correct. I grew up in the '80s, where kids could roam freely on bicycles and the only firm rule was that I had to be home before dark. I wasn't abused physically or sexually, and thank goodness there were no screens, iPads, or cell phones to stunt my emotional growth. This was a time when telephones were attached to the wall with a cord, and we were free.

But when I revisit my childhood, trying to understand why I turned to alcohol in early adulthood, it wasn't any single traumatic event that pushed me there—it was the absence of what I needed. I was so incredibly lonely. This was not the fault of my parents, but a result of how our family systems had begun to deteriorate in the past 200 to 300 years. For thousands of human generations, we lived nearby, or within the same teepee or thatch hut as our grandparents, aunts, uncles, cousins, siblings, and neighbors. We've all heard the phrase "it takes a village to raise a child," but these essential communal structures are so rarely intact anymore. Again, I was so painfully lonely. My father worked all day, six days a week, my mother also worked to support the family, and my brother avoided me like I had a permanent case of measles.

I was also one of the few non-Mormon students in my elementary school, and the only non-Mormon in my class, which led to another layer of isolation. I don't want to bag on Mormons, because I've met some great ones, but they are conditioned to believe that non-Mormons don't have a seat in heaven, which I was reminded of many times. I remember classmates telling me their parents wouldn't let me come over to play because I wasn't Mormon. On Valentine's Day, I'd get significantly fewer cards than the other students, even though we were instructed to make cards for everyone. In the second grade, my only friend in my class was the kid who crapped his pants. You know things are rough when you're begging the kid who shits himself during story time to hang out with you at recess. It was so brutal. I still remember the pain; I still carry the scars.

But like all living things, you have to figure out a way to survive, and for me, that was football. I practiced football every free moment I had and eventually went from last picked on the playground to first. On offense, I had a tremendous arm and was always the quarterback. On defense, I found it cathartic to smash into my colleagues, many of whom acted like I didn't exist at all, until I put my helmet in their sternum. Physically, I wasn't big, but I had a raging fire inside me, and football was a place to let all my frustrations out.

At the age of 12, my family and I moved to Edwards, Colorado, nestled high up in the Rocky Mountains about 10 miles west of the iconic ski town of Vail. On the first day of school, within minutes, I knew I was no longer in the bubble of Mormon land. Kids were using swear words, I heard Spanish for the first time, and a kid named Sergio with slicked-back jet-black hair said to me as he shook my hand, "Hey, you're the new kid, right?" I quickly realized this wasn't a friendly salutation as he had a safety pin concealed in his palm that stabbed me, and blood was now trickling down my forearm while I tried to find my first-period class.

I found my footing through the awkward middle school social hierarchy with football. I joined the team, earned the starting quarterback position, made friends with the cool kids, and eventually became one of the cool kids myself.

At the end of eighth grade, at 13 years old, three friends and I shoulder-tapped a bottle of vodka and began taking shots in my friend's basement while his parents were upstairs. We didn't understand that the effects of alcohol don't kick in immediately, so we kept on taking shots of vodka and lemon-lime soda until one of us said, "Hang on a second, I think my arms are going numb."

When I felt the initial waves of inebriation come on, it was like someone had just lit off the Fourth of July inside my brain. Every synapse was throwing its own little party, complete with sparklers and those whistling rockets that make you go "Ooooh, ahhhh." Years of rejection, shame, self-doubt, and existential loneliness that I didn't even realize I was carrying were escorted to the door, and I knew alcohol and I were going to be tight companions for years to come—hopefully forever.

When the smell of vomit wafted upstairs through the air vents, my friend's parents descended upon four remarkably drunk teenagers, none of whom were coherent enough to explain what was going on, but they quickly pieced it all together and made us phone our parents to come pick us up. I remember going on a walk with my mom the next morning, where she told me about my grandfather's drinking and how it had been a contributing factor to his early death just a year earlier. On that walk, part of me wanted to ralph in the bushes, but a bigger part of me felt vibrantly alive. Alcohol had opened a world I didn't know existed—one where it didn't matter what religion I was, where I could accept myself as I was, and, let's be real, where I loved the feeling of being drunk. Although I hurled the first time I drank—and it would be a precursor of what was to come—I wasn't addicted to alcohol from the first drink.

I had an absolute blast in high school—I played football, ice hockey, ran track and field, held a student council position, played electric guitar in the jazz band, was president of Future Business Leaders of America, and played several gigs with my own rock band Liquid Banana (I'm not sure what I was thinking with that band name). Alcohol only seemed to enhance my junior and senior years of high school. There were firm boundaries—ones that I didn't even have to set. If I had work or school the next day, I didn't drink. I didn't drink and drive, and I could easily shut it down after one or two.

Cracks began to emerge during my senior year in high school when my friends and I started throwing parties on Wednesday nights. On one Thursday morning when I didn't make it to class, my mom was notified. She then picked me up from my friend's house and drove me to my dad's glass shop, where she tried to make a point showing that if I chose to party over school, I'd be installing glass the rest of my life. That was a long day.

I finished high school with a potent arrow in my quiver called alcohol. It gave me superpowers, it put me on equal footing with everyone else in the room, my imperfections became far less imperfect, and it gave heaps more than it took. One late summer day in August 2000, while driving around Denver, Colorado, picking up furniture for my future dorm room, I saw a homeless man drinking a tall boy beer at 11:00 AM while stopped at a traffic light. While looking at this man who was wearing only one shoe, there was no empathy or compassion, just judgment. I remember saying to myself in a condescending tone, "Man, just stop drinking and get your life together." I couldn't fathom the idea of losing oneself in a bottle. It seemed like it took an eternity for the light to change from red to green, but maybe that was by universal design, and my gaze stayed with the desolate man as we drove off. "Could that happen to anyone? To me?" I asked myself. "Nah...not a chance."

In college, alcohol was a focal point in my life, but it wasn't running the show. I took 19 credits, played on the football team, was the lead guitarist for a hard rock band, and life was more than peachy. I did keg stands, organized beer pong tournaments, started a club called the Mathletes that soon became the largest social club on campus, and began using my band's speaker equipment to DJ fraternity and sorority parties. Playing early 2000s hip hop through 18" heart-pounding subwoofers to a packed dance floor was a spiritual experience enhanced by alcohol. I could read the room and knew exactly when to play Dr. Dre, "California Love," or "In Da Club" by 50 Cent.

I studied abroad in Granada, Spain, during the second semester of my junior year, and it opened my eyes to a nightlife I had never seen before. Showing up to a nightclub before midnight was a cultural foul, and the built-in "siesta" or national nap time from 2-5 PM wasn't just tradition—it was preparation. Like plugging my phone into the charger, those afternoon siestas supercharged me for yet another night of stumbling through cobblestone streets at 4:00 AM.

There was a nightclub called Camborio, built into the caves on a hillside that overlooked the Alhambra—the palace that in 1492 marked the end of Muslim rule in Spain and closed the book on 800 years of Moorish presence on the Iberian Peninsula. Leaving the club at first light, when the last stars were waving goodbye, I felt the familiar warmth of alcohol coursing through me, present but not in control. With the towering walls of the Alhambra glowing in the distance, I had never felt more alive.

When I returned from Spain that summer, three extremely difficult life experiences took place. My heart broke in half when I said goodbye to a Dutch girl with whom I had fallen in love, my rock band broke up shortly after, and alcohol began to change the terms of our relationship...

Chapter 5
What Addiction Isn't

Up until now, we've been talking mostly about alcohol—how it shows up in our lives and what happens when we remove it. But alcohol is just one expression of something deeper. To understand how to truly heal, we have to zoom out and look at the larger pattern behind it all: addiction itself.

Addiction isn't a choice that anybody consciously makes, nor is it a moral failure. It's not a lapse of ethical judgment or someone who has less self-control than others. It's not a weakness of character, nor a failure of will, which is how a large segment of society still views addiction. Addiction isn't an inherited brain disease, which is how the medical world tends to see it. Addiction, alcoholism, isn't the disease, but a symptom or representation of a deeper unrest.

Addiction isn't a life sentence that defines the trajectory of your life or determines your identity forever. It's not your destiny or something you're doomed to struggle with until your dying day. It's not something that makes you fundamentally different from other humans. It isn't a sign that you're broken beyond repair or that something is inherently wrong with your soul. Addiction isn't a reason to give up hope or to believe that you can't create a fulfilling life. It's not a badge of shame you must wear, nor is it something you need to apologize for existing with. Addiction isn't the end of your story—it's just a challenging chapter that will most likely turn you into a more resilient and compassionate human being when you emerge on the other side. Addiction isn't the problem; it's the messenger revealing the parts of our personalities that are out of balance. Addiction isn't a sequence of random cravings and neurons misfiring, but rather the soul, or deeper self, trying to communicate an important message to the body and mind of the person experiencing it. A message that something vital needs tending to, like a plant crying out through wilted leaves or stunted growth, begging for water, sunlight, or a shift in environment.

Addiction isn't a death sentence, not even close—it's the opportunity or invitation of a lifetime to step into the Dolce Vita or the good life.

Chapter 6
Addiction

One in 2 billion live to be 116 years old.
One in 10 becomes addicted to alcohol.

Addiction is one of the most fascinating topics I've ever come across. It represents a profound and complex enigma of human behavior—a subject that continues to captivate researchers, clinicians, and society alike with its psychological depth and neurobiological intricacy. It's a conundrum that the best minds of Eastern and Western medicine have yet to comprehend or solve with their arsenal of remedies and pharmaceutical interventions. For the past decade, I've devoted myself to understanding the addiction that nearly claimed my life.

Through interviews with over 550 individuals who have overcome addiction, I've sought answers to addiction's deepest mysteries: Why is it so hard to quit? Why is it so difficult to diagnose, and why do we spend so much energy hiding it? Why do self-loathing and shame so often accompany addiction? Why is simply "not picking up a drink" easy for some but impossibly hard for others? Why can certain people stop after one drink while others spiral, and what drives those with years of sobriety to relapse? How does alcohol erase the memory of its devastation, continuing to present itself as a viable option even years into recovery? Why has moderation failed for **every** single person I've interviewed? Why do we try so hard to control a seemingly uncontrollable thing? And ultimately, what does sobriety even mean—and why do those who heal from addiction often emerge more grounded, present, emotionally aware, and wiser than those who have never struggled with addiction?

Addiction remains the most captivating phenomenon I have ever witnessed, and perhaps its most surprising element is that, contrary to common belief, addiction is largely a modern phenomenon. Most anthropologists agree that before the Industrial Revolution, addiction wasn't anything like what we see today, meaning people rarely drank to excess or drank themselves to death. Of course, historical records of excessive drinking or addiction do exist. Historians believe Alexander the Great died of pancreatitis at just 32 in 323 BCE, likely from excessive drinking even by Macedonian standards. In medieval times, ale was often believed to be safer to drink than water, leading people to consume large quantities daily, yet few became addicted. Even the Bible references excess, reminding us that heavy drinking isn't new. However, addiction is part of a broader trend alongside conditions like chronic inflammation, chronic pain, morbid obesity, hypertension, autoimmune disorders, various cancers, deaths of despair, depression, and anxiety—all of which are becoming increasingly more prevalent.

Something alarming is taking place. The more I learn, the more people I interview, the more studies and data I come across, I feel like the characters in the movie "The Big Short," where in 2008 the data began to show a major financial crisis was on the horizon, then triggering the US Government to ultimately rescue the very architects of the downfall. This book is me ringing the bell that we are approaching a critical threshold of collective stress and lifestyle-related illness that is not far off. Towards the end of this book, I provide pathways out of this mess, but first, we need to bring our awareness to where we have come as a society and the blaring alarm that things are drastically out of balance: addiction.

The Textbook Definition of Addiction: The continued compulsive use of a substance or a behavior, despite harm to self and others.

Again, this is not a baseline human trait, but a recent occurrence with our species that is gaining momentum, and we are now seeing behavioral addictions that are equally destructive as substance addictions.

Addiction Through Lived Experience

Addiction begins as a quest to alleviate pain that most weren't aware they were carrying, or as an attempt to connect with ourselves, others, and something greater. Initially, alcohol serves as a lubricant, creating moments of warmth and belonging that feel genuine. The bottle offers what seems like a shortcut to intimacy and fun: conversations flow more easily, inhibitions fade, and the world feels more welcoming. But gradually, this connection becomes hollow. We need more to achieve less, yet paradoxically, as alcohol's ability to genuinely connect us fades, our reliance on it intensifies. This is addiction's cruelest trick—we remain tethered to something that no longer delivers what initially drew us to it, while it systematically dismantles the very connections we sought to strengthen.

From the outside looking in, it makes no sense—especially to someone who hasn't personally struggled with addiction. Here's a real example I witnessed while DJing a wedding:

> *Addiction is when your Uncle Rick makes you promise to stay sober at your cousin's wedding, yet you find yourself mid-speech, microphone in one hand, mysterious champagne glass in the other, eloquently slurring a soupy froth of words that make no sense. Meanwhile, the father of the bride is frantically making that universal "wrap it up" gesture across his throat like he's auditioning for a musical called "Please Stop Talking Now." Your brain is working at 7% capacity, yet somehow you're convinced you're delivering Shakespeare-level oratory while the DJ (me) slowly, preemptively fades in "We Are Family" to drown you out.*

In short, addiction is a total bitch…bringing heaps of pain and suffering to the person experiencing it and equally to friends and family who watch the destruction unfold. However, let's not paint addiction as the headless horseman because with it comes an incredible opportunity, and I strongly believe it 100% serves a biological purpose. In many languages, the word crisis (Chinese, Korean, Greek, Hebrew, Arabic, and more) is coupled with the word opportunity. An unchecked addiction will always reach crisis levels, which then presents a once-in-a-lifetime opportunity, or better said, the invitation to step into a healthier and more balanced way of living. I do not recommend aiming your cannons at the addiction either, because there is nothing to fight. Addiction is simply a messenger telling you something in your life is out of balance— and if you want to heal, you'll need to make changes. It's an intense pendulum swing into a theatre of darkness where we're forced to confront our fragmented selves.

We must then gather all parts of ourselves—the conscious, the unconscious, our inner child, the mind, body, and soul—and then create cohesion before we can step toward the light. We then emerge not merely recovered, but reborn as beings of unexpected depth, clarity, and wisdom.

Again, addiction, despite its initial appearance, contains hidden transformative potential. Addiction often arrives disguised as darkness, yet for those who fully surrender to the healing journey, this process can lead to profound illumination and personal radiance. Similar to how ordinary rocks transform into gems and crystals as their carbon molecules rearrange under intense, prolonged pressure within the darkness of the earth, people who have recovered from addiction emerge transformed. They become more anchored to reality, able to admit mistakes and learn how to ask for help. They build lives centered on helping others and, most importantly, they've separated or have become aware of the ego, likely for the first time ever. Another way to accurately describe addiction is as a path—albeit at first a destructive one—toward transformation. The Buddha taught that all humanity must cross the river of consciousness, separating from the ego. Addiction has the potential to force this profound change. I'm personally thankful for how alcohol, through destroying my former self, led me to become the person I am today.

Addiction in the 2000s

Stanford psychiatrist, addiction specialist, and author of the New York Times bestselling book *Dopamine Nation,* Dr. Anna Lembke, says the progression of addictions she has witnessed in her career has been staggering. While there are many causes, she attributes much of this to the overstimulation of modern culture, which keeps us chasing one dopamine hit after another.

The new millennium ushered in unprecedented addictions, evolving in waves while alcohol quietly tightened its deadly grip. The early 2000s saw patients falling victim to doctor-prescribed opiates, creating addiction where healing was promised (thank you, Sackler Family). Simultaneously, internet pornography transformed from the relatively contained world of print magazines into an unlimited digital stream, turning moderate consumers into compulsive users whose relationships and mental health deteriorated.

By the late 2000s, smartphones introduced the concept that behavioral addictions could rival substance dependencies in their power to hijack our neurochemistry. The 2010s expanded this frontier as parents began seeking professional help for children consumed by online gaming, with South Korea opening the first specialized treatment center for this emerging condition. By 2015, clinicians were regularly treating social media dependency, compulsive online shopping, and a surge of internet gambling problems.

Yet behind these headlines, alcohol—our society's most accepted and deadliest drug—sank its teeth in deeper. Throughout this period, excessive drinking soared, with 10% of Americans meeting the criteria for Alcohol Use Disorder (AUD). That's a lot of people struggling with alcohol.

When COVID-19 arrived, it accelerated these trends. A telling indicator of our collective alcohol dependency. Liquor stores were deemed essential businesses because, without access to alcohol, many people would require medical detox, occupying hospital beds that were desperately needed for COVID-19 patients.

In the 2020s, addiction is rampant. A Kaiser Family Foundation poll released in August 2022 received significant media attention. Among its findings: (1) Two-thirds of adults in the U.S. say they have been impacted by addiction either personally or through a family member; (2) nearly 1 in 10 adults in the U.S. has lost a family member to drug overdose; (3) the majority of people experiencing addiction don't receive treatment.

A *New York Times* article published in December 2023 noted in the headline that 48 million people in the U.S. experience addiction. 48 million. That would be all of California and 8 million more.

Today, according to a 2025 article in *NewsBreak*, mortality from alcohol-associated liver disease has doubled in the last 20 years across all demographics.

The scope of this crisis demands that we understand not just what addiction is, but why it's happening with such unprecedented frequency. In the coming chapters, we'll explore the complex web of factors that have created this perfect storm of human suffering—and more importantly, the path forward toward healing and transformation.

Testing for Addiction

Currently, there are no brain scans, biomarkers, or genetic tests for addiction, and there probably never will be. Despite scientists fully mapping the human genome in the 2000s, the so-called "addiction gene" was never found—because it likely doesn't exist. If they do find the alcoholic gene, would they then keep searching for the online shopping gene? Or the inability to stop playing Minecraft gene?

One concrete component of an addiction, which makes the diagnosis process incredibly difficult for individuals and creates an impenetrable wall for family and friends to pierce through, is denial. Recovery's first and most formidable obstacle isn't the addiction itself but the sincere inability to become aware of it. There seems to be a total lack of awareness. It's not deceit; it's blindness, even when friends, employers, or the law sound the alarm. Therefore, no progress, and I mean absolutely none at all, can be made until this denial is overcome. No diagnosis from a doctor, therapist, or self-assessment test will ever land unless the individual can recognize and acknowledge the problem themselves.

Another reason why addiction can be difficult to pin down is that people build their entire lives around it: Drinking can shape our daily schedule, social circles, where we work, hobbies (think ice fishing), where we live, and financial decisions. We become skilled at hiding it, or better said, not seeing it, because it's so tightly enmeshed in every aspect of our lives. We can internally justify our drinking because we can accurately tell ourselves, "I drink as much as my friends, the people I work with. I can handle it. My life seems fine." The reality is that it's nearly impossible to recognize a problem that's been carefully woven into the fabric of everyday life.

Seeing addiction clearly can feel impossible when it's enmeshed into the rhythms of daily life, but when awareness arrives, everything changes. This is where the real journey begins. Recognizing the truth isn't the end of the road; it's the start of reclaiming your life, one clear-eyed step at a time. In the chapters ahead, we'll explore how to keep moving forward—toward a life that feels grounded, awake, and worth living.

Chapter 7
Alcohol and Addiction:
The Modern Crisis

Before we dive into what causes addiction, I want to introduce you to the Monkey Scale—a simple rating system (created by yours truly) that indicates the relative importance of various addiction triggers. I call it the Monkey Scale because I love monkeys and remember in the introduction I asked us not to take ourselves too seriously...? While writing this chapter, I imagined monkeys in little white lab coats, trying to get to the bottom of this whole "addiction thing," and that always made me smile and relax.

According to the monkeys, addictions rarely stem from a single cause. Instead, they develop from a complex interplay of circumstances, some carrying more weight than others.

Rapid Fire - Causes of Addiction

The Monkey Scale: Understanding Addiction Factors

🐒

🐒 🐒

🐒 🐒 🐒

🐒 🐒 🐒 🐒

🐒 🐒 🐒 🐒 🐒

On this scale, a 5-Monkey rating identifies a major driver of addiction. Conversely, a 1 or 2-Monkey rating indicates a contributing element that, while relevant, is unlikely to cause addiction on its own.

Of Course You Have a Drinking Problem

🐒 🐒 🐒 🐒 🐒

A drinking problem is a totally normal and predictable response to living in a toxic culture. In fact, you should tell yourself "nice job" for finding a way to survive in a world where there seems to be a collective madness on display for everyone to see on the news, social media, the banned, and then unbanned TikTok. The way we are living is what is causing addiction, depression, anxiety, chronic pain, and inflammation to proliferate. We are at a high-water mark for collective pain that humans are living with, and the manifestation of excessive drinking, drug use, and compulsive behaviors are all ways to cope, or, better said, to adapt to this way of life. Another extreme example of this collective threshold of pain is when people feel like shooting up a Walmart or a concert venue is the only way out.

Humans are in biblical amounts of pain, and of course, we'll look for refuge in something that can alleviate or even drown this pain out: hello alcohol. This shared emotional and physical cellular pain our society carries at all times is what is forcing us to reach for something to ease the internal suffering, to forget it altogether, and to push our problems into another day. What's worse is we have been conditioned to put up a front that "all is good"—when shit ain't going well; at all. Author and spiritual teacher Eckhart Tolle says that what society has labeled as normal is actually insane, and it's getting worse. Author and historian Yuval Noah Harari makes a point in his smash hit *"Sapiens"* that although we are told tomorrow is going to be better than today, we've actually been in a several-thousand-year slow decline in overall happiness, which started with the agricultural revolution 12,000 years ago and is now accelerating in the industrial and technological age.

Despite living in what should be the "Golden Age" of information—where truth, centuries of research, and collective wisdom are merely keystrokes away—we find ourselves in a paradoxical reality. Many people are purposefully turning away from verifiable facts, choosing instead to inhabit echo chambers of misinformation. This phenomenon isn't accidental; it's engineered by individuals and organizations who have discovered that fabricating "alternative facts" is both profitable and powerful. Consider the absolute shit bag Alex Jones, who amassed millions by promoting the conspiracy theory that the Sandy Hook Elementary School shooting—where twenty children and six adults lost their lives—was a "false flag" operation designed to justify gun control. That such a claim could not only find an audience but create a lucrative empire reveals a fundamental breakdown in our relationship with truth and a blatant indicator that humans are headed down a perilous path.

When I saw the richest man in the world, at the 2025 presidential inauguration, give two very clear Third Reich Nazi salutes to the crowd in front of him, then to the crowd behind him, I immediately sold my Tesla stock and thought to myself—Damn… a drink would be nice.

While walking to the subway station in affluent Hoboken, New Jersey, just a short train ride to Manhattan, my friends and I were jumped by four soon-to-be gang members who we later found out were instructed to kick the shit out of white people as a gang initiation. While receiving stitches in my mouth at the emergency room from the oral surgeon, I remember telling myself, "When I get home, I'm getting completely fucked up," and that's exactly what I did.

Fires are burning in the Amazon rainforest, Glacier National Park will soon be glacierless, AI chatbots are replacing friendships with humans, hate crimes are on the rise, the Confederate flag appears to be making a comeback, misinformation and erosion of shared truth is rampant, oceans are becoming more acidic due to millions of tons of floating plastic in the seas, social media is hijacking the minds of our youth, and I can't seem to swallow the idea of spending $3 to 4K on childcare per month. There is constant pressure to be "productive" in a capitalist system that measures human worth by output. There is a 24-hour news cycle, with alluring graphics and tickers that bombard us with tragedy after tragedy without pause. There is a growing sense that systems are too broken to fix, creating an overall feeling of helplessness. Most are exhausted from having to curate perfect-looking lives on social media while deeply struggling privately. For most youth, the crushing weight of student loan debt will follow them for decades. We are expected to be constantly available via email, text, and messaging apps.

NO FUCKING SHIT people drink to excess. No mystery here. The pain of existing in today's world can be overwhelming, and alcohol offers a temporary escape valve that's socially acceptable and readily available.

It's Not a Drinking Problem, It's a Sobriety Problem

🐒 🐒 🐒

When MTV Jackass star Steve-O quit drinking, he said that he didn't suffer from alcoholism until after he quit drinking. The fact of it is that many people use alcohol as a way to make life tolerable.

Life is hard. Tremendously hard. Yes, there are miraculous moments, and at the end of this book, I'll try to drill the point home that we have already "arrived," that life is perfect just the way it is, but the fact of the matter is life can be an elbow to the groin at any time. The Buddha walked the earth for approximately six years as an ascetic, relinquishing personal possessions and wealth in hopes of learning the true nature of life. What he learned can be summarized in three words: life is suffering. Can you imagine coming home to family and friends, then being asked to share all about the adventures and travels that took place over the years, and the Buddha responds with "Guys, life is a total ass-kicking, and there's no getting around it. In addition, any attempts to sidestep this inevitable beatdown only result in more pain." This is actually his core teaching, and three of the four noble truths of Buddhism revolve around this concept.

In the book *When Things Fall Apart* by Pema Chödrön, the Buddhist nun talks about how addictions take hold when the edge of life is just a little too sharp and we lean on a substance or behavior for comfort. She uses the Tibetan word *shenpa* to describe this "sticky" hook—the moment we get caught in the urge for relief.

Yes, life can be a total bitch. There is a constant pressure weighing us down at all times. It could be your relentless boss, never-ending road construction, or the acceleration of pressure called gravity at 9.8 m/s^2, which is acting upon us at all times unless you find a way to leave the atmosphere. There is a spectacular phenomenon of birth and decay occurring in the universe at all times. Every minute inside the human body, thousands of cells multiply while thousands perish. Humans are born, and they die. Stars are born, then they die. Birth, expansion, retraction, and death are all expected components of the circle of life, which are all inextricably tied to suffering and pain.

However, life has always been like this and probably always will be. What has changed in recent history is that we are no longer sharing life's burdens with others. We're incredibly lonely. It's like we're all Texas Lone Rangers taking everything on the chin solo, which could be said is a death by individualism. We are social creatures, biologically wired for connection, and living life separated from the herd is excruciatingly painful for us, making the knife-edge of life just too sharp—especially when we live isolated lives. When we reach for a substance to dull or soften the edge of life, the foundational roots of an addiction begin to take hold.

The Growing Distance Between Us

🐫 🐫 🐫 🐫

Today, we are an incredibly lonely species, and it's getting worse. In the 1950s, the average American lived about 66 feet from their nearest neighbor. Today, that distance has increased to over 328 feet in many suburban areas. Meanwhile, the average American home has ballooned from about 980 square feet in the 1950s to over 2,400 square feet today—yet household sizes have shrunk. More people are living alone in larger spaces than ever before. We've literally built more walls between ourselves.

Our human bodies haven't gotten the memo that we're supposed to be independent islands of self-sufficiency. Our nervous systems are still operating on Stone Age software that expects us to be surrounded by our tribe. With increased solitude, stress hormones rise, and it turns out Netflix doesn't calm your cortisol like actual human touch. Studies show that immune systems weaken when we aren't surrounded by friends and family, causing us to be sicker—which we are currently seeing.

We've created a perfect paradox: we're constantly "connected" through technology while being physically farther apart than ever. We know that our old high school classmate's kid got third place in a wrestling tournament (thanks, Facebook), but we don't know our neighbor's name. The Western world teaches solitude and self-sufficiency, but one of the most reliable predictors of well-being and longevity is meaningful human connection. The Harvard Happiness Study, which started in 1938 and is the longest-running study on happiness, makes it abundantly clear that the quality and depth of your connections with other human beings determine your overall levels of happiness.

We are biologically, neurologically, and psychologically wired for connection, and we're not unique in this. Fish swim in schools, birds fly in flocks, prairie dogs kick it in colonies, and even trees have social lives beneath the surface where they share information and nutrients underground using fungal networks.

Humans...well, humans pay extra for detached housing and noise-cancelling headphones. When we don't authentically connect with other human beings, the release of oxytocin (the feel-good connection chemical, which is released when we form close bonds) diminishes, and serotonin production decreases in the stomach as the brain-gut axis is thrown out of balance. The brain's dopamine-driven reward system, which normally responds to genuine social connection, instead gets hijacked by external stimuli like TikTok—a terrible substitute for real human connection. Humans need connection for survival and wellbeing, and the data is in—thumb taps on your smartphone at 2:00 AM in hopes of connection don't even come close to meeting the requirement for human connection. We are pack animals living in our own oversized, self-imposed cages. No wonder more people than ever are turning toward alcohol, which, if I'm honest, at least in the beginning, provides a chemical substitute for connection. This intense feeling of separation at our core is what we are ALL trying to solve and soften.

The evidence is overwhelming: our modern way of living has created conditions ripe for addiction. We've built a society that maximizes stress while minimizing genuine human connection, then wonder why so many people turn to substances for relief. Understanding this context is crucial because it helps us see that addiction isn't a personal failing—it's a predictable response to an increasingly toxic environment.

But this is only part of the story. In the next chapter, we'll explore the biological and psychological factors that determine why these environmental pressures impact some people more than others.

Chapter 8
Alcohol and Addiction: The Biology and Psychology of Addiction

While environmental factors create the conditions for an addiction to flourish, individual biology and psychology factor in as well. In this chapter, we'll explore how modern alcohol has become a supercharged substance, why some people experience pleasure more intensely than others, and the fundamental biological drivers that make addiction to alcohol almost inevitable given enough time and exposure.

Supercharged Alcohol and How We Drink It

Two to three hundred years ago, alcoholic beverages weren't the ethanol-loaded rocket fuel that could launch a spaceship into orbit. Back then, beer was practically Mormon-approved, averaging a mild 3 to 3.5%. The ancient wine discovered at Göbekli Tepe ruins in modern-day Turkey (13,000 years ago) contained a modest 7 to 8% alcohol, and for thousands of years after, wine maintained this reasonable sip-to-buzz ratio. Hard alcohol? It barely existed as we know it today. The strongest drinks maxed out around 18-20%, basically hard seltzer by today's standards. Fast forward to now, a beer below 6% is practically labelled "children's menu." No self-respecting wine mom would be caught dead pouring anything less than 12 to 14% at a book club, and good luck finding college kids throwin' down shots of anything with less than 40% alcohol.

Just as the Industrial Revolution modernized everything it touched, it also revolutionized the alcohol industry. Using new machinery, techniques, and technologies, brewers, wine masters, and distillers learned how to basically double the alcohol content of the beverages in less time, with fewer materials, and, most importantly, with lower costs.

For the entirety of the Middle Ages (500 to 1500 CE), everyone from kings and queens to knights and peasants sipped on beer with a modest 3% alcohol content. Back then, yeast strains couldn't party hard enough to produce higher levels, and brewers struggled with temperature control. Fast forward to the Industrial Revolution, when beer makers got fancy with thermometers and hydrometers for precise measurements, while scientific discoveries shed light on the mysterious fermentation process. Today's brewmasters have access to overachieving yeast cultures specifically bred to create potent beers of 8% to 15% Alcohol By Volume (ABV), inspiring brutally honest names like "Delirium Tremens," "Liver be Damned," "Morning Regret," "Naptime Nectar," and "Blackout in a Bottle" that tell you exactly what you're in for.

With wine, same thing. For millennia, wine bobbed around 7 to 8% ABV. Only in the last 40 years have we seen the alcohol content rise from 10 to 12% in the 1980s to 13 to 14% in the 90s, and from the 2000s onward, wines in the 14 to 16% range—especially in warmer regions such as California, Australia, and parts of Spain. Specialized commercial yeast strains were developed that could tolerate higher alcohol environments. Previous yeast strains would die off as alcohol reached certain levels, making them alcohol's first victims. Grape growers found ways to delay harvesting to achieve higher sugar levels, and you betcha the grapes are genetically modified to yield a higher alcohol content.

With spirits (hard alcohol), it's actually an incredibly complex process to reach the 40% alcohol (80 proof) mark. Only at the turn of the 19th century had distillers figured out how to make drinks that bartenders could light on fire. Until about 1200 CE, hard alcohol maxed out at 25% using primitive stills and simple heat and condensation principles. By 1600, beverages reached 30% with the introduction of the alembic still and multiple distillation techniques. Then, in 1830, Aeneas Coffey revolutionized the industry with his continuous still, allowing for more efficient separation of alcohol from water. This made it consistently possible to produce spirits at 40% alcohol, establishing the standard benchmark for hard drinks we know today. With modern technology, distillers can create beverages with even higher alcohol contents—What's up, Bacardi 151.

The equivalent of giving anabolic steroids to our alcoholic beverages has yielded a dramatic rise in Alcohol Use Disorder (AUD) over the past 300 years—no surprise there. On top of that, how we consume alcohol as a culture has dramatically changed.

Drinking used to take place primarily in beer halls or alehouses and happened within view of the community, which created natural social regulation. Today, it is socially acceptable and even expected to drink in the following places: bars, restaurants, weddings, dinner parties, funerals, adult and children's sporting events, hair salons (men and women), on airplanes, on the toilet, in the shower, alone in the closet, in laundromats, fabric stores, bookstores, Zoom meetings (on or off camera), golf courses, mini-golf courses and yoga classes. Many also drink at home alone at night, during the day, and some get started upon awakening. Supercharged alcohol is now ingrained in every aspect of our culture, and we wonder why so many Americans struggle with alcohol use disorder…

Enhanced Dopamine Receptors

On December 17th, 2015, the podcast *Radiolab* released an episode titled "The Fix," exploring whether addiction could actually be treated with pills. At the end of the episode, almost in passing, they spoke about an evolutionary trait that gave some ancient humans a leg up, but ironically, in today's world, it can be a downfall. The concept they spoke about is what I call Enhanced Dopamine Receptors. There are 8 billion humans on the planet, and every single one of them feels pleasure (and pain) differently. Not everyone experiences the same level of euphoria when we take a drink, and when we sink our teeth into a maple donut, not everyone feels like they've been personally escorted to heaven's gates by a choir of angels like I do.

Past humans with enhanced dopamine receptors used to walk just a little farther to find shelter, warmth, and a mate. While the rest of the cave dwellers were like, "Eh, this rock is comfortable enough," our dopamine-charged ancestors thought, "But what if there's a cave over that mountain—with a south-facing view and granite countertops?" Dopamine plays a key role in learning and habit formation—it's the brain's way of rewarding us for repeating the same action over and over again. The catch is that "wanting" something isn't the same as actually "liking" it. What once helped us survive now backfires in a world where instant gratification is only a few clicks away.

I'm surprised more isn't written on this addiction theory. After I first learned about it, I thought I'd see more articles exploring how the sensation that alcohol gives us when we drink, for some, is almost too good to stay away from. It's like some of us got the premium cable package of pleasure sensations while others got the basic channels.

I've asked hundreds of people, both normal and problematic drinkers, what their first drink was like. Of course, all responses are different, but the common thread was that for normal drinkers, the experience of the first drink was a tepid to lukewarm experience—like sitting through a timeshare presentation. For many of those who later developed drinking problems, the experience of the first drink was like being handed the manual for life, and for many, they chased that feeling for the rest of their drinking careers. They hit the pleasure jackpot on their first pull and spent years chasing the initial high.

If someone has an enhanced dopamine system and lingering scars from childhood or whenever in life, then you have the prime ingredients for a major drinking problem. Imagine it's like following the world's most disastrous recipe: "Start with one hypersensitive pleasure system, add three cups of unresolved trauma, marinate overnight in your neighbor's Instagram feed who seems to have a perfect life, whisk together with a cup of generalized social anxiety. Let that sit for a decade while adding a daily spoonful of cultural normalization of heavy drinking and sprinkles of 'everyone else is doing it.' No baking required—just let sit until life crumbles."

Living life with an enhanced dopamine system is perhaps the rare case where genetics comes into play. A good way to describe this is saying that your genetics load the gun—you were born with a hypersensitive dopamine system—and the environment pulls the trigger, meaning you then encounter the right life conditions to become hooked on alcohol.

Fuck It, Let's Party

Addiction is complicated…or maybe it's not. Humans are biologically wired for pleasure, with sex for reproduction being at the top of that list. We're here for the party! This circuitry made things like a crisp apple or ripe blueberries taste divine. However, this wiring was built for a world of scarcity, and when we encounter abundance, our brain signals us to hit full send. For example, we have a genetic trait (CYFIP2 gene) that once instructed our early ancestors to eat every last wild cherry before a pack of raccoons could devour them first—and this same drive still operates in us today. Other mammals have this gene as well. Whales continue to hunt squid even when they are full and have difficulty swimming, squirrels are famous for caching way more seeds than they need, and grizzly bears have been observed taking naps during feasting because they can't seem to stop.

This tendency toward overconsumption makes evolutionary sense—in natural environments, food availability is unpredictable, so animals that maximize consumption when resources are available have better survival odds. Our brains developed reward systems that encourage this "feast when possible" behavior. The challenge for modern humans is that we've created an environment of perpetual abundance while still carrying these scarcity-adapted instincts, which leads to overconsumption of not just food but other substances and experiences.

The problem with non-stop hedonism is that the body and dopamine system aren't given time to properly reset. There's no scarcity phase after the feast. Modern humans are bouncing from one dopamine hit to another like pinballs in a machine operated by an over-caffeinated teenager. Maybe addiction is as simple as us trying to constantly "feel good" when our biological wiring actually expects and needs the phase of scarcity or rest afterward.

As humans who become addicted to alcohol, at first, we drank alcohol to feel good, then drank to feel normal, then drank to not feel like shit. This is dopamine's normal three-act play—from "WOOHOO!" to "meh" to "dear god, make it stop." Our dopamine system isn't wired to give us a 24/7 "Disneyland" experience. There are times when the party is supposed to suck. That's nature's way of telling us to go home and do our laundry.

Our ancestors had built-in boredom—no Netflix, no smartphones, no Spindrift variety packs. Their dopamine systems got regular breaks while they stared at clouds or waited for crops to grow. We've engineered a world where pleasure is available at the tap of a screen, but our stone-age brains haven't received the software upgrade. Humans at first thought we found the cheat code to "feeling good," but when we refuse to accept the natural rhythms of satisfaction and dissatisfaction, we're essentially throwing a temper tantrum against reality itself.

The 500-Year Theory

🐙 🐙 🐙

ALL humans would develop a dependency on alcohol if we lived long enough and alcohol were a constant in our lives. Studies show that very few people become addicted to the world's hardest drugs (alcohol included) if they try the substance only once. I once read that only 3% of cocaine users become addicted to the powerful stimulant after the first attempt. However, as renowned psychologist Sigmund Freud personally learned, cocaine becomes quite addictive if we repeat the behavior over and over. (Freud was an advocate that moderate cocaine consumption was beneficial to overall human health until he couldn't stop.)

I became physically and psychologically addicted to alcohol in my 20s; others in their 30s, 40s, and later in life. If humans lived for 500 years, and alcohol was a constant companion, then others would become addicted at age 153, 350, or 412. ("Sorry, I can't make your 400th birthday party, I'm checking into rehab...again.") The truth is that alcohol is an extremely addictive drug, and if you dance with the elixir long enough, coupled with the inevitable challenges of life, it will eventually pickpocket your soul, give repeated uppercuts to your liver, and deliver thousands of paper cut-sized wounds to your pancreas, which doctors would then one day tell you means you have pancreatitis. By that point, alcohol will have most of your organs looking like a well-used doormat at a frat house.

And here's the kicker—alcohol doesn't discriminate. It doesn't care about your job, your family history, or that you only drink "the good stuff." Given enough time, it'll have everyone raising a shaky hand at a meeting saying, "Hi, I'm [insert your name], and I'm an alcoholic." The only difference between the early and late adopters is just that—time.

While biology loads the gun and enhanced dopamine receptors determine how intensely we feel pleasure, there's another potent trigger that accelerates the timeline— pain and traumatic life experiences. Some people drink to celebrate life's victories, and others drink to numb life's defeats. In the next chapter, we'll explore how unresolved pain, childhood wounds, and life's curveballs can turn alcohol from a weekend companion into a daily companion, and why confronting those deeper core wounds is the key to freedom from the bottle.

Chapter 9
Alcohol and Addiction:
Trauma, Pain, and Healing

We've seen how modern society makes numbing agents, tranquilizers, and barbiturates feel almost essential for functioning. We've also learned that our biology isn't uniform—some of us are simply more sensitive to dopamine-driven "rewards," even though everyone falls somewhere on the same sliding scale. But what really drives us to seek relief in substances runs deeper: pain. Not just physical pain, but the profound emotional and spiritual pain of disconnection, trauma, and the human condition itself. In this chapter, we'll examine how pain fuels addiction and why, paradoxically, addiction might be exactly what some souls need to wake up.

The Precursor to Waking Up

🐒 🐒 🐒 🐒 🐒

In February 2019, I gave a talk at a Recovery Elevator conference in Nashville, Tennessee, and the point I was trying to make is that you are never on the wrong path, that it was the addiction that was trying to wake you up or show you a better way of life all along. I then went even further into the waters of woo-woo and said you chose this life path as an intense life curriculum for growth—or to wake up. When I walked off the stage, based on the amount of blank stares I received, I was like, "Well, bombed that one. I hope there are chicken wings at the buffet tonight."

Some of the attendees at the conference were there to save their marriages, one had recently received their third driving under the influence charge, and another had been bouncing from rehab to rehab without success. When we are in the throes of addiction, it's difficult to paint addiction with anything other than colors of doom: it's like being trapped in Freddy Krueger's nightmare or Skeletor's dungeon. But three years after that talk, someone in attendance told me how they finally understood what I was saying–that they now have an incredible life, one with less drama, more laughter, can roll with the punches of life more easily, and they have the addiction to thank for that.

If you go to recovery meetings long enough, you'll eventually hear someone say that they are a grateful alcoholic. The first time I heard this, my head sprang up from my slumped shoulders, and I was like, "What the hell did that guy just say?" And then he said it again, at the end of his share. In my mind, I was like, "Okay, I'll take care of this, everyone," and in my imagination, I walked across the room and double slapped the person who said they were thankful for becoming an alcoholic.

It was years before I understood and even realized that it was the addiction that destroyed me into the person I am today, and I'm extremely thankful for that. As I write this segment, I take breaks to look at the geometric shapes of palm leaves dancing in the breeze outside my office window in my home in Costa Rica, while I hear the laughter of my 10-month-old son as my wife and he play upstairs. I'm hesitant to label myself as someone who is "awake," but I can tell you I'm no longer asleep and simply going through the motions of life.

All the possible causes for addiction we have previously covered might be missing the bigger picture. Addiction is what sets fire to a way of life that is no longer bearing fruit, and then it could be said it's the catalyst that forces us individually and collectively into a more harmonious and balanced way of living. The twist: it's Freddy Krueger and Skeletor who have been cheering you on the whole time, even while they are trying to mess your life up—the villain of your story was actually the reluctant hero all along. You just had to give it time, make some shifts, and let the dust settle.

It's All About the Pain

🐙 🐙 🐙 🐙 🐙

19th-century German philosopher Friedrich Nietzsche coined the phrase "what doesn't kill you makes you stronger," which applies to basically everything, except childhood trauma or polio. Just like a tree sapling will carry a scar from childhood its entire life, humans also carry these emotional and physical wounds for a lifetime. You then discovered alcohol as a potent and highly effective way to alleviate or numb this lingering pain—and to that, I say nice job, you found a way. The source of this pain isn't your fault, but as quit lit author, Laura McKowen says, it is your responsibility to do something about it.

According to addiction expert, Dr. Gabor Maté, addictions are always a response to human suffering, with most experiences that make us prone to addiction happening in early childhood—sometimes even in the womb. He notes that all of his addicted patients in the Downtown Eastside in Vancouver (ALL OF THEM) experienced severe trauma in early childhood, such as physical abuse, sexual abuse, abandonment, or other forms. Loneliness is what I experienced in childhood, and I was amazed at how quickly the residual pain disappeared when I took my first drink at age 13. I thank the heavens that I wasn't physically or sexually abused as a child—if I had been, I'm certain I would have found relief in heroin or other harder drugs. Though alcohol is arguably the hardest drug out there.

In addition to painful childhood experiences leading to addictions later in life, traumatic experiences in adulthood can send us over the edge as well. A clear pattern has emerged after interviewing over 550 people with drinking problems. Many had seemingly normal relationships with drinking until a tragic experience occurred—loss of a parent, a job, personal injury, etc.—and then, like clockwork, their relationship with alcohol changed.

Almost every post-pandemic interviewee on the podcast said something like, "And then Covid happened." The pandemic, which absolutely qualifies as a major life stressor, pushed people's drinking over the edge.

These unavoidable life struggles are why I consider ALL drinking to be "gray area drinking." If we continue doing laps around the sun, it's only a matter of when life punches us in the Jimmy Britches, and if alcohol is a constant in our lives, there's a high likelihood that alcohol will be relied upon for relieving pain.

Again, all addictions are anchored to pain, serving as temporary escapes from suffering, and just plain boredom. We see this both on the individual and collective levels.

One myth I feel called to debunk in this book is the misconception that Native Americans have a genetic predisposition to alcohol abuse—nonsense. Indigenous tribes throughout the Americas and around the world knew very well how to make fermented beverages (it's quite easy, in fact), and many, such as the Anasazi Indians of the southwest, had incorporated alcohol into their ceremonies for thousands of years. The pattern of alcohol abuse only emerged after 85 to 95% of Native populations died from smallpox, measles, influenza, and typhus within 100 years of first European contact. Colonialism then forced them from their lands onto reservations without their primary food source, the buffalo, which was nearly purposefully hunted to extinction. They were then punished for speaking their own languages. Native populations faced unspeakable trauma and naturally turned to alcohol to mitigate this pain. No mystery here.

This is similar to why African American communities experience higher rates of addiction. Someone in their family lineage endured the horrific trauma of being forcibly taken from their home, separated from their family, and subjected to the brutal Middle Passage across the Atlantic, where millions perished from heat exhaustion, thirst, hunger, and disease. Those who survived were then sold into slavery, where lashings and beatings awaited them. This cosmic-level historical trauma has persisted through generations, affecting descendants for up to seven generations according to some researchers. Many African and Native Americans today still carry this inherited trauma while simultaneously navigating systemic inequities that create additional barriers to healing and advancement—a reality that would be irresponsible to recognize or deny.

Side note: In the book *Undaunted Courage*, the story of Lewis and Clark, there's a fascinating section about alcohol use among Southern plantation owners. The author describes how these slave owners stayed drunk from sunup to sundown—and they had to. How else could someone live with themselves while "owning" other human beings? Deep down, they knew it was wrong, so they numbed that knowing with constant alcohol.

If I were to describe the pain that leads us to addiction with one word, it would be disconnection, and if our symbiotic relationship with phones and technology continues, this disconnection or separation from our fellow humans and the rest of the living world will only increase. Specifically, in the last 300 years, humans have separated themselves from nature, from Mother Earth, from the soil, from food, from water, and fellow humans, and this causes a tremendous amount of unease (or dis-ease) within the human body. This is the primary reason why humans are suffering so much.

Millions of humans living in cities with polluted skies have yet to see the stars—those shiny glimmers in the night sky that connect us to our solar system, our extended home. 80% of Americans live with light pollution that prevents them from seeing the Milky Way, which the Incas called the sacred river–our spiritual tether to the heavens. When was the last time you felt soil between your fingers or sat in silence listening to birds instead of notifications? Our ancestors knew the names of plants that could heal or harm (there is no word for a weed in Quechua), felt the rhythm of seasons in their bones, and moved their bodies in harmony with the sun's journey.

This unprecedented disconnection humans experience daily is why our species is in so much pain. We reach for bottles instead of branches, scroll instead of stroll, and numb ourselves rather than feel the discomfort that is trying to guide us back to the pack. And it's not just the alcoholic or the addict. All humans bear the mark of this inescapable pain.

In 2016, author Johan Hari gave the TED talk "Everything you think you know about addiction is wrong," which shook up paradigms on how we view addiction. To summarize: the opposite of addiction isn't sobriety. It's connection. And further, the opposite of connection is disconnection, and we are an unbelievably disconnected species. Yes, we are more disconnected from our external worlds than ever, but this only mirrors the true source of the pain: the disconnection with the self.

It's a "Disease"

Before I begin this segment, I want to make it clear I'm not trying to convince anyone that addiction isn't a disease. The disease model is healthy for some, as it clearly states the severity of the situation and puts their drinking problem into a more manageable container. I'm also aware that in 1956, the American Medical Association classified addiction and alcoholism as a disease, so let's not forget that. The Affordable Care Act, passed in March 2010, views addiction as a disease and financially covers inpatient and outpatient addiction treatment, similar to other diseases such as cancer, asthma, and diabetes. When I first started the Recovery Elevator podcast over 10 years ago, I was in the camp that indeed addiction is a disease, and that alcoholism was a genetic trait that ran in families. However, the more I read, researched, and studied addiction, the more I came to believe these are adaptive or learned behaviors we employ as a way to survive in a batshit crazy world. In short, I don't think alcoholism is an inherited genetic disease, and this should come as good news.

The disease model somewhat falls apart when we try to put our finger on the disease. Especially when *The Big Book of Alcoholics Anonymous* mentions several times that drinking is but a symptom, meaning it's not about the alcohol, indicating the drinking, the alcoholism, is used to treat a deeper chronic disease or unrest…but what is it?

In 2015, I volunteered on a committee to help put on a three-day AA Roundup in my hometown. The committee was composed of members of Alcoholics Anonymous and Al-Anon, which is a 12-step group providing support to those who live or lived with alcoholic parents, family members, or friends. During one of the planning sessions, a gal from Al-Anon who doesn't struggle with alcohol said something about "her disease," and I remember my head jolting over with an inquisitive look, wondering, "Excuse me, what's the disease you have?"

The disease is not alcoholism—it's the human ego, or our thinking, which always sings a tune of unrest and is never fully satisfied for more than a brief duration. The baseline state of the thinking mind propels us to live in a chronic state of lack, fear, and scarcity. This perpetual unrest has been observed and recorded for thousands of years and seems to be intensifying in the modern age. When we lived in smaller packs and tribes, the group consciousness was almost a protective mechanism to keep the ego in check. But today, in our world of individualism and fractured communities, the ego is creating a wake of carnage, threatening the livelihood of the planet and all its inhabitants.

It's a disease of more—of always wanting more. What we have in front of us is never enough. Many Native American tribes had words to describe the chronic look of dissatisfaction on the white man's face, even after they gave them more and more land. However, the Native Americans also recognized their own ego, and in their legends, they created the fictional character of the Wendigo to teach the tribe to take only what they need and how overconsumption will eventually destroy us all. The Incas' word for this deep chronic restlessness was *pishtaco*, which roughly means "Boogie Man," and was commonly used to describe the Spanish Conquistadors who kept demanding more and more gold.

This insatiable hunger—whether for land, gold, or power—seems to be a universal human trait, at least for most who struggle with this "disease." Ancient wisdom traditions across the world recognized this tendency and created stories and warnings about it. The Buddhist concept of "hungry ghosts" with tiny mouths and enormous bellies symbolizes this same endless craving that can never be satisfied.

I think we are missing the mark and not directing our recovery efforts in the right direction if we emphasize Alcohol Use Disorder (AUD) as the disease. The true disease is the human ego, or our thinking. Again, this unrest seems to be accelerating. Remember how earlier I said that addiction is a modern phenomenon, something we have seen only in the modern world? Things are getting crazy—and not in a fun party way. However, I do feel we are not far off from the tipping point, usually prompted by pain, where we are forced to bring collective awareness to this insanity.

It's Genetic

You might be saying to yourself, "One monkey? Come on, Paul, it's clear that alcoholism runs in families." Even I have to admit, I've heard so many interviewees on the podcast say that one or both of their parents were alcoholics, and even I have a grandpa who was an alcoholic. This reasoning seems logical and also brings clarity to the whole "how the hell did I end up with a drinking problem?" question.

Earlier, I mentioned the idea of *enhanced dopamine receptors*—a biological sensitivity that might make some of us feel pleasure or reward more intensely than others. That's one small example of how genetics can *influence* susceptibility. But what I've learned over time is that influence isn't the same as predetermination. You can inherit a loaded gun, but it's the environment—and the pain we experience within it—that pulls the trigger.

I have, however, changed camps, and I no longer think alcoholism is genetic... This should come as good news, as you're not predetermined to struggle with alcohol forever based on your family history—nor are your children. What echoes through generations isn't a gene for alcoholism, but a cellular memory of chronic unrest—and alcohol is simply the salve we reach for to quiet the ache.

There are two main reasons why I no longer believe addiction or drinking problems are genetic. The first is the newer branch of science in developmental biology called epigenetics, pioneered by Dr. Bruce Lipton. He defines epigenetics as the study of how environmental signals—including thoughts, emotions, and beliefs—can modify gene expression without altering the genetic code. He emphasizes that cells read environmental signals, which then influence which genes are expressed. Lipton challenges the traditional view of genetic determinism, suggesting that our perception of the environment controls our biology more than our genes do. Further, according to current scientific understanding, only about 5 to 10% of diseases are purely genetic (predetermined). The vast majority—approximately 90 to 95% of diseases—are influenced by environmental factors and lifestyle choices. This includes conditions like heart disease, type 2 diabetes, and many cancers, which have genetic risk factors but are significantly influenced by environment, diet, stress, physical activity, and other lifestyle factors. This would also explain why many tribes in the Amazon basin of Peru, who share the same DNA as all humans, have yet to record a case of diabetes, metabolic syndrome, or multiple sclerosis, and their youth don't struggle with acne (think diet)—they have lower stress in their lives, don't eat processed foods, and don't make daily commutes on crowded freeways for 60-hour work weeks.

The second reason I no longer believe addiction is genetic is Dr. Gabor Maté's research and lived experience. As I mentioned earlier, he's made it clear that addiction stems from pain, not inherited genes. In fact, in his book *In the Realm of Hungry Ghosts*, he explores twin studies and finds that even identical twins raised apart can have vastly different relationships with substances. His conclusion? Our environments—not our DNA—determine how we cope, and pain, particularly in early childhood, is the common denominator.

It Doesn't Matter...

At the end of the day, it doesn't really matter what addiction is or what it isn't; you still need to do something about it. Even if you know exactly why you drink, or the drink seems to magically appear in your hand, you still have to move forward—ideally without alcohol.

I've spent years trying to understand the why behind my drinking, and that pursuit has become one of the most revealing journeys of self-discovery I've ever taken. But the truth of the matter is, I won't be able to ever fully pin down why I self-imploded with alcohol. Over the decades, I have sought many professional opinions, many who pulled the *Diagnostic and Statistical Manual** (DSM) off the shelf to tell me the exact ailment, disorder, or disease I have that seems to have derailed my life. All of these diagnoses turned out to be wildly incorrect. Turns out I didn't have "unipolar depression," "borderline personality disorder," or "bipolar disorder," but "beer for breakfast syndrome," and I needed to quit drinking.

I do think it's a noble and well-intentioned pursuit to uncover the nitty-gritty of why we drink, but much of that work consists of reflecting on the past. The healing journey is from here onward.

When we relentlessly scour the past for reasons why we drank, we take our energies from the only moment where true healing and peace reside—this very moment right now. It doesn't matter what you have, it doesn't matter what caused it—here we are, and now we have to deal with it. Your liver doesn't care if you're drinking because of childhood trauma or because you really like the taste of wood—bourbon. It's just taking notes for your next doctor's appointment.

I think now is a good time to remind you not to treat your addiction—or whatever you're facing—as something separate from yourself, and not to ignore it. Again, whatever you have doesn't really matter, but don't leave it in the car when you go shopping for groceries. Take your inner drunk to breakfast; just don't let it order mimosas. Befriend this part of you that seeks oblivion and self-destruction, invite it on your morning walks, and turn toward it with open and loving arms.

---

* *I think the Diagnostic and Statistical Manual (DSM) is one of the most dangerous books in existence because it will attach a disorder or syndrome to every single person who walks into a therapist's office, usually in under 10 minutes. One of the authors of the DSM-IV, Allen Frances, MD, later wrote a book about how the DSM is an out-of-control diagnostic tool that works in tandem with Big Pharma to overmedicate society.*

Remember, nearly all the causes of addiction listed above are attempts to escape the pain of separation or living a disconnected life. A drinking problem will go everywhere you go before you face it. It's a good idea to make peace with this part of your personality, name it, and become aware of when that part of you wants a double or triple gin and tonic. The "why" you drank, or what you "have," is revealed to you in real-time in the language of emotions and physical sensations. Many times I've said to myself, years after my last drink, "Ah, no wonder I became addicted to alcohol."

Another reason why it's partly a fool's errand to fully reveal the cause of our addiction is that there may be something much bigger taking place, something the human mind can't comprehend. We are looking for biomarkers or medical labels when there might be something taking place at the spiritual level. The addiction path may be what our souls choose in hopes of teaching us what really matters in life. Spiritual teacher Ram Dass, formerly known as Richard Alpert when he was a professor at Harvard University in the '60s, says our souls pick a life curriculum that gives us the best chances of waking up to our true nature. Many humans live an entire life without having to turn their gaze inward, but an addiction, if we choose healing, is what forces us to confront the thinking mind (ego) and then separate from it.

Whatever we are, or whatever we "have," is simply a snapshot of the collective tensions that have occurred in the past—and you have only a short snippet of the story since the forces that shaped your life were in motion long before you were born and before your parents were born. If we spend too much time dwelling in the past, in hopes of pinning down exactly where things went wrong, then our backs are turned from the only moment where healing begins—this moment right now. In fact, the addiction does everything in its power to pull you from the present moment.

Ruminating too much about what happened, what you have, and even how you're going to solve this is somewhat a fruitless effort. You have what you have, you are what you are. You have a yin to your yang, and a shoe to your foot. It's time to get busy living (alcohol-free of course), and maybe you're perfect just the way you are—there is nothing to fix, and you've never been on the wrong path. It's just the school of life. Unlike regular school, this one doesn't give you summer breaks or snow days, but the graduation parties are well worth it, and more people than ever are enrolling.

Understanding the role of trauma and pain in addiction is crucial, but it's only part of the journey. Now that we've explored why addiction happens, we need to address the practical reality: why is quitting so damn hard, and what can we expect when we try?

Chapter 10
Bar Owner in Paradise…

I returned to Granada, Spain, the summer before my last semester of college, with three friends, where we started the Granada Pub Crawl, a tour of the city's nightlife. I had a friend who was a wizard with Photoshop, so we created flyers, screen-printed some shirts, and within 10 days of arriving in Spain, we were taking 50-60 tourists to the best bars and clubs in the city for 10 euros ($12) per person. I said this in my last book, *Alcohol Is SH!T*. The Granada Pub Crawl should absolutely one day be its own book. We'd make 2,000 euros in four nights of the most epic partying one could imagine. On our days off, we'd rent a car and road-trip to places like Portugal or Barcelona and we flew Ryanair to Amsterdam on $18 one-way tickets.

One early morning, after a long night of leading drunk tourists through the windy Spanish streets from bar to bar, we arrived back at our apartment around 4:00 AM, where my three friends started drinking water. I wasn't ready for the party to end, and I remember looking at the water in my friend Sam's hand and then shifting my gaze to a bottle of vodka on the countertop. The progression into alcohol dependence is slow and steady, but that morning, my ship's sails caught a gale-force wind that sent me further into the waters of addiction, as this is when I started drinking solo nightcaps of vodka while my friends had called it a night.

Upon returning to America, my drinking returned to somewhat normal levels, and before graduating from college, I secured a job at an investment banking firm in Southern California. Three weeks before graduation, unable to sleep one evening, I realized I was completely uninterested in my future career as an investment banker, and the thought of wearing a suit and tie for the rest of my professional life was like a noose on the soul. While staring at the ceiling fan, I began reminiscing about the good life in Spain—where every night was a party, where I danced to the techno beats of Bob Sinclair, Daft Punk, and David Guetta in the best nightlife in the world, where music and alcohol brought everyone together, where the problems of the outside world didn't matter. Then it hit me, "Paul, screw this finance job, let's own our own bar in Spain." And that's what I did.

After graduation, I moved home to my parents' house in Colorado, where I worked three jobs and began saving as much money as I possibly could. Since I got my first DUI just five days after graduating college, the first $10K I made went to lawyer and court fees, but after that, my bank account started filling up as I was laser-focused on making my bar in Spain a reality.

My initial plan was to open a bar in the bustling metropolis of Barcelona. When I began researching liquor laws, I was astonished to learn that liquor licenses aren't even a thing in Spain. Want to sell hard lemonade on a street corner on a hot summer day? Go for it—even a kid can do it.

I still had contacts of bar owners from the Granada Pub Crawl summer, and I reached out to Rodrigo, who was the owner of our favorite bar where we took our inebriated customers on the Pub Crawl. When I told him my plan to open a bar in Barcelona, he let me know that his business partner was selling his shares in the bar and that I could be a 50% owner in the bar Dolce Vita, which is Italian for "The Good Life."

In less than 12 months, I saved $25K (thank you, Mom and Dad, for the free rent), borrowed another $15K from friends and family, then moved to Granada, Spain, where I was a 23-year-old bar owner in the most insane nightlife in the world.

Dolce Vita was small, maybe 600 square feet total, and we found our niche as a pre-party bar before going to the nightclubs. If you danced on the bar, you got a free shot. If you purchased a shot, you got Dolce Vita bucks that could later be exchanged for Dolce Vita shirts, hats, and even underwear. We set up deals with the nightclubs so that if they came into our bar and purchased a drink, they could get a discounted entrance into the clubs, and from 2:00 AM to 3:00 AM, we were completely packed.

The energy was electric. During peak hours, we had three bartenders, a bouncer, and a promoter in the streets passing out flyers. I'd bounce from serving sangria, shots, and *tubos de cerveza* to DJing a mix of hip hop, Spanish pop, and Euro House to our clientele from all over the world. After the bar closed at 3:00 AM, the Dolce Vita crew would head to the club, where we'd get ushered past the line of well-dressed partygoers like VIPs. There was always an endless supply of booze waiting for us, and I could invite anyone for a drink, for free, any night of the week.

The bar was thriving, I had a shoebox full of euros beneath my bed, and I was without a doubt living the Good Life. It seemed the party would go on forever.

After about three months of owning the bar, I thought it would be a good idea to scale back the drinking, especially during the week. I remember one Monday night bar shift, while walking to open the bar before 10:00 PM, I kept repeating to myself, "Paul, we're not drinking tonight. Paul, we're not drinking tonight." However, once I lowered the bar stools and played Lil Jon's "Snap Yo Fingers," I found myself with a beer in my hand just 10 minutes after opening. "Well, just one," I told myself. But then I had another beer in my hand when I played Snoop Dogg a few songs later—and keep in mind, there are no customers in the bar yet. I was already eight beers deep when the first customers rolled into the bar around midnight, and of course, I had to drink with them.

Within my first six months of owning the bar, I realized scaling back or taking breaks wasn't going as planned, and that's when I saw a flyer for the Granada American Semi-Pro football team. "That's it!" I told myself, thinking all I needed was a hobby to help tone down the drinking—and football had always been a rescue for me in life. So I went to the first practice, hungover, and made the team.

On the night of the first away game against the Barcelona Dragones, I worked at the bar but didn't drink. I closed the bar and hopped on the bus at 4:00 AM for the 12-hour bus ride to Barcelona, and about 30 minutes after leaving the bus station, I noticed I was the only one who wasn't sleeping. I was exhausted but couldn't sleep. It seemed like the bus's heater was on overdrive as beads of sweat dripped down my temples. I was about to ask the bus driver to turn off the heat when I noticed my hands began to shake. "Oh shit," I told myself as I realized I was withdrawing from alcohol while sitting next to a large Spanish defensive lineman who was sawing logs. When the bus seemed to come alive and get amped up for the game, I was in a cocoon of misery in the hood of my sweatshirt, wishing I was anywhere but there.

I seriously considered drinking a few beers before kickoff, which I probably should have done since I was in no shape to play a tackle football game against other large adults. While strapping on my shoulder pads, a teammate noticed I was already covered in sweat. "¿Todo bien?" (All good?) he asked. "Yeah, I just get nervous," I responded.

With each collision with another player, it was as if nuts and bolts were rattling loose inside me. I was almost thankful I separated my right shoulder at the end of the third quarter, so I didn't have to play anymore—but now I had a third-degree shoulder separation to deal with.

After the game, the team stopped at McDonald's before the 12-hour bus ride back home, and when I saw beer on the menu, there was no hesitation. With my right arm in a sling, my left hand shuttled four beers to my mouth before getting on the bus. When we stopped to refuel at 1:00 AM, I bought a bottle of vodka, which allowed me to time warp back to Granada. When I visited the doctor the following week, I learned the shoulder separation was serious enough that I would be out for the season—I was devastated and in a lot of pain.

When Christmas came that year, I told my business partner I'd paint the bar while he visited his family in France. On Christmas Day, I found myself alone, painting the ceiling and walls of Dolce Vita jet black—the same color my organs were turning. Before noon, I found myself with a paintbrush in one hand and a beer in the other. I then went outside and asked a homeless guy if he wanted to help me paint, and I'd pay him with beer. So until 11:00 PM, on Christmas Day, Javier and I painted a bar together while getting shitfaced. Surprisingly, Javier, who seemed to only speak in grunts and head gestures, was quite good with a paintbrush as long as I kept the beer flowing.

Looking back, that was hands down the loneliest Christmas of my life. And I wasn't even alone. I had Javier there, grunting his way through small talk and crushing it with a paintbrush as long as I kept refilling his glass with beer.

Within a year of owning Dolce Vita, I was drinking 20+ drinks per night, seven days a week. On Thursdays, we had a promotion called Power Hour, where for 15 euros ($20) you'd get a shot of sangria every minute for an hour. I would, of course, participate, and I'd have 60 shots of sangria, and then go on to drink another 15 to 20 drinks on top of that. By then, blackouts were nightly. Most mornings, I woke up with a dull fear, unsure if I'd even locked the bar. Yet, somehow, the door was always shut, the cash counted, the liquor restocked. My body kept functioning, even as my mind unraveled.

At 20 months in Spain, I was a full-blown functioning alcoholic. In the mornings, after getting one to two hours of sleep, I'd shuffle to the convenience store across the street that opened at 6:00 AM and buy two beers and a box of wine. I'd pour the two beers into a large glass, and while the beer was warming in the microwave so I could drink the beer faster, I'd chug the box of wine. I'd then drift off into a drunken stupor, where I'd wake up at 2:00 PM in a malaise of fog and pain before starting it all over again that night at the bar.

Sometime during my second year in Spain, I got my second DUI while driving on the Mediterranean coast. Since my tolerance was so high, when I blew an outrageous number on their breathalyzer, the Spanish Policía were like "Dios mío," and one of them said, "You know in America they'd take you to jail for this." I then said, "Well, what happens here?" The officers then pulled out a laminated graph that indicated I had to pay a 350-euro fine ($450) and how much time I had to sit in the car before I was safe to drive home. Since I had blown such a high blood alcohol content, they told me to wait in the car for at least six hours before I could resume safely driving the vehicle. Thirty minutes after the police left, I pulled back onto the freeway as the morning light crested over the Sierra Nevada Mountain range.

Like any drug, you need more and more of it to get the same effect, and my drinking hit new levels in my third year of owning the bar. On my days off, I'd drink entire bottles of vodka in my apartment alone, and most times, while blacked out, I'd go buy bottles that I didn't even remember buying or drinking. The binges killed my appetite, and before each bar shift, I had to force myself to eat a shawarma or street hot dogs.

One evening, after a multi-day binge, I sat alone in my sixth-floor apartment, staring at the open window across the room. Without thinking, I stood up and started running toward it. Somewhere deep inside, I knew exactly what I was about to do. But just before I reached it, my knees buckled and I collapsed onto the floor, gasping in panic. A part of me wanted out—permanently.

A couple of weeks later, in a binge while blacked out, I took four Ambiens and slept for two days straight. Ambien is an incredibly potent sleeping pill that can suppress the nervous system to such a point that a person stops breathing—think Hollywood star Heath Ledger, who died at age 28.

This was a major wake-up call for me, and I knew unequivocally that if I stayed in Spain, I wouldn't make it home alive. So at age 27, I walked away from Dolce Vita. I lost thousands of dollars, my pride and ego were crushed, but I was alive. Barely.

Those three years in Spain were simultaneously the best and worst of my life. On one hand, I was living an absolute dream. I was in my mid-twenties, owning a thriving bar in the heart of Granada's legendary nightlife, DJing at massive clubs until sunrise, and genuinely living "La Dolce Vita" in every sense of the phrase. The energy was intoxicating, the money was flowing, and I had visions of opening my own nightclub. For fleeting moments, I felt like I was exactly where I was supposed to be—young, fearless, and riding the wave of pure possibility.

But underneath all the glittering surface was a darker truth: I was medicating profound loneliness with ethanol, one shitty box wine and cerveza at a time. Being thousands of miles from family and everything familiar, I unconsciously and consciously turned to alcohol to fill the void. At first, it worked beautifully—it made my Spanish perfect, created instant connection, the perfect social balm for a nocturnal life. But ethanol is a terrible therapist. It promised to solve my isolation, but ended up creating a prison of its own. It became a desperate daily ritual just to function, and eventually, it nearly became my death sentence.

Sometimes I torture myself with the "what if" game. What if I hadn't become so undeniably addicted to alcohol? Would I have opened that nightclub? Would I still be living some alternate version of my dream life? But maybe—just maybe—the drinking problem was actually a form of protection. Maybe it was my soul's way of forcing me off a path that looked glamorous but was ultimately unsustainable. Maybe crashing and burning in Spain wasn't my failure—it was my rescue mission, guiding me back home to discover who I really was beneath all that liquid courage. Looking back now, I can see what I couldn't then—addiction had been the invitation all along. A painful but necessary wake-up call reminding me to live differently, to step into a better, truer version of the good life.

Chapter 11
Why Quitting Drinking Can Be So Hard

I want to keep this book real: Quitting drinking may feel like you're riding a unicycle through a hurricane, at least in the initial phases. It may feel like Mike Tyson is using your brain as a speed bag for a couple of months after you take your last drink.

A doctor may tell you that you have PAWS, or post-acute withdrawal syndrome. Nonsense—I call them healing symptoms. Your body is recalibrating without alcohol, sometimes overcorrecting, sometimes undercorrecting. Author Allen Carr said something similar about quitting smoking—once he viewed the sensations of withdrawal as signs of healing, he actually began to enjoy the process, going from a hundred cigarettes a day to none. I promise this period of discomfort will pass, and the pros highly outweigh the cons. Without a doubt. And like anything rewarding in life, it usually comes with a challenge.

Why is it so hard to quit drinking? I know it was for me. A rare few seem to spontaneously cartwheel into sobriety, but for most of us, the process takes years—from that first moment we recognize the internal voice saying, "Hello, let's please stop drinking poison," until the day we take our last drink. It's a roller coaster of stops and starts, more stops, even more starts, before (hopefully) we reach that permanent stop.

We are constantly in search of homeostasis. Seeking harmony is built into our biology—we've always been wired to return to balance. When we find something to help us achieve a more coherent vibration, aka feel less pain, we double-stamp the experience, and we never forget it. It gets triple-stamped when we repeat this behavior and get the same results. Drinking, or whatever makes us feel better, then gets inserted into the unconscious at a faster clip and always sits at the top of the deck—even if it's been years to decades since the last drink. When something becomes so effective, so reliable, so easy to acquire, and so socially acceptable that it delivers relief every time, the brain will always choose this option first for fast-acting relief, even if it's poisonous.

Quitting drinking is hard for many reasons, but at its core, it's about pain. You're going to feel pain in the initial stages without alcohol. As we covered earlier, Dr. Gabor Maté says addictions are always a response to pain, suffering, and trauma. In addition, he says that all addictions start and end with pain. There is no single reason why quitting drinking can be such an ass-kicking, but here are some factors that frequently come into play (keep in mind, the ass-kicking is only temporary, and there is a shame-free ocean of peace awaiting you on the other side):

Quitting drinking can feel like a total beatdown because alcohol is a highly addictive chemical. Your body will revolt like a toddler who's been eating ice cream every day, and then they're suddenly offered broccoli instead. This is called alcohol withdrawal, and a hangover is a prime example of this. The pain game of detox usually passes in the first 72 hours, but can go on longer. Side note: I mentioned this earlier, and I'll say it again because it's that important—alcohol is the most dangerous drug to detox from. R.I.P. Amy Winehouse. In severe cases, withdrawal can trigger seizures or delirium tremens (DTs), which can be life-threatening, especially for long-term or heavy drinkers. Each withdrawal episode also increases the risk of what's called the kindling effect—where symptoms become more intense and dangerous every time someone quits and relapses. While many people can quit cold turkey, please talk to a medical professional first—especially if you're a daily drinker.

It's hard to quit drinking because it becomes inextricably tied to the release of dopamine. If you've been drinking consistently for years, without many pauses, then your brain's reward system has been trained to await the introduction of alcohol before it releases dopamine—the feel-good (or learning) chemical. You'll eventually reach a point when you only feel good when you're drinking. When we stop drinking, it's a pleasureless state of anhedonia to the max, until your brain learns other ways to release dopamine.

The good news is that with the brain's ability to change (neuroplasticity), your brain's dopamine system will eventually become responsive to healthier activities such as reading a good book or going on a walk with friends. The time frame is different for everyone, but with time, your brain will return to its state where the simpler things in life bring the greatest pleasures. If you liked being a kid, then it's good news, as you'll be returning to a more childlike state where so little can suffice for happiness—like a snow cone.

It's hard to quit drinking because your subconscious is still clinging to those outdated myths that alcohol is somehow good for your health, your circulatory system, and will magically help you relax. Thank goodness, in the last five years, the truth about alcohol has finally started breaking through, and I can summarize it for you in three simple words: Alcohol is SH!T. It's not good for you. Not a drop, not a glass of expensive wine, nor a novel craft beer—none of it.

It's hard to quit drinking because it's a major change, and humans don't welcome change. The habit loop is powerful. Your brain has thousands of neural pathways saying "bad day = drink," "good day = drink," "Tuesday = drink." You're going to have to learn new routines, create new habits, and figure out a way to fill the time that used to be spent drinking. A big one here is boredom. You're gonna have a lot of extra time on your hands. But this also presents an incredible opportunity to explore new hobbies and go after your hopes and dreams. Want to be a professional bass fisherman? Go for it. Want to read all seven Harry Potter novels and remember them? Then go for it. Want to visit the seven ancient wonders of the world and remember the facts from the tour guide? Then go for it.

Quitting drinking can feel like swimming upstream in our booze-soaked world. From NASCAR races and school functions to funerals, alcohol seems to be the universal plus-one at every gathering. It's like you're trying to quit gluten while living in a bakery. But here's the truth: when you quit alcohol, you're not swimming against the current—you're finally going with the flow. It's everyone else who's paddling upstream, making life harder than it needs to be with their hangovers and 3:00 AM regrets. You? You're just gliding along, wondering why you didn't quit earlier. And, gratefully, the sober curious movement has seriously taken off in recent years as more people come to terms with the fact that alcohol is, indeed, sh!t.

Quitting drinking can be hard because you might be the only one on the block who doesn't drink. Social pressure is real. "Just one drink" is the phrase that's launched a thousand relapses. Friends don't understand that your "one drink" works like Pringles—once you pop, you can't stop. At first, you might feel lonely—but good news: my alcohol-free community, Café RE (mentioned back in the intro), is *THE* social app for sober people. And a note on "everyone is drinking"—this isn't actually true. A recent 2025 Gallup poll showed that only 54% of Americans now drink alcohol, which is the lowest in 90 years of tracking.

Quitting drinking can be hard because of the stigma. MAJOR good news here—the stigma is fake. At least that's been my experience with it in the last 10 years of telling thousands, well, millions, that I no longer drink. When you tell someone you no longer drink, the planets will not fall from orbit, and 99/100 times, you'll get a positive response. That 1/100 negative response is an indication that the person needs to be removed from your life (and could be an indicator that they also have an unhealthy relationship with alcohol).

Quitting drinking can be a reality check with brass knuckles because there's a mountain of emotions waiting to be felt. But, you'd rather face this on your own accord rather than have Mount Saint Helens erupt from your solar plexus while shopping at Costco.

Quitting drinking can be hard because stress doesn't magically disappear. That presentation still terrifies you, your in-laws are still coming to visit, and your boss still has unreasonable expectations.

Alcohol was your fire extinguisher for these problems…until it started spraying gasoline.

Quitting drinking can be hard because the identity crisis can be real.

"Who am I if I'm not the life of the party? The wine connoisseur? The beer pong champion?"

Quitting drinking can be difficult because you suddenly have to develop actual hobbies. Because drinking on patios doesn't count anymore.

Quitting drinking can be hard because you have to face reality—how do they say it in AA?—living life on life's terms. You miss the permission slip to check out from reality. Sobriety means facing life's uncomfortable moments without your liquid escape hatch. However, without booze in your life, you'll recognize you were fighting life problems with oven mitts. Problems still arise in an alcohol-free life, but you're better equipped to deal with them.

Quitting drinking is an epically challenging endeavor because the same person who got you into this conundrum is the one tasked to get you out of it. It's like hiring a plumber to fix a leak, and during the process, the plumber creates three more leaks. Then calling the same plumber to fix the original and additional leaks is like you being called in to solve the drinking problem. Now seems like a good time to insert the Einstein quote that says you can't fix a problem with the same level of consciousness that got you into the problem. This is why leaning into the support of a recovery group is so important—because your thinking, at the moment, is the problem.

Quitting drinking is a slap in the forehead because you're gonna find yourself with a refreshing surplus of time, money, and peace. Wait, that's a damn good thing :)

Quitting drinking is HARD, with a capital H, because even though you'll start to feel better, it will be so unfamiliar to you. It sounds strange, but when feeling like dog turds is your baseline, anything different is going to feel uncomfortable. This is a big one, and is linked to self-sabotage. Even if your baseline state caused by alcohol is depression, anxiety, and loads of guilt, this is still preferred over the unknown.

Quitting drinking is HARD because part of you wants to quit, but a near-equal part of you is clinging to that bottle like it's the last life jacket on the Titanic. We've had countless people sign up for our alcohol-free community Café RE, only to receive an email 47 seconds later asking for a refund. We've had one gentleman in particular who's signed up for almost every single Recovery Elevator retreat, then cancels moments before the cancellation deadline. He's basically our phantom retreat member. Part of us says, "YES, I'm ready to step into my new life!" While the other part says, "Nope, no fucking way. I'm building a blanket fort with my empty tequila bottles, and nobody can make me come out."

The Light at the End of the Tunnel

Yes, quitting drinking is one of the most challenging things you'll ever do. It requires facing pain you've spent years avoiding, rebuilding your entire identity, and learning to live without your most reliable coping mechanism. It means feeling everything—the good, the bad, and the unbearably uncomfortable—without your liquid escape hatch.

But here's what no one tells you about the other side: the person you become through this process is someone you could never have imagined. The clarity, the genuine connections, the ability to handle life's punches without falling apart—these aren't consolation prizes. They're the real treasure.

Nearly every person I've interviewed who has successfully quit drinking says the same thing: "I wish I had done it sooner." Not because sobriety is easy, but because the person they discovered underneath all that alcohol was worth every moment of discomfort it took to find them.

The journey from addiction to recovery isn't just about removing a substance from your life. It's about removing the barriers to becoming who you were always meant to be. And that person? That person is worth fighting for.

In the coming chapters, we'll explore exactly how to navigate this transformation—not just the practical steps of quitting, but the deeper work of building a life so fulfilling that you'll wonder why you ever needed to escape from it in the first place.

Chapter 12
Geographical Cure

Upon returning to America with my tail between my legs after walking away from the bar, I was detoxing from alcohol so severely that I had audible hallucinations for three weeks (which scared the absolute shit out of me). I thought I was going crazy and even asked people if they could hear bagpipes and trumpets…they could not. I'm thankful for my parents, who provided me a safe place to let my pride and physical body heal. I was hoping the drinking wouldn't follow me from Spain, but that wasn't the case. However, since I wasn't slinging drinks in a bar till 4:00 AM, I drank less, which my body thanked me for.

That year at my parents' house in Colorado, I found that it was easier not to drink at all than to drink and shut it down after one or two. However, when I did drink, I still found myself filling glasses with vodka for solo nightcaps, and I was blacking out nearly every time I drank. A classic trait of alcohol addiction is the blinders it puts on the individual consuming the drug. Even though, while owning Dolce Vita, I drank enough alcohol for several lifetimes and blacked out for probably a year total, I didn't consider myself an alcoholic. I even met with a therapist that year after returning from Spain, and she delicately asked if I thought alcohol was a problem in my life or if I had a drinking problem. I gave her a courtesy pause, then vehemently responded with "No, it's not." But yes, it most definitely was.

In early 2009, I was accepted into a graduate program at the University of Washington. That summer, I loaded up a U-Haul and moved to Seattle, hoping to once again leave my drinking behind. But when I found myself replacing my new roommate's bottle of Jack Daniel's for probably the seventh or eighth time, I knew something had to give.

On January 1st, 2010, with a pounding hangover, I walked into a Barnes and Noble and pulled the book *Beyond the Influence* by Katherine Ketchum, off the shelf, found a hidden nook in the store, and began reading. With an Owl City album playing through the bookstore's speakers, I read with shaky hands, sweat dripping off my brow, and with each passing page, I kept thinking, "Oh shit," I need to quit drinking and probably for good.

Now, if you had called me an alcoholic, I would have told you to pump the brakes and probably thrown a shoe at you, but the idea that I needed to remove alcohol from my life was landing.

The plan was to go 30 days without alcohol. Just a reset. A break. Let the body and brain recalibrate. But when that 30-day mark arrived, I felt...different. Not perfect, not "healed," but better in a way that was hard to explain. The fog had started to lift. My anxiety was no longer operating at DEFCON 1. I was sleeping through the night. So I decided to keep the feel-good train rolling—and to my surprise, I actually did.

I cruised past day 30 to 60, then 90. I didn't call it sobriety or announce it to the world—I just kept doing what was working. I focused on my health, exercised daily, cooked my own meals, and stayed out of the usual drinking scenes. And every night, I read *Beyond the Influence* like it was my personal quit lit bible. The pages were dog-eared and full of highlights. On rough nights, I'd revisit the same few chapters that helped talk me off the ledge.

When I did go to social events, I'd bring a dark beer bottle filled with water to avoid questions. I wasn't trying to fool anyone—I just didn't want to explain something I was still figuring out myself.

That same year, I landed a graduate assistant football coaching position at Montana State University in Bozeman. And it's not a coincidence that within ten months of removing alcohol from my life, I had a giant, bling-filled Big Sky Championship ring on my finger. The Bobcats had a hell of a season, and I got to be part of it. I finished my graduate degree with a 4.0 GPA, and without the chaos of drinking, I was finally able to show up for my own life.

For 2.5 years, I didn't touch a drop of alcohol, and my life transformed. But I was essentially just gritting my teeth through sobriety, never addressing the underlying wounds that had driven me to the bottle to begin with. This dry drunk phase eventually became incredibly boring and even lonelier—I wasn't throwing them back with my old friends, and I hadn't found any recovery friends either.

Around 900 days without a drink, my friend Anna reached out to me because she was struggling with alcohol, so we went to an AA meeting, which happened to be a first for both of us. I had it in my head that I was only there to support my friend Anna, and I was already cured, because after all, I had just gone a couple of years without a drink. With each passing share in the meeting, an electrical current began to grow inside of me. I heard stories of job loss, traffic accidents, divorce, homelessness, bankruptcy, jail time, and someone even served a long prison sentence for killing someone while driving under the influence. None of these things had happened to me, and despite the firestorms of pain alcohol had brought me, the idea of "hold on a second, maybe I don't have a drinking problem," took hold. I drank two days later, and the plan to just have a couple turned into 25+ drinks.

The first word out of my mouth the next day, when I woke up shortly before noon, were "S...H...I...T..." It was a wake-up call that I didn't have anything under control, and the beast alcohol hadn't been tamed at all; in fact, the claws seemed sharper than before.

After that drunken night in August in 2012, I got back on the sobriety train and logged another 10 months, then 4 months, then 6 weeks, then 2 weeks, then 8 days, then 3 days—then hello merry-go-round from hell, as I found myself on a vicious cycle of day ones, over and over.

Looking back, I thought the hardest part was behind me. I'd proven I could quit—hell, I'd done it for almost three years. I figured it was just a matter of willpower and white-knuckling my way through the cravings until they disappeared forever. But what I didn't understand yet was that sobriety without healing is just holding your breath underwater.

Eventually, you have to come up for air. Each relapse was like a fever spike, my soul's way of saying "school is still in session."

The biggest battle wasn't going to be fought against the bottle. It was going to be fought in the depths of my own heart, in places I hadn't even discovered yet. Places where the real reasons I drank were hiding, waiting for me to finally have the courage to look.

Chapter 13
A Toxic Culture

"Some poor phoneless fool is probably sitting next to a waterfall somewhere totally unaware of how angry and scared he's supposed to be" - Comedian Duncan Trussell

No Kidding You Have a Drinking Problem

Using alcohol as a tool to navigate a toxic culture is totally normal. I would even go so far as to say that you should congratulate yourself for finding a way to survive in a world that has lost its compass. What we've collectively labeled as normal—our cherished societal structures and daily rhythms—is actually a carnival of madness masquerading as sanity.

The gleaming facades of our wealthiest nations mask a growing epidemic of inner turmoil. Beneath the surface of our technological utopia, a raging storm has been intensifying: anxiety and depression surge, cancerous cells multiply, autoimmune disorders flourish, chronic pain becomes increasingly prevalent, and suicide claims more lives than ever, all while addiction tightens its grip.

These afflictions aren't random outliers but interconnected symptoms—warning flares from bodies and minds rebelling against the unnatural cadence and toxic foundations of our modern existence. In today's fast-paced world, all of these conditions of extreme unrest are manifestations of a toxic way of living.

How do we fix this? Just like we can't do anything about our drinking until we become aware of it, we first have to recognize our own collective and individual bullshit. This awareness won't come from the top down—it will come from the bottom up. I still have a sliver of hope that the internet, the greatest invention of our time, might actually help facilitate this transformation. Ironically, it's the rapid rise of addictions that could spark the next leap forward for humanity, since it's often the intense pain that forces us to turn our gaze inward.

For us, we chose alcohol—for others, it's sex, gambling, crack, heroin, fentanyl, shopping, work, incessant scrolling, caffeine, sugar, food, exercise, narcissism, hoarding, perfectionism, codependency, self-harm, cutting, picking, pulling, purging, binge eating, and that's the short list.

And when people reach their breaking point where nothing seems to relieve their pain and desperation, they shoot bullets into concert venues, drive cars into crowded areas, or—now more than ever—point guns at their own heads and pull the trigger.

In 1972, Dr. Bruce Alexander conducted the infamous Rat Park experiment, demonstrating it's the environment, or way of life, that creates the conditions for an addiction to take hold. Alexander placed a lone rat in a cage with drinking water and then another bottle of drinking water laced with cocaine. It was only a matter of time before the lonely rat overdosed and died. Every time. Sad face emoji. You take that same rat, place him in a cage with water, cocaine, friends, potential mates, running wheels, caves to explore, a tiny drum set, and Netflix, and the rat will sample the intoxicating elixir once or twice. But invariably, he'll abandon the fleeting high for something far more potent: the warm press of fur against fur, the gentle chatter of his companions, the irreplaceable chemistry of connection. Given paradise with all its temptations, our small protagonist chooses community over chemistry every time.

Current behavior displayed by humans in the cage of planet Earth, at least in the rich modern world, indicates we are a sad, lonely lot who are constantly seeking wholeness in chemicals, which temporarily do help, but in the long run only bring us pain, increased dissatisfaction, and extreme unease.

It's worth noting that the most insidious addiction facing humanity right now isn't even a substance—it's our relationship with screens and technology. Unlike a bottle, you can't simply put your phone back on the shelf. This dependency weaves itself into nearly every part of our lives, and in time, it may be the river all of humanity is forced to cross together.

In a fictitious world, if a psychologist could analyze all 8 billion humans and give a psychoanalytical diagnosis, it would be *species-wide disconnection syndrome* with *maladaptive coping mechanisms*, coupled with *planetary attention deficit hyperactivity disorder*—with a side of *"I'm the main character" syndrome.*

Psychologist's notes: Patient presents with bizarre, contradictory behaviors, including creating social media accounts to feel connected while becoming increasingly isolated; developing life-saving technologies while simultaneously inventing more efficient ways to destroy each other and the earth; amassing absurd wealth while complaining about insufficient resources; and spending decades learning how to communicate—primarily to argue with strangers online.

Patient exhibits a remarkable ability to quickly recognize insanity in others while remaining completely oblivious to their own.

Notable symptoms include: building massive climate-controlled structures to avoid nature while paying premium prices for "natural" products; declaring themselves the most intelligent species while requiring warning labels not to eat laundry detergent.

Prognosis: Given the fact that the patient has waged a full-scale war on the very thing that is keeping them alive—Planet Earth and Mother Nature—patient will most likely end up in self-destruction mode, killing themselves and probably all other humans. This psychologist recommends an immediate reality check and follow-up appointment scheduled ASAP (if the patient is still alive). This case is grim—the grimmest of all. At this point, an evolutionary leap may be the only solution, as all traditional remedies have failed.

All addictions are born out of chronic unrest and are representations that we are living wildly out of sorts with how humans are wired to live. Native Americans viewed these diseases of unrest as canaries in the mine, signaling to the tribe that something is out of balance and needs to be corrected ASAP.

The 600+ mass shootings and 83 school shootings that took place in America in 2024 are a whole flock of canaries saying, "Yo, something is fucked here—as in drastically broken." The 50% increase in new cases of depression from 1990 to 2017, seen mostly in the richest countries, is a BLARING RED FLAG indicating our value systems are fundamentally wrong. America, the richest country in the world, is now experiencing a drop in life expectancy that doesn't seem to be reversing.

Fire season has grown by 80 days since the 1970s, and Inuits in Alaska are having to invent new words for species they've never seen before, like a robin, which used to never travel that far north, because the planet is heating up at a faster rate than normal. According to paleontologist Dr. Kenneth Lacovara, we are in the middle of a mass extinction where Earth has lost 615 species in the last century—more than 100 times the natural extinction rate—and there are 70% fewer animals and fish on the planet today than there were in 1970. Mammals, fish, birds, reptiles, amphibians, sharks, the Bornean orangutan, the leatherback sea turtle, the black-footed ferret, the African wild dog—they're all peacing out.

According to author Dr. Zach Bush, chemical farming, or our modern food system, isn't building complete human beings. Further, if you follow the standard American diet (SAD), you'll find yourself with a chronic condition such as high blood pressure or diabetes. In 2024, author Jonathan Haidt published the book *The Anxious Generation*, written about Gen Z (born between 1997 and 2012), focusing on how smartphones and social media have critically impacted their psychological development and well-being.

None of this level-ten bullshit is separate from your drinking—in fact, using the powerful depressant ethanol to seek relief or to numb out these painful realities is almost predictable.

In 2022, Dr. Gabor Maté and his son Daniel Maté published a siren call titled *The Myth of Normal*, which was one of the hardest books I've ever read because it's 497 pages of revelatory doom and gloom that makes it unequivocally clear that our way of life is what is causing all these unprecedented levels of disease, unrest, and addictions.

There are many reasons we drink, but the primary reason is we're looking for connection in a world that is becoming increasingly more disconnected. Studies show people's self-reported rates of loneliness have doubled in the last 20 years. The average time spent engaging with friends was 60 minutes a day in 2003 and decreased to 20 minutes a day in 2020. Single-person households accounted for 13% of all U.S. households in 1960—it more than doubled to 29% of all households in 2022. According to the Cigna Corporation, 43% of Americans feel they don't have someone in their life to talk to about serious issues. Apparently, loneliness wreaks havoc on your health and is the equivalent of smoking 15 cigarettes a day, according to former US Surgeon General Vivek Murthy, who in 2024 issued a distress call saying we are now in a loneliness epidemic.

No mystery here, problem solved. You have a drinking problem because we are living in a society where numbing agents are expected, almost required. Our species is limping along, hoping the next technological or scientific breakthrough will put an end to our chronic unhappiness, but it has only added to the problem. We are living wildly out of balance, and this is why addictions are skyrocketing.

But a Symptom

In the Big Book of *Alcoholics Anonymous*, the most profound line, in my opinion, is "drinking is but a symptom." The DJ just did a back spin on the record and on the microphone just announced, "Yo, this has nothing to do with alcohol." We are using alcohol to address the feelings of deep disconnection and dislocation from our fellow humans, the land, animals, the food we consume, and most importantly, ourselves. We are using alcohol as a third-party substance to backfill unmet human needs in today's world of chaos.

In the Americas, there's a shared collective memory of the trauma indigenous groups endured when ripped from their lands that still causes pain for both white and Native. Black people in America, although thankfully no longer in chains, still face racial injustices that create suffering for all. This seemingly unsolvable pain makes everyone want to reach for a drink. Black, brown, white, yellow—we are all in pain.

I was lying on my back next to a fire at an ayahuasca retreat. Behind me, an African American woman I had never met, well into her journey with ayahuasca, appeared to be meeting God for the first time.

"Is that you, God? You're so beautiful," I heard her whisper as she wiped tears from her face. Then she added, "What's that? Them? Ah, they are. Indeed, I see it also."

She suddenly made a 180-degree turn, sat beside me, and placed her hand on my bare chest. "The white man is in so much pain," she whispered aloud while gazing into the heavens.

Of course we are. Only someone so disconnected from self and universe, living in constant fear, could put other human beings in chains and rip Indigenous peoples from their lands. One particular strategy was to kill all 30 to 50 million buffalo (bison is the correct term) in hopes of starving them out. They managed to kill all but 340 American bison. We are ALL in pain–including the bison.

All drinking problems, addictions, and diseases of the modern world are symptoms of this shared chronic pain. We're never satisfied for more than fleeting moments before this deeply seated unrest bubbles to the surface again. Modern economies have thrived in this environment, birthing consumerism as a way to distract ourselves with products that promise eternal happiness yet inevitably come up short. The bottle promises relief, community, and joy—only to leave us more isolated and in greater pain than before. This cycle of temporary escape followed by deeper suffering keeps us trapped, much like our ancestors who inflicted harm from their own wounded places. Recognizing this pattern is our first opportunity to break free.

Drinking is but a symptom of something much deeper. It's a simmering brew consisting of the Religious Crusades, the burning of millions of women at the stake, the Spanish Inquisition, the Transatlantic Slave Trade, Mao's Great Leap Forward where nearly 30 million died from starvation, the gas chambers in Auschwitz, the systematic destruction of Indigenous cultures and their spiritual practices—forcing entire peoples to abandon their sacred connection to the land and ancestors—and this concoction of unresolved trauma and pain is coming to a boil as the uncertainties of artificial intelligence, nuclear war and rapid climate change are added to the near boiling brew.

Most are in total denial of their own pain and completely blind to how we're all connected in this suffering. I once mentioned to a friend the massive floating islands of trash in the Pacific, and he cut me off mid-sentence, saying, "Yeah, but they haven't found the trash piles yet." No, they have. The National Geographic website has plenty of videos and images showing boats navigating through trash for days, but as they say, ignorance is bliss.

We suffer from intense denial. Jesus recognized this, too, saying we are quick to point out the splinter in someone else's eye while remaining oblivious to the plank sticking out of our own eye. This denial serves as a powerful defense mechanism, allowing us to avoid confronting uncomfortable truths about ourselves and our collective responsibility.

In August 2023, my wife dragged me to the movie *Barbie*, where I surprisingly found myself laughing out loud several times. There's a scene when Barbie first leaves Barbieland, and while walking on the street, she starts audibly talking to herself about a pulsing sensation of fear with no specific object. A woman passing by interrupts with, "Oh, that's anxiety. I have it too." All humans in the modern world live with a baseline state of anxiety that we have accepted as normal.

The Chapter I Looked Forward to Writing Most

When my family and I went to Costa Rica in January 2025 for three months, I packed an additional bag filled with highlighted and dog-eared books so I could continue writing in Costa Rica. Many of these books are filled with Post-it notes and highlighted sections, showing that our culture is wildly toxic. I've been saving articles and passages from audiobooks in a note in my iPhone for over three years, "proving" that our society is like a wretched, moldy banana.

I brought the book *The Comfort Crisis* by Michael Easter with the thesis that our species is losing its resilience and becoming remarkably soft. All the comforts and inventions of the modern world—air conditioning, memory foam, power steering, espresso with the touch of a button, tacos delivered to your door in under four taps on your smart device—have not improved our lives at all. Quite the contrary: it's made humans remarkably soft, and not the good kind of soft referenced in Daoism.

I packed the books *Dopamine Nation, The Anatomy of an Epidemic, Braiding Sweetgrass, The Anxious Generation,* and, of course, the giant hardcover copy of *The Myth of Normal,* in hopes of writing the most profound chapter ever written on how living in the early 21st century is like licking 80-grit sandpaper after eating a bulk-size box of Lemondrops.

I'd love to write another 8 to 10k words, all backed with scientific studies and data, proving my point that today's unprecedented levels of bullshit are what is causing our modern-day addictions. But I won't. I can't. For three years, this was the chapter I was most eager to write, to reinforce my own ideas about how the world is the problem and not me. And that may be the case (probably not), but I do recognize my external view of the world is a mirror of my internal world. I'm sick just like everyone else, and I have a plank the size of a full-grown piñon pine sticking out of my own eye, but I'm at least aware of it—or partly. My eagerness to write this chapter was slowly replaced by apprehension. A tension of sorts was building, and I found myself postponing the chapter I was most eager to write.

The reason is, I have to be careful where I place my mental energy. Humans have a brain that leans toward negativity. This is an evolutionary negativity bias that makes us fix the roof when it's not raining. However, if I ruminate in the muddy trenches of society, I'll get stuck there.

In addition, I'm ready to move on, to begin the healing process, to focus on the good, and to show others how to do the same. If we are to heal in a toxic culture, we cannot do so if we're glued to the idea that society has become perpetually unhinged, because in reality, things are how they are.

So, I'm inviting you to drop the addictive and possibly true idea that our world is broken and do two things:

1. Tell yourself that nothing is wrong with you, that you are not fundamentally flawed, and that a drinking problem is a normal manifestation of a disconnected culture.

2. Continue reading with the awareness that we are canaries in the mine signaling that our culture is out of balance, and that the healing trajectory you find yourself on is also what heals the world. The world heals through you.

Chapter 14
2014: The Fire Swamp Part 1.
South America

The Summer From Hell

In the 1987 classic film *The Princess Bride*, Westley and Buttercup enter the Fire Swamp to escape Prince Humperdinck and his soldiers. Few survive this hellscape due to the hidden sand pits, sulfur gas pockets that spontaneously combust, and let's not forget the rodents of unusual size. The summer of 2014 was my Fire Swamp. I barely escaped with my life and even made a conscious effort not to make it out alive.

The summer of 2014 was LONG. Partly because it started early—in April of that year, I flew to the southern hemisphere to Peru, where it was already summer. One of my best friends from high school, Brady, had asked me to chaperone a trip to Machu Picchu, where he was taking 12 of his social studies students who had recently completed a unit on the Incas. I was so thankful for this date on the calendar as it was a "Paul, get your shit together date." I didn't want to let my friend and his students down. I logged a couple of alcohol-free nights the week before the trip, but that's about all I could manage.

I remember boarding the plane for the 10-day trip thinking, "Finally, my sobriety starts here," only to find myself drinking seven beers at 2:30 AM during the layover at Lima International Airport, followed by three glasses of wine on the early morning flight to Cusco. When I collected my bags, I saw a taxi driver holding a placard with my name on it. Since I knew he had no idea who I was, I wheeled my luggage within five feet of the driver and went straight to the airport bar, where I chugged two more beers.

On the taxi ride to meet with Brady and the students, I told the driver I needed to use the restroom, thinking we'd stop at a convenience store where I could throw down a couple more beers. We stopped at a small café that didn't sell alcohol, but when leaving the café, I looked across the street and saw a cantina that seemed to be pulling me like a magnet. I looked at the taxi, then at the cantina, and said to myself with an incredible amount of shame, "Fuck, Paul. C'mon, man, just get in the taxi."

When I arrived at the hotel, my friend Brady took one look at me and said, "Oh shit, man." He knew right away I was tanked. Instead of showing up fit to be a chaperone, I was drunk, smelled like a dead possum, and the hangover I had been trying to fight off had already landed in my temples. I felt like absolute dog shit in every possible way. I had let myself down, and more importantly, Brady and his students.

However, I didn't drink on that trip, and with each passing day, the bloating, puffiness, sweats, feelings of worthlessness, and explosive shits (more on that later) dissipated as I began to heal. With each mile walked in the Andes on the Inca Trail, I began to recognize myself again, and the feeling of dread was slowly replaced by hope. As I saw waterfalls cascade off 18,000-foot glacier-filled peaks, it became so abundantly clear again that alcohol had no place in my life. Toward the end of that trip, I even felt glimmers of happiness that had been absent for so long. Hello Paul—welcome back.

I planned to continue traveling in South America after the Peru trip as a chaperone. I felt so good as I gave a heartfelt goodbye to Brady and the students when their shuttle left for the airport and they began their journey home. As I watched their bus merge with traffic, I knew that I was done with alcohol. I felt amazing. It had been 10 days since my last drink, and I had an incredible itinerary ahead of me. Lake Titicaca, La Paz, the Amazon, Argentina, and Chile were the next stops. I was ready for the adventure of a lifetime! I was drunk three hours later.

That same night, I was almost arrested by the Peruvian police because I was too drunk to follow orders during a random nighttime drug raid. The police busted into the hostel room, flipped on the lights, and with machine guns in tow, ordered everyone out of bed and into two single-file lines. In only boxers, I managed to climb down the bunk bed ladder and stumble into line. The girl across from me looked familiar as I had a vague recollection of making out with her in the hostel bar earlier that night... As the police were searching bags, I found refuge in a lower bunk bed nearby, where I was abruptly woken up again by shouts from the police officers. After this happened a second time, I saw the officers convene and discuss whether or not to take me to jail. Thankfully, they did not.

I woke up the next day around 1:00 PM with a "Fuccccckkkkkk." I had slept past checkout, and all my bunkmates were off to their next destination. My initial plan was to stay at the hostel for one night before traveling to the highest freshwater lake on the planet, Lake Titicaca, cradled at 12,500 feet in the Andes. Three nights and three hangovers later, I arrived at the lake and took a boat to a remote island where I checked into a small hotel carved out of the mountain rock.

While it seemed the other travelers at the dinner table didn't have a care in the world, I was experiencing mental warfare. As they were talking about exploring the lake on kayaks the following day, I was giving myself a pep talk: "Paul, you can do this. We are not drinking tonight, or for the rest of the trip." As if the devil were listening, the next moment, a gal at the table said, "Should we see if we can get some beer?" I responded before anyone else at the table with "GREAT IDEA."

Now I believe the "self" is composed of many parts: the conscious, subconscious, body, mind, soul, spirit, and inner child. When there is a battle going on inside your head, it doesn't matter who wins—you lose, with the inner child taking it on the chin. This inner kiddo, who just wanted to hang out with me and go on an adventure, was crushed when he heard me say "GREAT IDEA" to getting beer. When we went to the hotel lobby, which sold snacks, souvenirs, and beer, I was so thankful to see metal bars and a padlock on the beer cooler as the reception area had closed for the night. All parts of me let out a collective sigh of relief, knowing that I wouldn't or couldn't drink that night. I rode that momentum and didn't drink the following two days and nights at Lake Titicaca.

The next day, on the bus ride to La Paz, the capital of Bolivia, I overheard a couple of travelers talking about a secret cocaine bar in the city that changes location every couple of weeks or months to keep its location secret, or after being busted by the police. I told myself, "Paul, let them do their thing. We have two days of sobriety. We are checking into the hostel and going to bed—keep this momentum going." Surprisingly, even after owning a bar and all the late nights as a DJ in bars and clubs, I had never seen or done cocaine. I reaffirmed to myself, "Nope, not happening." Plus, ironically, I had just read the book *Marching Powder,* which was about a foreigner who ended up in a Bolivian jail after being busted with cocaine. Not a life experience I wanted. I was seeking sobriety, not experimenting with an amphetamine laced with who knows what for the first time.

After checking into the hostel, I went to the attached restaurant, and while waiting for my food to arrive, two attractive girls from Holland asked if I wanted to go with them to this mysterious cocaine bar as they didn't feel comfortable going alone. Forty-five minutes later, the three of us were on the other side of La Paz, ducking under a metal gate that a bouncer had lifted. It shut with a loud thud behind us as we entered the bar. I'll save you the details, but when I walked out of a Bolivian strip club at noon the next day (at least I was accompanied by the two Dutch girls), a pit in my stomach the size of Jupiter reminded me I was sinking deeper into the Fire Swamp.

How does one pull out of a nose dive of this magnitude? I should have boarded the next flight leaving La Paz for America. Perhaps I stayed due to pride, or possibly the idea that I could still "get my shit together," or maybe it was the Guns N' Roses flyer on the wall announcing a concert two days from now on April 10th, which was my birthday. I went through a huge Guns N' Roses phase and still love their music today. The solo at the end of "November Rain" by Slash is one of the reasons why I learned to play electric guitar, and I spent countless hours in my teens trying to master the solo. I bought my ticket to the concert, as well as the "Death Road" mountain bike tour for the following morning at 6:00 AM to give myself an extra reason not to drink because mountain biking hungover is terrible. Neither fun nor safe.

While walking to the concert with four Israeli travelers, I did something smart. When they stopped to buy beer, I told them I wasn't going to be drinking that evening. I made my intention of not drinking clear to other human beings before we entered the soccer stadium. I later came to learn this is **THE** most effective strategy anyone can use when it comes to ditching the booze: burning the ships. This is best described as radical honesty about our drinking with another human being which eliminates any option of turning back - you can't unsay it.

When we are clear and direct with our intention not to drink, we create accountability, which then turns into a deeper connection (community) with others. In addition, I believe 99% of humans are good people and want to help you achieve your goals.

The concert was awesome! I know this is a poor analogy for a book about sobriety, but the lead singer Axl Rose's voice is like a fine wine and has somehow improved over time. The band took multiple breaks since La Paz sits at nearly 12,000 feet, and we all felt short of breath after dancing to each song, especially when they played "Welcome to the Jungle." The Israeli travelers drank the entire concert yet didn't offer me a single drink, and I felt included in the group. I was rocking out to one of my favorite bands of all time, on my 32nd birthday, in South America, and I was sober.

In addition, I'm not that tall, but Bolivians are quite short, so I had a perfect view of the stage when the piano riff for "November Rain" began. I felt tears of gratitude streaming down my face before they even hit the first verse. It had always been a goal of mine to see Guns N' Roses live, and my goodness, what a journey it took to get here. When Slash began the iconic solo at the end of the song, I stopped moving as a current of electric energy pulsed through my body. I looked up at the stars, saw a sliver of a moon, and it was as if I could feel the universe conducting the beats of my heart. I found the brightest star in the sky, said thank you for this moment, and then let the heavens know my intention of sobriety. April 10th, 2014, my birthday, at a Guns N' Roses concert in Bolivia—what a great day to begin my new life with Slash stamping my intention of sobriety with the best guitar solo ever written.

Unfortunately, when we got back to the hostel and someone invited us out for drinks, the Bruno Voice took over, immediately said "YEP," and all sober intentions (declarations) floated away into the Andes.

So, when the shuttle driver entered my hostel room at 6:05 AM the next morning, asking if there was a Paul Churchill who signed up for the Death Road mountain bike tour, my eyes opened with a FUCKKKKK, knowing that I was still drunk and hadn't even set an alarm. I quickly gathered what I needed and found myself on a shuttle full of happy travelers who were pumped to mountain bike down what is infamously known as the most dangerous road on the planet.

The Death Road tour begins at 15,091 feet and continues for 40 miles until it reaches the Bolivian jungle at 3,900 feet. Before the Bolivian government built a safer two-lane highway in 2006, the Death Road was the only route connecting La Paz to the jungle. For 70 years, roughly 300 to 400 people, each year, rolled to their deaths at the bottom of the canyon.

When I got on my bike, I looked to my left and saw snow about 100 feet up. I was freezing. I had no gloves, was wearing a light windbreaker with only a T-shirt underneath, and since I knew warmer temperatures awaited at lower elevations, I started pedaling—oh yeah, I was still drunk. As I coasted down the single-lane dirt road with numb hands, I could see the carnage below, and in one particular area, I saw multiple cars and buses piled on top of each other.

The discomfort of a hangover showed up around mile 15, but it was the mental anguish that was torturing me. While the other cyclists were constantly stopping to take selfies and group photos with the impressive drop behind them, I couldn't stop thinking about riding my bicycle off the cliff and becoming the latest casualty of Death Road—the idea brought me peace. It would have looked like an accident. I was losing hope, and the word to describe that day, and the Fire Swamp summer of 2014, was despair.

What I didn't know at the time was that the only place the pain could begin to soften was the present moment, and perhaps that's why the universe had me sign up for this high-adrenaline tour, but I kept missing it. I was incessantly thinking into the future about how to fix my life and how to get my drinking under control, meaning stopping altogether. When my mind wasn't in the future, it was ruminating in the past, and none of the voices were pleasant.

With each passing mile, the Bruno Voice kept chiming in with "You dumb fucking idiot, you're ruining this trip and your life," and "You had one job, and that was to not drink." All addictions will take you to a point where you lose your seat inside your body as you don't know which voice to identify with, and you no longer know who you are. I would later learn it was none of these voices, but I wasn't there yet.

While gravity took me to the jungle, I must have repeated to myself, "I'm never drinking again," at least a thousand times. I probably even said it to myself while drinking the celebratory beer with the other cyclists before getting into the shuttle to return to La Paz. Of course, that night was a booze fest at the hostel, and when I woke the next morning, I realized my cell phone charger had been stolen while I was sleeping.

An interesting thing about La Paz, Bolivia, is that the government doesn't allow big box stores, so I couldn't just pop over to Walmart, Target, or the Apple Store and pick up an iPhone charger. Instead, I purchased several black-market chargers, and none of them worked. Somehow, one of the faulty chargers managed to suck out the remaining charge I had left. When I connected the phone to the cable, I saw the battery display go from 5% to 4% to 3% in a matter of seconds before I quickly pulled the charging cable from the phone. Now I was traveling alone in South America, and alcohol had done a fantastic job of isolating me even more. When my phone died shortly after, I experienced a loneliness that few authors have ever been able to adequately describe. I sat on the market steps, the sun setting in the distance, dead phone in hand, and sobbed uncontrollably.

I was glad to leave the bustling metropolis of La Paz and head to Rurrenabaque, Bolivia, for a 4-night tour in the Amazon jungle. I have always felt a sense of peace in nature, and the Amazon is nature on steroids. For hours, we navigated tributaries of the Amazon River on a small boat until we reached a lodge on stilts deep in the jungle. I didn't drink the first three days or nights of the tour because alcohol wasn't available, and I even met a gal who let me borrow a proper iPhone charger for a couple of hours each day to charge my phone from the generator so I could take pictures.

While lying in bed under the mosquito net, trying to fall asleep, it was the crickets that kept me company. I wondered to myself why they sang in the first place. I'm sure some of them are looking for mates, or perhaps claiming territory, but there has to be something more to the nonstop cacophony from sundown to sunup. The soundtrack of the Amazon, anchored by crickets at night, then birds and monkeys during the day, did wonders for my nervous system. I began to settle.

I've mentioned crickets a few times already, and that's not by accident. When crickets sing, they're not just calling to mates or marking territory—they're inviting you into the moment, the universal party. The first time I truly heard them was a recording of their calls slowed down roughly 400 times, or to the equivalent of a human lifespan. I was floored. What emerged wasn't noise. It was harmony. A layered, rising-and-falling chorus comprised of angel-like voices that seemed to breathe in sync with the Earth itself.

It brought tears to my eyes, and I've never heard crickets the same since. That sound—so ordinary it fades into the background—is actually an invitation. A reminder to drop whatever spiral you're stuck in and join the dance. The soundtrack of crickets is the soundtrack of life, and every night they sing, they're saying: you're part of this too. You belong here. And that is exactly how I felt as I eased my body back to some sort of homeostasis in the belly of the Amazon rainforest.

We caught piranhas, watched capybara (true rodents of unusual size) swim from one riverbank to the other, swam with playful pink dolphins, and our flashlights reflected dozens of caiman eyes glowing in the darkness on a nighttime tour. We came up short on our quest to find an anaconda, but simply being on the river that months earlier had passed by Machu Picchu before joining this same river calmed me. You'd think I would have been terrified being waist-deep in murky water, surrounded by piranhas, caimans, and being on the food chain menu myself. But it was the opposite—I felt connected. What I breathed out, the trees breathed in, and what the trees breathed out, I breathed in.

Despite being over 6,000 miles from home, I felt at home in the Amazon. It's hard to explain why, but if you sit in silence long enough, it seems as if the trees, birds, monkeys, and iguanas are calling you home. Many Indigenous cultures, as well as biologists, have recognized the Amazon as the heart, lungs, and pharmacy for everyone on the planet, containing plants, barks, herbs, and vines that can heal any ailment. In just three days in nature, and of course without alcohol, my heart, lungs, body, soul, mind, and spirit began to respond to the healing frequencies of nature, and I felt optimistic about the future. I still had a killer travel itinerary in front of me and was gaining confidence. Throughout the days, I kept confirming to myself that I was done with alcohol and it had no place in my life. None.

On the fourth day in the Amazon, we took the boat to a home on stilts that sat in front of a clearing so we could see the sunset as a group on the balcony. A fellow traveler came to the sunset deck with a candy bar and a Gatorade, and when I asked where he got them, he said, "The family sells snacks and drinks below inside their house." I walked downstairs and asked for a Snickers bar, and the woman asked me, "Algo para tomar?" which means "something to drink?" I responded with, "Yes, what do you have?" At the end of a short list was the word cerveza, which landed with a thud, as if it had physical mass, and the inertia of the word kept reverberating in my brain.

Now you may be reading this, going, "Dude... NOOOOOO... have a Coca-Cola, a Snickers bar, and go enjoy a sunset in the Amazon." One voice in my head, with a delicate and soothing tone, said, "Paul, buddy, let's think about this—not a good idea." Another voice said, "Paul, you just went three days without alcohol; therefore, you do not have a drinking problem." Now true, I did just go three days without drinking, but as I mentioned earlier, it wasn't an option—it wasn't available. I'm sure many of you have already surmised that this type of thinking is far from rational, and I'm trying to give you a real-life example of what an addicted mind looks like. "Fuck, okay, but it will be just one."

I bought all the beer in stock and drank the three liters, about nine beers, in under 30 minutes, since it was supposed to be a quick stop for sunset, and they needed the one-liter glass bottles back. Later that night, back at our lodge, I was lying on a dock about two feet above the water, attempting to pet a caiman/alligator who was sleeping below the dock.

As I mentioned earlier in this chapter, I should have gone home. With the non-stop mental warfare between my ears, I wasn't enjoying myself, and in all truth, I was losing myself to alcohol. But since I had only 3 weeks left of traveling, and perhaps it was pride that kept me on the road, I stayed.

After the Amazon, I took a tour south through the Potosí salt flats, where one day I was too hungover to even get out of the car. With my forehead pressed against the Jeep's window, sweat dripping down my temples, I could see the other travelers from New Zealand, Russia, and Belgium taking epic pictures and having a blast. I was in an absolute hellish Fire Swamp and had no clue how to escape. The playbook seemed so incredibly simple, containing just one play: don't drink. Yet the problem was that while 10 players were inside the huddle repeating the play—"Don't drink on two, ready, break"—the Bruno Voice, or the 11th man, was compulsively rationalizing a way to drink.

After traveling south through the Potosí salt flats, I arrived in the San Pedro de Atacama Desert in Chile, which, according to many stargazers, is the best place on earth for viewing the heavens. Remember, even when we are navigating our own Fire Swamps, there are still moments of repose and peace built in. I signed up for a stargazing tour, and as the astronomer pointed his green laser toward Jupiter and Venus, which seemed to make a horizontal line toward the middle star of Orion's belt, I felt a remembrance of sorts. A knowing that even though I was taking direct blows to the goat blocks daily from alcohol, I was still on the correct path. That I was being supported and guided as my soul traversed this seemingly impossible human curriculum. Conceptually, none of it made sense, but while lying on my back, staring up at the Milky Way, a quiet recognition stirred—like I was coming home to something I didn't know I'd lost.

From the southern tip of Chile to northern Alaska, almost all indigenous cultures believe that when we depart from Earth, our soul is released into the Milky Way after a quick stop at the middle star of Orion's belt. The same messaging is written across Egyptian hieroglyphs, and the three pyramids of Giza are aligned with exact precision to replicate the three stars of Orion's belt, with the largest pyramid in the middle representing the middle star.

On that cool, cloudless Chilean night in the desert, accompanied by the hum of crickets at nearly 8,000 feet, my brain—which has roughly the same number of neurons as the Milky Way has stars—stopped trying to "figure out" or "fix" my life, as it knew it was pointless. Not because I was beyond fixing, but because a quiet knowing emerged, hinting that there is nothing to fix in the first place and that we are all exactly where we are supposed to be in this very moment.

Looking at stars on a clear, moonless night should be added to everyone's recovery portfolio, especially when you need help calming the thinking mind. Two trillion galaxies are what our current telescopes can see, and when the thinking mind tries to make sense of it all, it's like I can hear Snoop Dogg say, "Bitch, please." The longer I look at the night sky, the less my mind tries to categorize, solve, and fix, and the more I lean into the idea that everything is exactly as it should be. While looking at the glimmering stars, the soul began whispering, "We'll be home soon enough," and there was comfort in that.

I took a 13-hour overnight bus ride from Chile to Argentina, which crested the cordillera of the Andes at nearly 15,000 feet. Since I rarely sleep on planes or buses, the Bruno Voice convinced me I should get some alcohol so I could sleep on the bus. In the middle of the night, I woke to what sounded like Plinko chips from *The Price Is Right* going dink, dink, dink, and I quickly realized it was my empty bottle of vodka that had fallen from my seat and was now rolling down the middle aisle of the bus, clinking off the metal rails of the seats behind me. At the same time, I recognized the familiar smell of bile and shame. I looked down and realized that while in a blackout, I had vomited all over my shirt, pants, and bag below. When I exited the bus, the driver looked at the patches of dried vomit on my clothing and laughed, saying, "Windy roads, eh?" Oh, how I wished it was just nausea from the curvy roads of the Andean mountain passes, but it was something much worse: I was losing my soul to the spirit of alcohol.

When I arrived in Salta, Argentina, after the overnight bus ride from hell, I checked into my hostel, threw away my shirt, took a nap, and then met an Irish woman named Rochelle at the hostel, where we came up with a plan to rent a car and drive south through the wine country of Argentina.

When we got into the car, I blurted out, "I know we're planning on touring wineries, but I'm not going to be drinking." Part of me questioned whether I had said that out loud or not, but it was well received, and on the long drive, I opened up about my struggles with alcohol and how it was ruining this trip and my life. It was so liberating to talk openly about what was shredding me inside. Rochelle asked questions, listened intently, and asked how she could help as we drove deeper into the Argentinian countryside. I said, "No matter what comes out of my mouth in the following days, this is me saying I don't want to drink. Please don't offer me a glass of wine, not even one." Ship burned.

To my surprise, that conversation was all I needed, as I didn't drink for three days and nights while visiting wineries in Argentina, and it was quite enjoyable. Rochelle drank wine. I drank soda. She kept asking me in her Irish accent, "Are you doing alright?" "Are you okay being here?" The power of accountability is real. If it were just me and myself trying to stay sober, the Bruno Voice would have had me bent over the first wine barrel we saw, but I did something so incredibly simple, yet so hard at the same time: I asked for help. What I didn't know at the time is that human beings are biologically wired to help others, and feel-good chemicals like oxytocin are released when we ask for help and when we help others. This is me strongly suggesting you ask for help with your own goals of sobriety because there are people in your life who want to help you. Maybe do it right now.

On the morning of the fourth day, while having breakfast with Rochelle at a fancy hotel before checkout, something caught my eye on the other side of the restaurant. It was an extra-large display bottle filled about two-thirds with a clear liquid, flanked by wine bottles. When Rochelle excused herself to use the restroom, my eyes honed in on the mysterious bottle as the neurons in my brain began to fire and the Bruno Voice started to speak up.

Bruno - "Hey Paul, just to let you know, you went three days without drinking in wine country. Someone with a drinking problem couldn't do that."

Paul - "Great point Bruno. You're totally right."

Before Rochelle could return from the restroom, I walked through the nearly full restaurant and, without pause, picked up the bottle, unscrewed the cap, and started chugging for at least 5 seconds— probably more like 10. It nearly all came back up as I felt the fire ignite in my throat and stomach. I had no clue what I was drinking, but it contained alcohol and a lot of it. I can only imagine what it looked like to the other guests eating breakfast to see someone chugging the contents of a decorative bottle before 8:30 AM. As I walked back to my table, I did my best not to make eye contact with some of the diners who had just watched me chug hard alcohol like it was water. I sat down at the table, and when Rochelle returned 30 seconds later, I said, "Well, should we go?"

Now I want to take a time out here and remind you to focus on the similarities and not the differences. I'm guessing you haven't chugged hard alcohol in a restaurant, in front of the other diners, at breakfast time. But I want you to ask yourself, what's your decorative bottle chugging equivalent? Where the Bruno Voice takes you to a completely irrational place, leading you to act in ways never before imagined? Okay, back to the story.

As I drove, I felt tipsy, then drunk. I was driving intoxicated in a foreign country with a passenger in the seat next to me. The shame began to pierce through the weight of the alcohol, and once again, I was reminded that I was indeed still in the Fire Swamp. I kept driving, windows down to hide the smell of alcohol on my breath, and didn't mention anything to Rochelle about my solo mission of getting annihilated before driving 6 hours back to Salta, Argentina.

If you struggle with your drinking at all, I'm sure you can relate to this sentiment: I start drinking, and I find it nearly impossible to stop. When we made a stop to refuel, I saw Rochelle walk up a small hill to use the restroom in a building detached from the gas station. When I went inside to pay for gas, there was no way I could miss the bottle of Fernet behind the cashier, which Argentinians sip as a strong aperitif to aid with digestion after a meal. I told the clerk to pour me a double. He turned to look at the bottle, which turned out to be another decorative bottle and not even for sale since it was a gas station and not a bar. When he turned back to me, I spoke before he could say anything, and my tone assured him I wasn't taking no for an answer. "Sí, este." "Yes, that one." As the clerk pulled the bottle off the shelf, I saw Rochelle exit the bathroom and begin walking back down to the main building. I had less than 20 seconds. "Llénalo," "Fill it," I said in a stern yet still polite voice. "¿Así está bien?" "Is this good?" said the clerk. "Más," "More," I said, as I slid $20 worth of Argentinian pesos across the counter. I then chugged probably 10 ounces of 80-proof Fernet in less than 3 seconds, setting the glass down an instant before Rochelle entered the gas station.

I tried to let alcohol take me to a happy place for the remainder of the drive, but it wasn't happening. I was not only fucked up, but it had become abundantly clear, for the thousandth time, that I had a major problem on my hands, and my whole life would be fucked if I didn't get a handle on this. Thank the heavens that guided the steering wheel safely back to the rental car return office, which was housed inside the bus station where Rochelle had a bus ticket for departure that evening to her next destination. As I walked Rochelle to her bus terminal, I told her that I had been drinking that day, all day, and had driven drunk. I could see anger change the color of her cheeks, but the old soul inside of her took over, and she responded with a hug. She said she believed in me and that I could do this. Sixteen months later, I would receive a random card in the mail postmarked from Ireland. It was a note from Rochelle congratulating me on one year of sobriety.

The remaining couple of weeks of the trip were a blur. I did manage to log a couple of nights sober, but I was losing the war to alcohol and losing myself. At least in Argentina, I was able to find a proper iPhone charger, and I used my phone to look up an AA meeting at 8:00 PM that evening. I walked 40 minutes to the meeting location, which put me at the steps of a large church, but the door was locked and the lights were off inside. "That's okay," I told myself, as I had arrived 10 minutes early.

While waiting on the church steps, it seemed like everyone who walked in front of me had it all figured out and knew where they were going. There's a certain gait that someone walks with when they aren't losing their shit inside like I was. My anxiety was a hard 9.5/10, and I wondered when the hell the doors to the meeting were going to open, but they didn't. At 30 minutes past the hour, which seemed like 74 years of torture, knowing there was no meeting, I put my head in my hands and once again began to audibly cry. I just wanted to go home—not geographically home, but back to the Milky Way, to the stars, to the heavens, anywhere but there.

I cried for a long time on those steps. I probably would have cried until the sun came up, but I felt a hand on my shoulder, and when I looked up, an older woman said, "Hermano, ¿qué pasa?" "Brother, what is wrong?" There was no fabricated story as the inner child answered first between heaves and sobs with, "There was supposed to be an Alcoholics Anonymous meeting here tonight at 8:00 PM." After wiping tears from my face, I showed her my phone screen, and she said, "Oh dear, there are two Rosary Churches in this town. You're at the wrong church." She told me to go to a new location in two nights, and I would find my people. Before she left, she put a hand on my shoulder, looked directly into my swollen eyes, and said, "Tú puedes, lo sé con todo mi corazón." "You can do this, I know it with all my heart." Looking back, it was clear the universe had been guiding and protecting me at all times, even when I was in the hellish Fire Swamp. An angel had just sent me a message. "I can do this, I can do this," I repeated to myself as I walked back to my hotel.

Two nights later, I found myself at a Spanish-speaking AA meeting, and even though I didn't understand much of it since the Argentinian accent and slang were way different than what I was used to, I felt less alone. If you find yourself in the middle of your own Fire Swamp while reading this book, do your inner child a favor and go to an AA meeting or Café RE chat. While at the AA meeting, my nervous system was able to calm down enough for me to think somewhat clearly.

"Fuck this trip," I told myself. I needed to get home ASAP. Two days later, on the long flight back to America, I found myself journaling the same line over and over: "I can do this. I can do this."

One good thing that came from that brutal trip to South America was the idea of sober travel. I kept telling myself during the trip that I wished I were traveling with other people who didn't drink alcohol, and four years later, I would lead my first sober travel trip back to where it all started: Cusco, Peru.

Chapter 15
2014: The Fire Swamp Part II

Before we pick up the story back in America, I want to highlight a key component of addiction: the mind splits, and there are two voices. One voice has logically concluded, based on clear past evidence, that alcohol is extremely toxic to the system and needs to go. Then you have the Bruno Voice—the addiction—which gives you 55 reasons why drinking is a good idea. The main reason this voice is so convincing is that it speaks to you in your own recognizable voice; it has the same tone, cadence, sense of humor, slang, and vernacular. This voice is also intelligent, as it invents convincing stories based on logic about why drinking is a good idea.

For example, earlier in the Amazon, when alcohol wasn't available and I would have had to ferment my own if I wanted to drink, the Bruno Voice convinced me I wasn't an alcoholic since I had just gone three days without alcohol—and someone with a drinking problem couldn't do that. I believed that reasoning each time. It's incredibly difficult to discern which voice is speaking, and you eventually forget which voice is you. This is primarily how you lose yourself to an addiction.

I think the first step of *AA* should be revised. Instead of "We admitted we were powerless over alcohol, that our lives had become unmanageable," it should focus on thinking. We are powerless over our thinking because we reach a moment when we don't know who is thinking and what to believe. Admitting we are powerless over our thinking (or alcohol) is the only step one has to master to quit drinking and take back control, but as the Big Book of *AA* says many times, drinking was but a symptom of a deeper unrest: the ego, or thinking.

I would later arrive at the knowing that I'm neither of these two voices, and it's the biological mechanism we call addiction that prompts us to split from ALL the voices in the head and become the observer of these voices—that is, of course, only if we quit drinking, which is usually prompted by heaps of pain, unthinkable suffering, and a series of rock bottoms. We stop identifying with any of the mind chatter in the head and begin to recognize thinking as a function of the brain, not who we are at our core. Said another way, we identify more with the ocean and less with the constant crashing of waves.

Imagine you've been playing basketball for as long as you can remember. You've identified yourself as a player, the court is your home, the ball is your rock, and as far as you're concerned, nothing but a curtain of blackness exists off the court. Just like drinking was fun at first, so was playing basketball, but eventually you roll an ankle, one of your teammates never passes the ball, there's a scandal with the towel boy, and the team starts fighting with each other. It soon becomes so painful to stay on the court that you take a peek behind the curtain of darkness.

What an addiction is trying to get us to do, with biblical amounts of pain, is to leave the game altogether, find a new seat high up in the stands, and become the observer of the game taking place below. An alcohol addiction, or any substance or behavioral addiction, can lead to an essential reordering of consciousness.

Nothing exists in this universe without a purpose—this is called endowment theory in biology—and I feel an addiction, albeit extremely painful, is a potent driver that can wake us up if we surrender to the addiction process. It's the invitation, if we are to listen, to a healthier, more balanced way of living where we are no longer slaves to the incessant stream of thoughts in the brain. This is true freedom.

A drinking problem can force us to stop relying on the thinking mind for salvation for three main reasons. First, we are not our thoughts. We have incorrectly placed our seat in the mind; we aren't a happy self or a sad self, we are beings. Second, if we choose to recover, we'll soon realize the thinking mind has many pitfalls: it's rooted in the past, is obstinate to change, and has an intense negativity bias. Third, and this is most important, it's impossible to think yourself into a better state of being since thoughts exist in time and are anchored in either the past or future.

The only moment you can be anything at all is this very moment right now—not at the end of this chapter, book, or in five years.

Splitting or detaching from the voices in the mind is the most radical thing that can happen to us in a human life. The Buddha calls this the river crossing of consciousness. The Buddha mentions—and this is not metaphorical—that all of humanity has to make this evolutionary leap in consciousness if we are to survive as a species. He is referring to the ego, which is the most dangerous thing on the planet by far, and it's the addiction that allows a small percentage of us to pierce through it, or better said, to sidestep it altogether, recognize its insanity, and no longer identify with it.

The ego lives in a constant state of lack, is never satisfied for more than a short duration of time, and abundance is a concept that it furiously rejects. The human ego is on the precipice of destroying mankind and perhaps all life on the planet. The three most pressing issues that humans face today are nuclear war, a warming planet, and technology/artificial intelligence. All of them are manifestations of the core problem: the human ego. We are an incredibly intelligent species, but we split the atom not to create limitless energy, but to kill our fellow human beings.

Christianity recognized this insanity of the human mind and called it original sin, which means to miss the mark or to miss the present moment. Jesus told his disciples to stop seeking salvation in the future and to observe the lilies toiling in the wind, for they are not concerned with the past or future—they just are. In Buddhism, the baseline state of the human mind or ego is called Dukkha, which translates to suffering, pain, dis-ease, or straight-up dog garbage. In Hinduism, it's called Maya, which means "illusion."

It is said that Siddhartha Gautama, the Buddha, obtained enlightenment or nirvana after meditating for 49 days under a Bodhi tree (Ficus religiosa). Jesus did something similar when he fasted for 40 days and 40 nights in the Judean desert. Through these experiences of intense pain and suffering, they were able to see the mechanics of the ego as an insatiable entity that always looks to the future for salvation. With this realization, they both obtained a higher level of awareness called Buddha and Christ consciousness.

Apparently, this consciousness was no joke, as these rare flowers of humanity performed miraculous healings, and it was rumored that when the Buddha or Jesus entered a village, spontaneous healings would happen within a 15-30 mile radius.

The Buddha sat cross-legged under a tree for seven weeks, Jesus fasted in the desert for nearly six, and you've most likely experienced years of emotional rock bottoms that would make the Buddha and Jesus say, "Eh, no thanks." You have suffered enough.

Spiritual teacher Eckhart Tolle, in his book *A New Earth,* makes his point very clear: we are here, on this planet, in this very moment in time, to overcome the human ego, enlighten, awaken to our true nature, or we will perish as a species. This transformation of consciousness, which, according to Eckhart Tolle, can be sparked by intense pain and suffering, is what many spiritual teachers indicate as being the most important task at hand for all of us. Countless volumes have been written on the subject of awakening, but there is no set pathway or sequential set of steps to break free from the ego, and as Jesus says, it may come to the sinner before the saint. It may come to the addict before the good Samaritan.

Many ancient cultural texts, including Native American legends, the Bible, countless prophecies, and the Mayan calendar, point to a time when we are to break free from the chains of the ego, and that time is now. On December 21, 2012, the Mayan calendar marked a new period for humanity, one that has already started to bring intense change and transformation for humans that is expected to last for about 80 years. I don't know about you, the reader, but I feel we are on the precipice of something big as paradigms and egoic totalitarian states are beginning to crumble.

So what is this colossal change or shift I'm referring to? It may not seem like much on paper, but again, it's the most radical thing that a human being can experience in a lifetime. It's a tipping point we hit where we begin to place more emphasis on the present moment as opposed to the past or future. It's knowing the only moment for wholeness is now, and we consciously choose to be anchored in whatever experience we are facing now.

This may not sound like much, but it can and will transform the planet—in fact, it has already started. Just one human being who embodied this new consciousness was more powerful than all the Roman Legions combined, and before he left the planet at the young age of 33, he taught humans the concept of forgiveness. This person was named Jesus Ben Joseph. All human souls are on the trajectory of awakening, enlightenment, or realizing the ego only leads to an all-you-can-eat buffet of turd sandwiches. It's not those who fight an addiction, but those who accept an addiction as the messenger that something is gravely out of balance and surrender to the energy of the addiction to create a way of living that now flows with the current of life.

Again, in the summer of 2014, I knew none of this. I kept searching for "me" in some region of the thinking mind, and it only ended with more suffering.

This chapter was difficult to write as I found myself crying for the old self who was so alone and in so much pain. But I'm also thankful for the intense life curriculum that has birthed the life I have today.

Chapter 16
2014: The Fire Swamp Part III.
Utah and Montana

"If you're going through hell, keep going"
- Winston Churchill

At this point in my sobriety journey, I knew damn well that geographical cures don't work. But I also knew my chances would improve back in a familiar setting—surrounded by friends, family, and daily walks or runs with my dog, Ben. On the way back home to Montana, we had a family trip planned to my favorite place in the world: Lake Powell, which is a 185-mile-long reservoir carved deep into the red rocks by the Colorado River in southwestern Utah. It's where the Paiute, Anasazi, Utes, and Navajo Indians called home.

If you explore the vast network of canyons long enough, which has more coastline than the coast of California, you'll come across Indian ruins, petroglyphs, or arrowheads. The stars, the red canyon walls, and crickets always made me feel at home in that area of the country since the majority of my childhood vacations were spent at Lake Powell and other iconic destinations in southern Utah, such as Moab and Zion National Park. I had just logged a couple of sleepless, sweat-filled nights without alcohol, and on the drive to Lake Powell, I was feeling a sliver of optimism and kept repeating what the Argentinian woman told me a few weeks earlier: "I can do this. I can do this."

I arrived at the houseboat at Lake Powell with my parents and dog Ben a day before my brother Mark and my two friends Rick and Sam. Accountability was already in place for the trip since everyone knew I had quit drinking in 2010. Yes, I'd had some slip-ups and had just taken an epic ass-kicking on the chin while in South America, but I was confident all that was behind me. As the sun slipped behind the towering canyon walls, my mom received a call from her sister notifying her that her father had just died. Yes, I was sad—my grandpa was no longer with us—but being the empath that I am, I could feel my mom's pain, and she was obviously a mess. The Bruno Voice didn't even have to speak; the bottle was in my hand before I even knew it, and I kept it a secret.

For the first five days of that trip, I woke up one to two hours before everyone else so I could drink three to four beers before the sun rose in the east. During the day, I would sneak beers into the bathroom and hide the cans for later. In the evenings, after everyone had gone to bed, I took strategic pulls from the lone bottle of rum on the boat, drank a few beers, and walked around collecting the hidden empty cans. One day, while drinking root beer floats at the marina, my friend Rick, while opening a Corona, said, "Man, that's crazy you're doing this whole lake trip sober—good on you." But I wasn't doing it sober. And I desperately wanted to let everyone know. I was dying inside.

One afternoon on the trip, we were walking back to the houseboat after a long hike, and when we were about two miles out, I started to jog, thinking I could arrive 10 to 15 minutes before the others so I could chug some beers without them knowing. My friend Sam saw this and took it as a cue to race back to the boat. Although alcohol wasn't doing me any favors physically, I was still in my early thirties, and there was no way I was letting Sam get in front of me and my drinking. The moment I saw him run to catch up, I bolted. I found a couple of shortcuts, jumped into a small slot canyon, and I was GONE! When I arrived at the boat, I took three beers to the bathroom and started chugging. I was drinking in an attempt to calm the category 5 hurricane inside of me, but it didn't do much, as every beer I drank and hid only amped up the anxiety, shame, guilt, fear, sadness, self-criticism, desperation, and despair.

On the second-to-last night, my brother, Rick, Sam, and I were seated around a campfire on the lakeshore. Rick said he was going inside to get some beer, and the others asked him to bring some out for them as well. Now, alcoholic math is a real thing. I knew exactly how many beers were left at the bottom of the extra-large Igloo coolers: zero. The only remaining beers on the boat were hidden, and I was planning to consume them alone later that night and the next morning. When Rick came back with the somber announcement that there was no beer left, Sam said, "Are you sure? I thought we bought enough for the whole trip." Then my brother chimed in with the amount of beer he had brought for the trip, and all three of them surmised there was no way they should have run out of beer. You would think my blood pressure would rise, knowing they would eventually figure out that 35 to 40 beers were missing, but I felt a sense of peace, knowing the gig was probably up and I would have to come clean with them around the campfire. But here's the thing with normal drinkers: all three of them were like "oh well," and they continued the night drinking Pepsi and bottled water. I wanted to be found out so badly...

The next morning, after I finished my fourth beer as the stars of the night sky began to fade away along with the chorus of crickets, I did something smart. While the Bruno Voice was still sleeping, I walked downstairs to my parents' bedroom on the boat and knocked on the door before 7:00 AM. When I entered, my mouth opened, and it all came out—I burned the ships. I told them everything. I told my dad that it wasn't Rick who liked his rum so much, it was me. I told them I had been drinking the entire trip: how I'd wake up at 4:00 AM and start drinking, then continue when everyone else was asleep. The words "alcohol is ruining my life" came out of my mouth multiple times. My parents are wonderful people, and they said all the right things. Later that day, I burned the ships with my brother Mark, and he also said all the right things. A few months later, I would also tell Rick and Sam that I was the reason they ran out of beer on the trip. I offered to reimburse them, but they declined and said all the right things.

On the drive home from southern Utah to Montana, I kept finding myself with a death grip on the steering wheel, saying, "I can do this, I can do this." Although I was still in the Fire Swamp, I felt lighter since I had recently offloaded the weight of my struggles with alcohol to my parents and brother. The three most important people in my life at that time were now up to speed on the true depths of my struggles with alcohol. I poured 100-proof alcohol on the mast, the hull, and the deck, and set the ship ablaze. I was unable to take those conversations back, which the Bruno Voice was pissed about, but as I mentioned, the intensity of the problem had slightly dissipated since I no longer carried the burden alone. I strongly feel burning the ships is the single most important thing we can do for ourselves if we wish to quit drinking. Step one of Alcoholics Anonymous is the equivalent of burning the ships and is the only step one has to get perfect: We admitted we were powerless over alcohol. Ship burned with the self, and that's the first and most important ship to burn.

When I arrived home in Montana in mid-May 2014, I had just started a new job at a crisis management facility called "The House of Hope." This is where people landed if they were experiencing a mental crisis or were suicidal, and this is where authorities would take someone after a failed suicide attempt. It was also a bridge to the state mental hospital, and as I learned, if someone said something like, "I'm going to kill every last one of you," they'd shortly be escorted there in a police cruiser. I thought this job would be good for me since I enjoy helping others and could put my own problems aside and focus on helping patients.

This should have been a good plan, but the Bruno Voice had me on a repeated cycle of day 1s, and each time I arrived at work to clock in, there was a serious inner debate that took place: "Paul, you need help. Check into the facility as a patient, not as an employee." This happened for about 30 seconds every time I clocked in for work. How the hell was I supposed to support patients in distress when inside of me, there was a volcano of pain erupting at all times? I think the universe placed me at The House of Hope for a couple of reasons: first, to show me how much worse things could actually get, and second, to assist a couple of individuals who really needed help.

One afternoon on a shift, I was outside with a young man who was detoxing from meth when he received a call that the state was going to take his child away from him since he was currently in treatment, and the mother had recently died from an overdose. When he hung up the phone, there were three seconds of calm before he exploded. I have always been good in emergencies, and something in my body told me this was a delicate moment. I knew exactly what the man was hoping to accomplish when he took off in a sprint toward a large rock. I saw the angle, bolted in his direction, and as he dove headfirst like a torpedo to smash his head on the rock, I was able to get a hand on the side of his face and direct his body into the bushes instead. For the next 30 minutes, I kept him safe from himself as he purged generations of pain and suffering from his system.

On another occasion, shortly after clocking in and not checking myself in for help, a patient came to the front desk to ask for the TV remote. Now, we were instructed to memorize all the patients' names, and since there were only six beds, this wasn't too hard, but on this occasion, I got this guy's name wrong, which he was not pleased with... at all. I said, "Hello Stanley, sure thing, let me get that remote for you." "What did you say?" the man replied. "Uh, sure thing, I'll get that remote for you," I cautiously responded as I already felt the energy in the air shift. "It's Steven, you piece of shit," the large, bearded man growled. The man's breath suddenly began to quicken, and when I looked at the other staff member who had been employed there much longer than I had, the color left her face since the previous couple of times this had happened with this man, it was a full-on DEFCON level 10 emergency where police, fire, and paramedics had to come in and take over. My gut intuition also instantly notified me we were on very shaky ground.

I calmly but briskly walked from behind the front desk and, in a slow and reassuring tone, said, "Follow me to the TV room, Steven." As Steven followed me, I made sure to keep an eye on him in my peripheral vision, which was a good idea because he took a swing at me. The punch flew over my head as I ducked, and his momentum landed him on the couch I was trying to take him to in the first place. I quickly put up my hands and said, "Steven, we're cool, man," and pulled up a chair next to him. One of the staff members brought a bag of carrots and a peeler and signaled with their head that it was for him. Steven's breath indicated he was about to plunge into the depths of an irreversible panic attack, and I quickly held out a carrot and the peeler. Apparently, this method, which they didn't cover in the two 8-hour crisis management training sessions two weeks prior, had helped soothe Steven in the past, or at least bought time until paramedics arrived.

As I watched Steven ferociously peel carrots as he rocked back and forth on the couch, I realized I wasn't much different from Steven. We were both in an extreme amount of pain, but I was somehow able to keep my pain on the inside. I could feel the situation with Steven deteriorating as some of the swipes with his peeler were now taking off skin from his hand, and there was blood. As I desperately tried to think of what to do, I found my left hand on his shoulder and my right hand on his non-peeling forearm, and I started focusing on my breath. Intuitively, I knew I had to anchor both of us, and I put all my energies into my breath and the peculiar present moment we both found ourselves in. To my surprise, several minutes had passed, and Steven was beginning to calm down. To my left, over my shoulder, I saw the paramedics with a stretcher in tow, ready to take over, but something inside of me shook my head left and right as I called off the big dogs.

I lasted five weeks at The House of Hope before quitting, but I'm incredibly thankful for my time there and the lessons learned. On one of my last shifts at The House of Hope, while I was entering patient notes on a night shift around 3:00 AM, there was a window cracked open by the computer where I could hear the soft hum of crickets. I stopped typing, opened the window even more, then leaned back in the chair and let the chorus of nature usher in a deep sense of peace. Yes, I was profoundly struggling and losing hope overall, but the crickets sparked a dormant remembrance that everything is perfect just the way it is, and I was still on the right path...

My time at The House of Hope made it abundantly clear that things could indeed get much worse, and I 100% needed to step up my sobriety efforts if I were to get sober and have anything of a life worth living. I started going to AA meetings daily, got a sponsor, scheduled sessions with therapists and addiction counselors, read more quit-lit books, listened to recovery podcasts (I think there were fewer than five recovery podcasts at that time), and spent significant time hiking in nature with my dog Ben.

I do want to remind you that at this time in my journey into an alcohol-free life, I was done with the moderation phase. All of my mental energies were going toward building a life of abstinence, but the Bruno Voice kept coming at me hard with all the classic lines: "Paul, it will be different this time," "Of course you can have just one," "Paul, everyone else your age is drinking," "You need to have a little fun." And when I did manage to get one, two, or three days away from a drink, the Bruno Voice would fully convince me that someone who really was an alcoholic wouldn't be able to do that.

This time in my life was a level 10 ass-kicking, and I still wasn't done with the gauntlet of the Fire Swamp yet. I kept wondering what it was going to take to stop drinking. In terms of classical Newtonian physics, an addiction is its own mass of energy that moves recklessly forward until acted upon by an equal or greater force. I was hoping the third law of Newtonian physics would not hold, meaning that I wouldn't need a fiery rock bottom to curb the addiction that clearly had control of my life. I was out of control, my life was out of control, and I had no idea how to stop it.

One might wonder where God, or a higher power, comes into play during this chapter in my life. In all truth, I was an atheist at the time, but of course, there were countless generic foxhole prayers of "Dear God, please help," which were on repeat over and over. However, the spirit alcohol had so dimmed and nearly fully severed my electrical current connecting me to the universe that I was alone and drifting further into the abyss.

One mid-June Saturday morning, I drank two beers in the parking lot before attending an AA meeting. I was so sick of saying "My name is Paul and I'm an alcoholic," after they asked if there was anyone in their first 30 days of sobriety, but I knew I had to be honest and keep going. After that meeting, I drank two more tall boys in the parking lot before driving 1.5 hours to Helena, Montana, where I had to DJ a wedding later that evening. While wheeling my equipment into the venue, one of my speakers fell onto the wooden dance floor and left a small crack. The following Monday, I got an email from the venue saying that I needed to replace the broken dance floor panel, which cost $575. I was paid $600 for the wedding, and at first I said "No way," but I sent a check and accepted full responsibility. I've DJed hundreds of weddings and events, and only twice have I dropped equipment—both times I had been drinking.

One morning in early July that summer, while lying in bed hungover, I found myself repeating what the Argentinian woman said to me: "I can do this, I can do this." Without my knowing, the verbiage suddenly switched, and I found myself saying, "I am doing this, I am doing this." I felt a sudden surge of energy, and this was a monumental step forward in my journey for two key reasons. First, I was already well into the process of quitting drinking—it was a journey I had already started long ago. The massive container ship called my addiction had already been nudged towards the waters of sobriety, and in reality, I was closer to the finish line than the start. Second, "I am doing this" places us more in line with the universal nature of time. "I can do this" is a noble statement, but inherently incorrect because it places a quit date in the future, and the only time I would ever be able to quit drinking was in the moment that I found myself in. As quantum physicists understand, time is an illusion, and the only moment we have for doing anything is the moment we find ourselves in now.

"I am MOTHERFUCKING doing this," I heard myself say. From that moment on, it was "I AM DOING THIS. I AM DOING THIS." I kept building my alcohol-free life in my head, on paper, in journals, with other people, through mantras in the shower, and that spark, which I had ignited long before, began to accumulate a mass and momentum of its own. It still wasn't near the force of the addiction, but I kept visualizing a life without alcohol, hoping a tipping point would eventually be reached.

Another critical step forward for me that summer was when I stopped trying to fight the addiction, which may sound strange to you since there was still a fierce storm system of raccoon turds called addiction swirling around me at all times. At one AA meeting that summer, on a Friday night, I heard a powerful passage on page 417 of the Big Book of *AA,* which can be summarized as "Acceptance is the answer to all my problems today." So much of my mental and physical energy had been dedicated to fighting what "is," and I had yet to explore the idea of accepting or surrendering to things as they currently are. My takeaway from that Friday night meeting was that it's useless to fight what "already is," and I began to welcome the idea of accepting or surrendering to whatever life circumstances I was facing. With this new concept came the idea that perhaps the addiction wasn't necessarily something bad, but rather, perhaps it was there to tell me something— that I needed to make certain changes in my life. We've all heard the line "don't shoot the messenger," and I began opening up to the message.

I did my best to stop viewing the drinking problem as something to fight, but rather as something to turn inward toward and explore. The drinking was a misdirected cry for wholeness. Again, it was an invitation of sorts. This new thinking gave me the courage to turn my body, mind, and spirit toward the addiction and pain, instead of sprinting away from it.

I remember on several hungover mornings and sweat-filled sleepless nights, I tried to let all 120 trillion cells of my body relax into the pain and not contract from it. I was even daring enough to start asking questions: Why was I drinking so much? Why couldn't I stop? Why the pain? What does the universe want me to learn through these experiences? Although I was still keeping Big Alcohol in business, I was no longer running. I was opening up, releasing, and asking for more help.

Whether it's incoherent foxhole prayers hurled into the heavens by an atheist drunk (myself) or strategic life planning sessions involving vision boards with an addiction counselor, it all still works. When we ask, we always receive. This universal law shows up everywhere—in religions, spiritual teachings, mystical traditions, and even from my Pop Warner football coach. It's a core teaching in the Bible, too, straight from the book of Matthew: *Ask, and you shall receive.* This always holds true; it's just the timeline and the size and shape of the delivery that we sometimes struggle with.

When I say timeline, we see time going in one direction and think our petitions to the universe follow the same trajectory. For example, I ask the heavens for a hoagie sandwich on a Tuesday, and I find myself eating one on Friday later that week. In reality, it works more like this: we can ask for something in the year 2014 and receive it in 2013. In addition, we often have a predetermined idea of what the summoned help should look like, and we think it has to be a human being holding a sign saying "I'm here to help" or a clear image of Jesus emerging from the tile pattern on the bathroom floor as we sit on the toilet.

The universe had been answering my requests all along. After returning from South America, I was accompanied by my 10-month-old red standard poodle named Ben, whom I had gotten as a puppy in September 2013. Many mornings in the summer of 2014, before opening my eyes, I would start praying or asking the universe for help, only to have these desperate requests interrupted by nonstop licks to my face that wouldn't stop until I got out of bed. Even though I'd turn over and cover my face with a pillow, he wouldn't let up. I missed all of this at the time, but that prayer had already been answered in the form of a fluffy 45-pound (now 70-pound) soul containing infinite love. This guy got me out of bed on those hungover mornings, and looking back, it was Ben who took me on walks. Even though I was struggling to feel anything but hatred toward myself for breaking my own heart daily, Ben's affection toward me never wavered, and his unconditional love began to challenge my deep-seated inner self-loathing. There were times in the morning when I couldn't remember if I had fed Ben the night before while in a blackout, yet Ben would still act as if I were the brightest star in his galaxy. I don't think it's governments, currencies, or institutions that keep the fabric of society intact—I think it's the animals inside our houses that do their best to teach us humans daily how to live life from the heart. I do not doubt that it was Ben who got me through the Fire Swamp in the summer of 2014, and as I write this, Ben is now 12 years old, doing great, and sporting a haircut that makes him look like an African lion.

Chapter 17
2014: The Fire Swamp Part IV.
Rock Bottom and My Final Day 1

In mid-July 2014, I got a DUI while driving to work in the afternoon. During the roadside test, I mentioned I was suicidal, which landed me in a suicide-proof jail cell, and the booking officer exchanged my clothing for a massive padded muumuu designed to keep me safe. I remember lying awake in the jail cell around 2 or 3:00 AM with peace, knowing that this was FINALLY it. I had just been pulled over for driving under the influence at 3:30 PM—I had hit my rock bottom. Thank goodness! I called my mom the day of the arrest to notify her of what had happened, and when I walked out of the Livingston, Montana, jail the following day, my brother, who had flown in from Seattle, was there to meet me. I needed to see a familiar face so badly, and I'm forever thankful that he dropped everything in his life to come and help his little brother. My mother flew in the same day, and they both created a safe container for me. We ate home-cooked meals, watched movies, did puzzles, and I didn't drink while they were there because I had hit my rock bottom...right?

I dropped my brother and mom off at the airport in the evening and jumped right into bed around 9:00 PM, which was the plan I had discussed with both of them on the way to the airport. As the hours passed without sleep, I could hear the Bruno Voice start chirping: 11:00 PM, 12:00 AM, 1:00 AM. The battle was real, and I was losing. I had the idea to search for a sobriety group on Facebook at 1:55 AM in hopes of finding support. I entered "Sober Group" in the search bar, and at the top of the page, before I could even see the search results, was a Bud Light Lime-sponsored ad. "You've got five minutes," yelled Bruno, and I was in the car driving to the gas station where I stood at the checkout at 1:59 AM with two Bud Light Lime tall boys—one minute before they could no longer legally sell alcohol. This was how the idea of Café RE was birthed, which is the non-profit alcohol-free community I still run today.

The next day, I woke with a "FUCK ME" with a capital F and called my therapist to see if I could get in later that day—thankfully, they had an opening. When I showed up, it was a gentleman named Dr. Chuck who was filling in for my normal counselor, Melissa, because she had a sick child at home. Melissa had previously prescribed me 2 to 3 benzodiazepines at a time to calm me down and help me get a couple of days away from alcohol. Although benzodiazepines (Xanax, Librium, Valium, Klonopin, Diazepam) are basically alcohol in pill format (and I wouldn't recommend them to anyone for anything, as they are also highly addictive), they usually allowed me to get a night or two away from alcohol, which was at least something I could build on.

When I picked up the script at the pharmacy, I looked at the bottle and immediately said "oh shit" as I saw it contained 25 tablets of 10 mg Diazepam when I was expecting and hoping to see only 2 to 3 pills. I knew right away this was going to be a problem—and that was confirmed the next morning when I opened my front door and saw a fresh dent in the right front fender of my truck. I had no memory of how it got there. Luckily, upon inspection of the dent, I could see parts of tree bark lodged into where the fender meets the wheel well, and I felt relieved knowing I didn't hit a car or person. I don't think I drank the night before, but who really fucking knows. For the rest of the day, I felt an impossible weight on my shoulders, and as I searched the depths of my soul for strength to continue, I found none.

Later that evening, when I walked into my room, I saw a framed picture of myself on top of a mountain I had summited years before. "That dude is long gone," I heard the Bruno Voice say. "There is no way you're going to beat this," the Bruno Voice said sternly, and I found myself nodding my head in agreement. It wasn't planned or premeditated—there was no written note. I had had enough suffering, and there was no fight left in me. I walked into the bathroom, took the remaining 20 or so benzodiazepines along with a handful of other pills, gave my dog a long hug, and went to sleep.

When I woke the next afternoon, there was no "Hurray! I'm alive!" Instead, it was an "Oh fuck, I'm still in this nightmare called my life." I later spoke with a doctor who said just the amount of benzodiazepines alone should have done the trick twice over... But yet there I was, still breathing air into my lungs and still in the Fire Swamp. What got me out of bed around 3:00 PM that day was, once again, the answer to my prayers: my dog Ben licking my face. I later took several laps around the neighborhood, Ben glued to my side, trying to process what I had tried to accomplish the previous night. I was still groggy from the combo platter of pills I had taken the night before, but a deeper part of me chimed in, saying, "Paul, that's not how it's going to end. No way. We can do this. We ARE doing this. WE ARE MOTHERFUCKING DOING THIS." To be honest, I didn't really believe the pep talk, as I had no idea how I was going to stop this level 10 ass-kicking.

On Saturday, August 23, 2014, I went to a Broncos preseason football game in Denver, Colorado, with seven of my best friends at our annual Fantasy Football draft. I managed to stay sober the previous two nights, which was a feat, but as I climbed the concrete steps to our seats in the very last row at the top of the stadium, I could feel the familiar tensing in my body. There was beer everywhere I looked, and I knew without a doubt that I was going to be drinking in the very near future if I stayed. So two minutes into the first quarter, I told my buddy I'd be right back, and I left the stadium. I sat on a bench, pulled out my phone, and sent probably the most important text message of my life to all the members of the Fantasy Football League. I said, "Hey guys, I'm going back to the hotel. You all know I don't drink, but to be honest, it's been a major issue in my life lately. As in, it's ruining my life. I know if I stay at the game, I'll end up drinking and probably end up naked on the JumboTron. Have fun, and we'll connect later." Ships burned.

Again, I want to highlight that burning the ships is the most impactful thing you can do. Now I did drink again—in fact, it was 45 minutes later at the hotel room where I finished every beer in the room, probably 12 to 15 beers—but it was progress. Well, not the drinking part, but me burning the ships. My friends are good people, and they all asked how they could help. One of them, named Pedro, even left the game early to come check on me at the hotel. When he arrived, he saw all the empty beer cans and sarcastically said, "Ah, pulled an audible, eh?" I'm thankful for the conversations we had that night, and Pedro is still a good friend in my life.

The following week was more of the same. I'd drink, wake up the next morning, give myself the normal pep talk of "I AM DOING THIS," only to find myself drinking later that afternoon. That Saturday, I found myself driving drunk with a broken taillight to DJ and emcee a wedding. During the ceremony, there were only three songs I had to play, but my vision was so blurred that I had trouble seeing the computer screen, and I even covered one eye with a hand so I wouldn't see double. I recall saying to myself, "Oh fuck, I think it's this song...wait, it's 'Amazed' by Lonestar...fuck, isn't it the Wedding March?" Miraculously, I picked the correct song for the wedding party entrance, then the right song as the bride walked down the aisle with her father, and then, through process of elimination, I knew what song to play for the recessional at the end of the ceremony. The disc jockey gods were kind to me that afternoon, because as far as I know, I was the only one who knew I was totally shitfaced during the ceremony. Thank goodness the bride didn't have to correct my song selections.

During cocktail hour, as I snatched four full glasses of wine off the trays when waitstaff passed in front of the DJ table, I knew I was in trouble. There was a low probability of me finishing the evening, let alone doing a good job, and a high chance I was going to ruin a wedding. As "Neon Moon" by Brooks & Dunn was playing for the second time in a row on repeat, I sat down in my chair behind the DJ console, and the gravity of the situation hit me. I had just risked my own life and the lives of others while driving drunk over an hour to the wedding venue. I hadn't even begun dealing with the legal repercussions of the previous DUI just five weeks prior, and I was driving drunk again, with a broken taillight. In that moment, it became abundantly clear to me that I was still out of control, about to ruin a wedding, and needed help. The universe agreed, and the stars lined up.

I had a DJ company at the time, and one of my DJs had just finished an event about 15 minutes away from me. Despite me telling him the wrong wedding venue, he still found me, and I was relieved of my disc jockey duties within 30 minutes. I called my friend Kristin, and she came to pick me up. On the drive home, I cycled through calling my mom, dad, and brother until one of them picked up so I could announce I was going to rehab. After about 15 calls without an answer, I rolled down the passenger window and screamed so loud that every wolf, elk, grizzly bear, and bison in Yellowstone National Park turned my way. And then another scream, and several more, until there was nothing left.

Upon awakening the next morning at my friend Kristin's house, I remember hearing the birds for the first time in a long time through an open window. When my parents called, they asked if everything was okay, and I told them "NO," but I'd get back to them about rehab because something felt different that day.

Looking back, while in Kristin's car, I had surrendered to the moment, stopped fighting, and had given my body permission to purge or release a colossal amount of energy that Mother Nature gladly received as we drove down the winding canyon road back to Bozeman.

The following weekend, on Saturday, September 6, 2014, I went camping with some friends. After setting up my tent, shortly after sunset, I cracked a beer and joined the group. I took a sip, then noticed my dog Ben was steadfastly staring at me. I paused before taking the next drink, noticed the crickets, and knew unequivocally that if I drank that beer, I would soon be dead. Although all moments in time are beautiful works of art, there are moments in our lives that are more important than others. Every part of my being knew that I was at a critical juncture in time. My dog Ben was still staring directly into my eyes, and I felt the hairs on my arms rise. My inner child, with the help of my soul, was calling me deeper into the present moment. A light breeze passed through the soon-to-fall aspen leaves. A Brewer's blackbird sang from a nearby Douglas fir. It seemed the chorus of crickets intensified. There was a vibration of peace in the moment that was not compatible with the Bruno Voice, and I dumped out the rest of the beer, packed up my tent, said goodbye to my friends, and went home. September 7, 2014, was my day one.

Author's note on the Summer in The Fire Swamp

This was a damn hard chapter to write. I still haven't fully processed many of these asskickings, and as I wrote this chapter, I realized there are still many electrical charges of pain and suffering stored in my body that came to the surface as I wrote. As I mentioned in the intro, writing is part of my healing journey, and I found myself crying several times while writing about the summer in the Fire Swamp since these suppressed memories needed to be processed. It's also a damn good reminder of where I don't want to be again, and I need to STAY THE COURSE. While writing, when painful memories came to the surface, I made a point to stop and send love and warm energies to the younger Paul, who was in so much pain. I'm so proud of that guy in his early 30s for never giving up—he moved forward with so much courage and strength. I love that version of myself so much. And now I'm crying as I write this. Dammit.

Chapter 18
A Dying Molecule

If aliens were to visit planet Earth and observe a species drinking a toxic substance that had no health benefits and left that species incapacitated the next morning, I imagine they would be scratching their heads in total confusion. If they had the chance to speak with this *Homo sapiens* (sapiens means wise), I imagine it would go something like this.

Aliens: Hello, Earthling, on the weekends, we see you drinking a liquid that does not hydrate you, it seems to zap your intelligence, your decision-making skills disappear, and you have trouble getting out of bed the next morning. We feel we are missing something. Can you please explain?

Wise Human: Yeah, that sounds about right. Oh, wait, we also drink it on weekdays, even if we have to get up early for work the next morning. Don't forget Holidays, sporting events, concerts, graduations, birthdays, funerals, work events, book clubs, while cooking dinner, yoga, and some drink in their bedrooms upon awakening and throughout the entire day, even while at work, despite the boss saying it's company policy not to drink at work.

Aliens: Okay…then we assume this makes you happy or feel good?

Wise Human: For a couple of hours, maybe, then you come back down and feel worse than when you started, which is called a hangover. Oh, and if you drink too much, the room will start spinning and you'll end up barfing up your lunch, dinner, or both.

Aliens: We imagine you stop then, correct?

Wise Human: Well…perhaps for a bit, but some resume drinking immediately to avoid the hangover and to suppress a whirlwind of uncomfortable emotions like anxiety, depression, and the current state of the world.

Aliens: Interesting…well, does it give you magical powers?

Wise Human: Most definitely, yes! It makes you think your jokes are funnier, that you're better looking, that your life is in a better state than it actually is, that you're a better dancer, that your finances aren't fucked, and you're good in bed.

Aliens: Is any of that true?

Wise Human: Well, no…not really.

Aliens: Would it be correct to say your species routinely, with predictable regularity, drinks a toxin that drastically diminishes your chances of survival in a universe that is already challenging to survive in?

Wise Human: Um, I never thought of it like that.

Aliens: We assume then it's free?

Wise Human: No, not exactly. Wait, unless someone gives it to you as a gift.

Aliens: Wait a second, you're telling me humans purposefully gift this poison? As in with a good intention? Hang on, we don't think our translation machine is working properly.

Wise Human: No…well, yeah…you've got that right.

Aliens: Wise Human, we have spoken with the Emperor Penguin, the Douglas Fir, the Andean condor, and two banana slugs; we feel you have much to learn from your earthly counterparts. In our explorations throughout the galaxies, we have yet to meet a species that purposefully makes life more difficult by consuming large quantities of poison. In addition, it seems that when someone chooses not to drink this poison, they have to repeatedly explain why to their friends and even family members.

The Truth Is Emerging

In 2010, British doctor David Nutt was tasked by the British government to put a harm score on 20 of the world's most dangerous drugs. What came in as the most dangerous drug wasn't crack, heroin, cocaine, or meth—it was alcohol. This finding was so incongruent with how society viewed alcohol at the time that Dr. Nutt was shortly sacked from his government position after releasing his report. When a reporter asked the British government why Dr. Nutt was fired, they said, "He was let go because he cannot be both a government adviser and a campaigner against government policy at the same time." This is total bananas. B-A-N-A-N-A-S.

In January 2023, the World Health Organization (WHO), which for several decades supported the stance that one to two drinks per day is beneficial to overall human health, put out a statement saying "No Level of Alcohol Consumption Is Safe for Our Health," citing that alcohol is a toxic, psychoactive, and dependence-producing substance. In that same month, *The New York Times* published an article titled "Even a Little Alcohol Can Harm Your Health," citing that even low levels of alcohol can raise the risk of high blood pressure and heart disease. In December 2023, men's publication *GQ* released an article with the title "The Year We Realized Any Alcohol Is Bad for You." In Canada, the Canadian Centre on Substance Use and Addiction (CCSA), in new guidance, argued that the ideal amount of alcohol that someone can drink is NONE. They also make a clear point, saying that a daily drink increases someone's risk of cancer, cardiovascular conditions, and liver disease.

The U.S. government agency, the National Institute on Alcohol Abuse and Alcoholism (NIAAA), which for the first 45 years of its existence stated that 1-2 drinks per day was not only safe but was good for your overall health, now states that drinking less is better than drinking more. They also recommend that individuals who do not drink should not start drinking for any reason because "evidence" indicates that among those who drink, there is a higher level of death from all causes. The NIAAA has done a complete 180 in the last decade. In 2017, with secret funding from Big Alcohol and your taxpayer dollars, the NIAAA conducted studies showing that daily alcohol consumption was good for you, which is complete level 10 bullshit.

Thank fucking heavens the correct information about alcohol is coming to light and people are starting to make healthier choices about what they drink. I take full responsibility for every alcoholic beverage I have consumed in my life, but when the DARE (Drug Abuse Resistance Education) officer came to my school in the late 80s and early 90s, there was little to no discussion about the true gateway drug: alcohol. While growing up, it was a hard "Just say no" to heroin, crack, and cocaine, while alcohol was a benign liquid that delivered cardiovascular health benefits. Total bullshit. In April 2017, I delivered a TEDx talk titled "Duped by Alcohol," which now has over 700,000 views on YouTube, about how my experience with alcohol was not as advertised. Again, I don't want to paint the picture that I'm a victim, but there was a major lack of transparency about the serious potential dangers of alcohol, and worse, it was marketed and stamped by the very institutions that were created to keep us safe, that alcohol would enhance our overall health and well-being.

I Ain't Touching That Shit

Despite decades of billion-dollar marketing from Big Alcohol and government agencies selling booze as a life-enhancing elixir, drinkers have begun to connect the dots. In the age of information, the truth is harder to bury. In August 2022, Stanford neuroscientist Andrew Huberman of the *Huberman Lab* podcast released an episode titled "What Alcohol Does to Your Body, Brain & Health," which was the #1 downloaded episode on Apple Podcasts for nearly two years. To put that into perspective, there are over 4 million podcasts in existence, with more than 200 million total episodes. I can guarantee you Big Alcohol execs were saying, "Fuck, fuck, fuck—when is this episode going away?" For 120 minutes, Huberman tells it how it is: alcohol is shit.

Again, I am so thankful that accurate and correct information about alcohol is now being disseminated to the public, and people are making better choices based on this information. In 2024, over 40% of Americans reported plans to cut back on alcohol, according to data from NCSolutions. That number increases to 49% for millennials and 61% for Gen Z. Just one year later, in 2025, nearly half (49%) of Americans planned to reduce alcohol consumption, and they are making good on their plans. According to a 2025 Gallup poll, only 54% of Americans now drink alcohol, marking the lowest point in 90 years of data. In 2023, it was 62%.

With wine, sales fell 8% in 2024 due to changing consumer preferences, prompting producers to focus on non-alcoholic offerings for growth. Global wine consumption from 2017 to 2023 decreased to the equivalent of around 3.5 billion fewer bottles of wine, and vineyards worldwide are ripping out their grapevines because it's no longer a good use of land. Acquerello, a San Francisco restaurant with a wine cellar of 15,000 bottles from across the globe, reported a 24% decrease in wine sales from 2023 and says that 2025 is going to be their worst year on record, according to their wine director. In 2024, France opened its first industrial wine de-alcoholization center. Holy shit, I had none of this on my alcohol-free bingo card.

On December 16, 2024, *The Prof G Markets* podcast, hosted by market expert Scott Galloway, released an episode discussing how the stocks of major alcohol companies are down. Boston Beer has fallen 9%, AB InBev—think Budweiser and Corona—has fallen 15%, Jack Daniel's is down 20%, and Walmart reported beer sales declined 11% in the past year. The host Scott Galloway is invited to give a yearly talk to the board of AB InBev, and he says his message to the board this year is, "You're fucked, and you're fucked even worse."

"You're fucked," meaning that people have already started to drink less. "You're fucked even worse," meaning that your future customers aren't even drinking. He then continues to say in the episode that Big

Alcohol companies are the new cable companies, where their business models are becoming obsolete and will have to radically change, or similar to how their products killed millions, they themselves will perish.

Non-alcoholic (NA) beers basically didn't exist until commercially branded NA beer made its way into tens of thousands of bars and grocery stores in the 1990s as part of a legal defense against Mothers Against Drunk Driving (MADD) and the rise of the Designated Driver movement. Turns out, mothers who lost their children to drunk driving have the power to ignite real change—and thank God they did. So beer giants made NA beer to mollify the rightfully pissed-off mothers, but they had zero intention of scaling this segment of their business, and I've read in the past that they purposefully made the beer taste bland.

Big alcohol didn't plan on growing their alcohol-free offerings because alcohol consumption impairs inhibition and often generates rapid repeat purchases, which is why you'll occasionally see some drunk idiot buy a round for the entire bar. We've all seen our tab at the end of the night and said to ourselves, "What the fuck happened?" I once bought a $700 bottle of vodka in a Vegas nightclub while blacked out. So the alcohol industry had no interest in hampering the most profitable arm of their business, which is why they put NA beers in obscure locations on the shelves in bars, did zero marketing, and really didn't want anyone to know about the alcohol-free option.

In 2013, hedge fund manager and ultramarathon runner Bill Shufelt quit drinking. Finding the selection of non-alcoholic drinks at the time to be unsatisfactory, he sought out John Walker (not Johnny Walker), a brewer from Santa Fe, and the two of them launched Athletic Brewing in 2017 with only two beers, which were available in only a handful of stores in the New England area. Shortly after, they expanded their distribution to all 50 states, and Athletic's sales grew from $2.5 million in 2019 to $15 million in 2020 to $51 million in 2023, then a whopping $130 million in 2024. The company is now valued at $800 million, is the second-fastest-growing food and beverage company in the U.S., and its brand has recently surpassed others such as Tecate and Jack Daniel's. Athletic Brewing has managed to buck a 5,000-year trend, saying that a beer has to contain alcohol, and the top-selling beverage at Whole Foods in 2024 was a beer that contains zero alcohol.

According to Bump Williams Consulting, an agency that specializes in the alcoholic beverage industry, the NA beer market, which is currently valued at $22 billion, has been growing every year by 30 to 40% since 2019 and shows no signs of slowing down. When Heineken released its first true zero AF beer in 2017, the Chief Marketing Officer, Jonnie Cahill, was skeptical and said, "Are we sure this is really a thing? Is this going to work?" In 2022, the 0.0% AF beverage accounted for $83.6 million in sales for Heineken. Data also shows that NA beer accounted for 2.2% of all grocery store beer sales in 2023, which admittedly may not sound like a lot, but there was a time, not that long ago, when NA beer sales made up 0.2% of all grocery store sales in the mid-2010s.

I have personally seen this rapid expansion on shelves. There's a gas station chain in Montana called Town Pump, where in 2013 they had one shelf dedicated to NA beers, and in 2025 they now have three full coolers (32 shelves) that contain only alcohol-free options. White Claw now offers an AF option; you can now purchase AF sake, and I'm sure AF moonshine is the next million-dollar idea. I'm not sure an AF Colt 45 or King Cobra will take off, but things are changing, and they are changing fast.

Another indicator that personal tastes are evolving is the number of alcohol-free bars and even nightclubs that are popping up across the country and around the globe. In our alcohol-free community, Café RE, we have a resource section where we list AF bars. At first, it seemed like we were adding one new bar per year, but now we have dozens listed, and we're having trouble keeping up with all the new AF establishments. In episode 455 of the *Recovery Elevator* podcast, I interview Chris Marshall from Austin, Texas, who could be credited with America's first AF bar, which opened in 2017. A true pioneer, Chris was driven by his own struggles with alcohol to start serving AF drinks—and he's found tremendous success.

Establishments that serve alcohol have a lower vibration, especially dive bars, meaning the energy in the building is dense and is usually accompanied by a pungent, moldy smell that makes the hairs inside your nostrils recoil. Customers are opting out of these environments like never before, and it turns out most patrons prefer places where some drunk baboon won't spill a drink on them or try to spark a conversation with slurred words.

I used to own a vending machine and arcade business across the state of Montana that did incredibly well. The further away I got from my last drink, the harder it became to enter the locations that served alcohol—not because I was tempted to drink, but because of how my body physically responded upon entering. One day, when going to service the arcade games in a college dive bar, around four years after my last drink, my body told me a change was needed. When I walked through the service door in the back of the bar around 11:00 AM, well before the bar opened for customers, I felt a sudden uneasiness in my stomach and chest area. It was like my lungs and entire body began to contract. It made me stop just inside the doorway, and I intuitively walked back outside, where I immediately began to feel better. About a minute later, I entered the bar again, and boom—same thing happened. I instantly felt like shit again. I returned outside and quickly began to feel better. When I walked into the bar for a third time and smack, I was met with the intense feeling of dog turds. I said to myself, "Oh shit, this is no longer going to work for me. I have to sell this business."

For the last eight years, I had built a business that brought in $20 to 25K a month, but in that moment, I knew I was no longer a vibrational match for it. I couldn't keep forcing my body into spaces where it would physically contract from the energy in the building. In 2018, I sold the business—but made sure to include one important clause in the buy-sell agreement: I still get to play the arcade games for free across the state of Montana.

What's Really Inside the Bottle

In January 2025, CNN did a full 20-minute segment with U.S. Surgeon General Vivek Murthy, where he made the case that alcohol labels should carry the cancer risks associated with alcohol. His statement to Congress included recent data showing that alcohol causes roughly 100,000 alcohol-related cancer cases and about 20,000 deaths each year from cancer alone. Currently, the government warning on alcohol labels is this:

> **GOVERNMENT WARNING:** (1) According to the Surgeon General, women should not drink alcoholic beverages during pregnancy because of the risk of birth defects. (2) Consumption of alcoholic beverages impairs your ability to drive a car or operate machinery and may cause health problems.

How I read that is: if you're not pregnant, nor operating machinery or driving a car, alcohol is completely benign. There absolutely should be something mentioning the link between alcohol and cancer, with a broader statement mentioning that if someone consumes alcohol (the most dangerous drug on the planet), they can expect to see an overall decline in health and life expectancy. Maybe the label should mention that your chances of ruining a wedding drastically increase when consuming this beverage, or perhaps that you have a higher chance of taking a nap in the snow after drinking. Now Congress still has to act, and if they don't act, we should act with our votes and our decisions to purchase beverages without the poison. I can't think of any reasons why Congress wouldn't act...oh wait, here's a reason: Big Alcohol has been throwing dirty money via lobbying efforts at the government for decades.

Dirty Money

I say dirty money because that's what it is. Normal drinkers don't keep the lights on for Big Alcohol. There's a rule in business called the 80/20 rule, where 80% of your profits come from 20% of your customers or efforts. With Big Alcohol, it's more like the 95/5 rule, where 95% of their profits come from 5% of their customers: alcoholics. The Molson Coors company, based out of Boulder, Colorado, doesn't turn a profit off the guy who buys a six-pack of Coors Light, drinks two beers, then places the remaining four beers in the back of his refrigerator until the following weekend. That customer doesn't pay the bills. It's the person who drinks a 30-pack on Saturday, then again on Sunday, and loads of beers throughout the week. This is the same for ALL alcohol companies. The addicted customer is buying 95%-98% of the product, and they know it. This is the same with wine—it's not the customer who has a glass of wine for dinner that keeps them in business, but the drinker who finishes two bottles a night.

A couple of years ago, one of our Café RE community members invited me to go rock climbing in the foothills just outside of Golden, Colorado. After climbing to the top of the bluff, I had a clear view of the Coors factory about 1,000 feet below me at the base of the mountain. It was a sight to see. I could hear the low rumble of freight train cars dropping off raw materials and ingredients to be turned into beer. I saw trucks being loaded with pallets and others pulling out of the facility to begin making deliveries. I was flooded with emotions as I viewed this factory that appeared to be at least the size of 10 football fields. I was surprised when I heard myself mutter an audible "Fuck you" to the Coors factory since their product nearly killed me and has killed so many others. I was also filled with gratitude and relief that I no longer consume their product. But wow, what a machine—I have to admit, it was quite impressive. We hear so much about drug cartels south of the border, yet here was a massive factory selling the most addictive drug on the planet in plain sight.

Now I would insert a paragraph here about how these companies are the devil, and the individuals that work there should feel horrible about their career choice, knowing they are selling a chemical that destroys the fabric of society, but I would be a total hypocrite since I used to own a bar and I sold a shit ton of alcohol. I was no different than the alcohol companies. As a bar owner, I didn't make my money on the customer who nursed a beer for an hour, but the foreign exchange student who bought 10 shots, then danced on the bar, and then probably slept through class the next morning. However, we are designed to grow, as individuals and as groups. As I became addicted to alcohol and started to learn more about what alcohol actually is, I departed from that soul-sucking business model and later quit drinking.

I'd like to think that Big Alcohol will eventually accept the fact that their product is total dog shit with fancy graphics on the can or bottle, but I don't think that will happen. In fact, I think they are a malignant cancer in America and across the globe, selling a product that has the capacity to suck the life energy out of its customers. Let me be clear: I'm not suggesting we make alcohol illegal. We tried that from 1920 to 1933—Prohibition—and it didn't go well. The problem wasn't just alcohol itself, but that the U.S. government went after the supply without addressing the demand. I absolutely think alcohol should remain legal, but there are a few changes we could make that would *definitely* help.

Advertising.
No advertisements on TV, film, radio, magazines, social media, billboards, bus stops, inside subways or trains, ski lifts, gondolas—none. Anywhere.

Design and Packaging.
Limited fonts and colors can be used on the can and packaging: black, white, and possibly red. Font = Times New Roman, no larger than size 24.

Labeling.
Studies show that when cigarette manufacturers are required to put pictures of black lungs or holes in throats on packaging, sales go down—shocking, right? Labeling for alcohol should be just as accurate and explicit about health risks, especially cancers. Honestly, there should probably be a skull and crossbones ☠ ☠ ☠ ☠ on every alcoholic beverage sold.

Environmental Responsibility.
Big Alcohol is trashing the planet. At Recovery Elevator retreats, we do service projects where we clean up the area we visit, and our cleanup bags are always disproportionately filled with alcohol bottles. Alcohol

containers make up a huge portion of beverage waste in our oceans. A fixed percentage of alcohol revenues should go toward cleaning up roads, parks, waterways, and cities. Big Alcohol is shitting all over the planet and not doing a thing about it.

Treatment and Recovery.
Alcohol companies should be required to contribute to the treatment and recovery of their addicted customers. This starts with higher taxes. Speaking of taxes…

Bent Over a Barrel

In fiscal year 2023, the U.S. federal government collected approximately $10 billion in alcohol excise taxes from distilled spirits, wine, and beer.

Wow, that's a lot of money! I imagine the U.S. government is using that cash to invest in education, infrastructure, renewable energy, homeless shelters, and more. But wait—there's a number we're missing: the cost of alcohol use in America, or more precisely, the burden that alcohol places on society.

Based on available research, alcohol-related costs in the United States total approximately $250 billion annually. This breaks down to about $35 billion spent on healthcare (40 to 60% of occupied hospital beds have connections to alcohol), $25 billion on the criminal justice system, $16 billion on motor vehicle crashes and emergency services, and a whopping $179 billion due to lost workplace productivity.

So, let's do the math: the U.S. government brings in $10 billion in tax revenue from alcohol, but it costs $250 billion to clean up alcohol's wreckage. American taxpayers make up that $240 billion difference. Canadians are getting a slightly better deal but are still getting hosed— the Canadian government brings in $13 billion in alcohol revenue while alcohol costs Canadians $19 billion, leaving taxpayers on the hook for $6 billion.

Let's break down that $250 billion into bite-sized pieces. Every single day, the social and economic damage that Big Alcohol companies aren't paying for costs Americans $685 million. Every hour? $28 million. Every minute? Nearly $250,000. And every second that ticks by, alcohol causes almost $8,000 worth of damage across America.

In the time it took you to read that last short paragraph, nearly $40,000 in alcohol-related costs just hit American taxpayers like you and me..

On its website, the National Center for Drug Abuse Statistics (NCDAS) has broken down this deficit by state, calculating how much taxpayers have to spend to cover the shortfall for every drink consumed. Take Texas, for example: Lone Star State citizens had to cover an $18 billion deficit as a result of alcohol's mess. They calculated that for every drink consumed in Texas, an additional $2.69 in taxes needs to be collected to pay for alcohol's true cost.

Here's how wild this gets: when someone orders a Michelob Ultra at a Texas Roadhouse in Dallas, some random taxpayer in Fort Worth is essentially forced to chip in an extra $2.69 on top of that drink. The drinker pays for the beer, but everyone else pays for the cleanup.

When I averaged this out across all 50 states, the number that should make everyone's eyebrows shoot up is this: $2.66 per drink. That's the additional amount taxpayers are on the hook for every single time alcohol is consumed in America. For every Budweiser cracked open, every glass of merlot poured, every whiskey on the rocks ordered—$2.66 in tax revenue has to be collected somewhere, from someone, to clean up the mess.

Here's the bottom line: Big Alcohol is paying around 4% of what they should be paying in taxes, and you and I are picking up the tab for the other 96%. They've got all of us bent over a barrel. Think about this absurdity—a 40-ounce bottle of King Cobra malt liquor costs less than a bottle of water at gas stations. How does that make any sense?

The price of alcohol should be at least doubled, maybe tripled, with every penny of that increase funding the real costs: healthcare systems, addiction treatment, literal trash pickup, and educational programs. But that's not happening, and there are zero signs it's going to change anytime soon. This is institutional rot at its finest.

Big Alcohol operates like a carcinogenic tumor in society—they make their money off addicted customers, collect their profits, and vanish when it's time to clean up the wreckage. The only real difference between Big Alcohol and Drug Cartels? Official paperwork, above-ground distribution routes, and government approval stamps.

The Future of Alcohol

Alcohol is going the way of cigarettes in the next 10 to 20 years. For decades, tobacco giants had us convinced that inhaling smoke into our lungs was safe. Look how much we've evolved when it comes to cigarettes. Can you imagine sitting next to a chain smoker on a flight from Los Angeles to New York? *Insert hand-to-face emoji here.*

Today, it's abundantly clear that smoking causes lung cancer and is the leading cause of preventable death in the U.S., with around 500,000 deaths per year. Smokers used to be viewed as elegant and sophisticated. Now, when I see someone smoking outside in the cold, I look at them with pity and always send them heartfelt energy to beat their addiction—because they are addicted, and for many, it will cost them their lives. Big Tobacco is marking out gravesites for itself and its future neighbors in the cemetery: Big Alcohol.

I had a brief stint with smoking, which I'm thankful for. In January 2017, I volunteered at a rehab facility in Thailand, and after being offered a cigarette for the 76th time, I said okay. I planned on it being just a Thailand thing, but during my layover in Japan, I found myself buying a pack of cigarettes, and then again a couple of days later at a gas station in Montana. I was hooked—addicted before I even knew it. Within six months of starting smoking, I was up to a pack a day.

In August that year, I was registered to run the iconic 23-mile Jim Bridger Ridge Run, and I had an honest conversation with myself: "Paul, dude, if we're going to run this race, we have to quit smoking cigarettes." At the end of June, I stopped smoking cold turkey, which was absolutely brutal, but I'm thankful for this experience because now I have so much empathy for smokers. When I see a smoker outside on the street, I always say a prayer for them, sending them liberation and clean air for their lungs.

The alcohol industry is currently tanking across the board. Wine, spirits, and beer sales are all declining—fast—with the only growth area being non-alcoholic offerings. Even worse news for alcohol companies? Their future customers aren't buying what they're selling. Young people are drinking significantly less, and many aren't drinking at all.

In the annual Monitoring the Future survey published in 2024, around two-thirds of 12th graders reported they hadn't used alcohol in the last 30 days—the largest proportion of abstainers since the survey began tracking abstinence in 2017. And here's the kicker: a record 80% of 10th graders said they hadn't touched alcohol in that same period.

Currently, we still live in a world where we have to justify why we're not drinking poison, but that chapter is coming to an end. I think it flips in another 5 to 10 years, and people who choose to consume alcohol will have to explain and justify why they're drinking a chemical that puts them and others at risk.

It may seem that part of the alcohol-free explosion is being driven by Big Alcohol itself, but that's not accurate—customers always tell businesses where to go. Heineken recently launched an ad campaign titled "0.0 Reasons Needed" for why we're not drinking. The biggest driver of this movement is consumers who are waking up fast to what alcohol actually is.

Similar to how Joe Camel is now seen as a sad, lumpy ungulate with tar-filled lungs, I don't think we're far from viewing the Most Interesting Man in the World (Dos Equis) as someone who regularly makes poor health decisions. In less than 10 years, the Captain Morgan pirate will be viewed as a dejected, sorrowful drunk, and frat boys who insert tubes into their assholes to buttchug beer will be the losers on campus.

Does all of this make me happy? Kinda. I try not to focus on Big Alcohol's world too much, but I do feel this information is relevant for this book since I'm trying to show that things are changing with how we view alcohol. True, I do mutter a "take that bitch" when I come across an article saying wine sales dropped by nearly double digits in 2024, but

I need to be careful where I place my energy. I don't want to waste time fighting Big Alcohol or rallying my listeners to grab their pitchforks and head to the Molson Coors factory.

If I go that route, I'll come across as a sad, resentful, angry podcaster full of bitterness—and after all, I have alcohol to thank for pushing me into the Dolce Vita, the Good Life. I do have to call out Big Alcohol's putridness in this book, but my bigger goal is to share the correct information about how alcohol is the Headless Horseman that has a high probability of derailing your life if you consume it long enough.

Now I take full ownership of every drink I consumed, but when people are better educated about alcohol's damaging effects, they can make better decisions for themselves and are better equipped to intervene when they see friends or family drinking to excess. I should have had dozens of mini to major interventions, but 10+ drinks a night for a college student and 15+ drinks a night for a bar owner was viewed as totally normal.

When I was a full-blown, raging alcoholic, only three people commented on my drinking. One was a girl I dated briefly who didn't drink at all, and I didn't take her warning seriously because, well...she was a non-drinker. The other was a friend named Zak, who called me after a boating trip in my early twenties. He said, "Hey Paul, I saw you drinking vodka out of the bottle around 7:30 am, and wanted to make sure everything is okay." I told him I was fine, which I honestly thought I was, but I definitely wasn't.

The only real forceful pushback I received was from my bouncer Ricardo, when I owned my bar in Spain. We had just closed at 3:00 AM, and when he came back into the bar to get his jacket, he saw me filling up an empty glass bottle with probably 5 to 6 ounces of vodka. Ricardo said, "What's that for?" "It's for the walk home," I shot back. Ricardo, in a very serious tone, said, "Paul, you can't do that. If you keep that up long enough, you'll become an alcoholic." While walking home through the empty Spanish streets at 3:30 AM, I thought about what Ricardo had just told me. "Nah, I'm a bar owner, it's all good," I confidently told myself. But in reality, I was already fully addicted to alcohol and had a long road ahead.

NA Beers and Recovery

For many people, including myself, NA beers (or mocktails) are not triggering and can even help satisfy cravings for alcohol. In fact, I have trouble drinking more than one or two NA beers in a sitting before my stomach begins to reject them. For others, NA beers can light the neuronal alcohol pathways in the brain ablaze and can be triggering.

Your sobriety—your alcohol-free life—is the most beautifully important, fragile seed you are cultivating right now, and my recommendation is to steer clear of NA beers in your first year away from alcohol.

Yes, there are trace amounts of alcohol in non-alcoholic beers (less than 0.5%), but you'd have to drink around 25 to 30 of them to reach a 0.05% to 0.08% blood alcohol limit, depending on your body size. Drinking 25 NA beers would be incredibly uncomfortable. I saw an Instagram video of a guy who drank three NA beers, then blew 0.00 into a breathalyzer. He drank three more and still blew 0.00. He continued blowing 0.00 up until 12 NA beers, when he finally registered a 0.01.

I once heard a story where a wife told her husband that the only beers he was allowed to have in the house were non-alcoholic beers. The man stocked up on NA beers and found himself drinking 20+ NA beers nightly in his garage alone to get the same effect as one or two normal beers.

I know that in recovery circles, especially in the rooms of Alcoholics Anonymous, consuming NA beers can be contentious because there are trace amounts of alcohol, and they can be triggering. Again, I recommend that someone always err on the side of caution when it comes to their sobriety, and there are hundreds of other true alcohol-free options I'd recommend someone start with first—like an ice-cold lemonade.

However, if we're concerned with trace amounts of alcohol, consider this: a hamburger bun contains around 1.18% alcohol, fruit juices in your refrigerator, like orange juice and apple juice, contain anywhere from 0.05% to 2.0% alcohol, and a banana begins to ferment as it ripens, leading to an alcohol content of about 0.2% to 0.4%.

My favorite NA beer is from a Chicago-based brewer called Go Brewing, which launched in 2023. One of our community members in Café RE connected me with the owner, Joe Chura, and I pitched the idea of a beverage collaboration. He said, "Let's do it." On their award-winning pilsner, we put the *Recovery Elevator* logo and tagline—*Find Your Better You*—with a QR code leading to the *Recovery Elevator* website.

One reason I wanted to partner with an NA beer company is that many people buy NA beer as a step towards quitting drinking. A QR code leading them to a community for support is way better than the verbiage "drink responsibly," which puts all the blame on the consumer and none on the company selling a product that roughly 10% of their customers become addicted to. I hope to explore more beverage collaborations with Go Brewing in the future—we sold 180 six-packs in less than two weeks, and it was a great feeling drinking an NA beer with the *Recovery Elevator* logo on the side.

I've thrown out the idea on the *Recovery Elevator* podcast that I'm open to partnering with Big Alcohol because there definitely needs to be something more than the shaming "drink responsibly" on bottles and cans. The podcast has been downloaded over 10 million times, so I'm almost certain some Big Alcohol executive or employee (who are perhaps struggling with alcohol themselves) has heard the pitch, but no takers yet. However, I don't think Big Alcohol would ever list a resource on their cans to help addicted customers quit drinking because it means fewer profits for the company, even though it's the ethical and moral thing to do. I know there was a time in my drinking career (which I pray to the heavens is over) where, after my tenth beer alone on the couch, my drunken gaze would have come across a message on the can suggesting a lifesaving change.

Chapter 19
Healing

Getting one day of sobriety, is harder than two.
Two days, harder than a week.
A week, harder than a month.
A month, harder than a year.
A year, harder than 10.
And 10 years, harder than 40.
- Robby H.

It's no surprise that the human body reverts back to a much healthier state after we stop ingesting a Class 1 carcinogen. What is surprising is how expansive the healing is. I came across a list from a Reddit user of what he no longer suffers from now that he has put the bottle down:

Anxiety
Depression
Bloated belly and face
Swollen fingers
Tingly feet
Dry hair and nails
Acid reflux
Crippling heartburn
Food sensitivity
Dry skin
Redness
Droopy eyelids
Fatigue
Lack of motivation
Zero self-respect

Constant self-deprecating jokes
Red eyes
Foggy vision
Lack of self-control
Anger
Stress over nothing
Impatience
Short fuse
Stirring in the middle of the night
Waking up tired every morning
Spiraling thoughts
Sweats
Stinky body odor
Huge pores on the nose and cheeks
Short-term memory. Gone.
Poor money management
Uncomfortable in everyday social situations for no reason
Shortness of breath
Feelings of worthlessness
Inability to feel any positive feelings whatsoever
Suicidal ideation
Inability to think long-term
Inability to live in the moment
Sore aching muscles
Stiff joints
Dry mouth
Bad breath
Bleeding gums
Inability to make decisions
Lethargy
Sloth-like behavior
Explosive shits
Dehydration
Inability to focus on a single task for long

Light sensitivity
Runny nose
Shaky hands
Dizziness
Nausea

On the flip side, this shows you how potent and psychologically destructive and addictive alcohol is—that someone can experience this cornucopia of pain daily and yet return to the bottle over and over.

I hosted a virtual chat in our alcohol-free community (Café RE) and brought this expansive list of healing as the topic. I found it hilarious that, of all the nagging ailments listed, such as halitosis, feelings of worthlessness, and shaky hands, the chat attendees honed in on the explosive shits, which I think was referenced several times during the chat and throughout the week.

Hyper-referencing explosive shits is a wonderful thing. First off—no more explosive shits. I was at a bachelor party in Dijon, France, when I turned to my brother with a puckered face and demanded, "Give me your key." As I waddled through the narrow cobblestone French streets with clenched everything like an emperor penguin, I knew I was in trouble. While fumbling with the key to my brother's apartment, I felt a lego-sized turd roll down my leg, then another. "Why the fuck is the bathroom on the second floor?" I cried out. Fiery, cantankerous, unholy, belligerent, explosive shits on every single step of the spiral staircase leading to the second floor. I didn't make it.

Another reason why referencing explosive shits is a glorious thing is that it represents a return of humor and laughter in our lives—and we all know that laughter is the best medicine. It's been over ten years since I've had bouts of explosive shits, nearly the same amount of time since I quit drinking—go figure. That alone makes this journey worth it.

Healing: What to Expect When
You Put the Bottle Down

A question I'm often asked and see posted in Café RE is what to expect when we put the bottle down. Alcohol first kills us spiritually, mentally, and then physically. But when you stop drinking alcohol, your body heals in reverse: first physically, then mentally, then spiritually. Of course, there is overlap; it's not quite this linear, and honestly, the healing never really stops. Putting the bottle down will heal your family for generations to come.

I recently asked *Recovery Elevator* Instagram followers to summarize sobriety, or the healing that takes place after we quit drinking, in three words. The three most common responses were: energy, peace, and presence. Who would have thought? Billions of dollars are spent on prescriptions, pills, oil diffusers, counseling sessions, weighted blankets, serums, pastes, diets, wraps, meditation apps, Himalayan salt lamps, foam rollers, sound machines, and adaptogenic drinks—all to achieve more energy, peace, and presence. Go figure—removing alcohol, which is advertised as a benign liquid promising energy, peace, and presence, actually results in the very things we were chasing: more energy, more peace, and a greater sense of consciousness. I'm glad we're on this side of things.

There's a concept in the recovery world called the 'pink cloud,' which represents the soul and inner child skipping through grassy fields holding hands now that you've stopped drinking alcohol. Life seems more doable, detoxing is no longer part of your morning or daily routine, and you now have the energy needed to step into the life you've always wanted for yourself. And when I say step into, it's more about allowing that life to come to you. The pink cloud isn't necessarily guaranteed, but if it does arrive, welcome it, you deserve it, and enjoy the ride.

Although the timeline looks wildly different for everyone, here's what healing can start to look like—physically, mentally, and spiritually—once you remove alcohol.

Physical Healing

First Week: The Most Intense Healing Symptoms

- Withdrawal symptoms peak within the first 1 to 3 days and begin to subside.
- Heart rate and blood pressure begin to normalize.
- The cells in your mouth, esophagus, stomach, and intestines start rejoicing as they begin to recover.
- Sleep patterns start improving (although the first three nights can be rough).
- Hydration levels improve as your body stops losing excess fluid.
- Overall, inflammation begins to reduce.
- Tears—like the first rains after Simba reclaimed the throne, the tear ducts are clearing out toxins.
- The liver begins initial repair work by reducing fat accumulation and begins to process the backlog of toxins that took a back seat to alcohol. (Side note: the liver can repair 2/3 of a damaged liver, or can fully heal if not more than 2/3 of the liver is damaged.)
- The dopamine system begins recalibrating: There's a small chance you may crack an authentic smile at the end of this week, especially if you hear someone pass gas.
- Confidence rises knowing you are taking control of your life again.
- Self-assurance returns knowing you did something you didn't think you could do: Go 24 hours without alcohol, and this builds with each 24-hour cycle we add to it.
- At the end of this week, there's a chance you'll start feeling like a human again. The flood of emotions confirms this. Feeling a wide spectrum of emotions is the normal human experience.
- You stop looking like something that washed up on shore after a particularly rough storm.
- Explosive shits become a distant memory. Good riddance.

First Month:

- Your overworked liver should stop sending you hate mail. Significant liver function improvement as the body is now processing toxins at a normal pace. Bile production returns to normal, carrying away fats and other waste.

- Reduced facial puffiness and improved skin appearance. Your friends will stop wondering if you're retaining water because secretly you're a pufferfish.

- Weight stabilization as metabolism adjusts since drunk nacho nights are no longer a thing.

- Color and light begin returning to the eyes—this is a big one.

- White blood cells emerge from hiding, and improved immune system function throughout the body begins to take place.

- Blood sugar levels begin to stabilize, and your pancreas no longer threatens to write a tell-all memoir.

- Nutrient absorption improves when your gut isn't distracted by processing poison.

- Reduced acid reflux and stomach inflammation—your stomach stops its nightly impression of a volcano documentary.

- More consistent energy levels throughout the day. You may find you need less caffeine to get your day started.

First Six Months:

- The hypothalamus, pituitary, and adrenal axis settle down, and you begin to feel less stressed. A flat tire is now just a flat tire and doesn't have the capacity to ruin your day or life.

- Cortisol levels in the blood begin to balance, and your body no longer acts like it's being chased by an invisible bear.

- The brain is well into the genesis of generating new neurons. Little baby brain cells start tentatively building connections while looking over their shoulder to ensure alcohol truly is gone.

- Liver enzymes continue trending in a positive direction. Your liver, having downgraded from "imminent strike" to "cautiously optimistic," starts remembering what its actual job description was before becoming a full-time alcohol processor.

- The staircase that used to leave you winded now makes you wonder where the Rocky steps are.

- There's a new depth to your eyes, and people may start saying there's something different about you, but they can't pinpoint exactly what it is.

- Skin regeneration and repair are fully underway, resulting in what could be called a "glow" or, better said, the light your organism naturally emits is no longer blocked by the portable bar you were carrying around in your bloodstream.

First Year:

- Liver tissue regeneration continues, and liver values return to normal in most (and many extreme) cases.

- When you come across words like 5K, 10K, half marathon, marathon, you pause and say to yourself, "Hmm… Maybe we should sign up."

- Cardiovascular health improves with reduced risk of heart disease; 365 days without an arrhythmia means no more passive-aggressive notes from the most important organ in your body: the heart.

- Risk of alcohol-induced cancer drops significantly across multiple organ systems. Your cells stop playing Russian roulette every time they divide and instead focus on their actual jobs, like supporting a human who's finally treating them with the respect they deserve.

- Skin renewal is complete, resulting in an overall healthier appearance.

- Overall, improved hormonal balance gives your endocrine system the feeling of a job well done.

- Weight and metabolism have fully stabilized.
- Better sleep quality becomes consistent, and your relationship with your pillow becomes a loving partnership.
- Reduced risk of diabetes as insulin sensitivity improves—your pancreas unclenches for the first time in years.
- Pupils are no longer sending S.O.S. signals, and light has fully returned to your eyes.
- You may have had people ask what's your secret—the irony that your "secret" is actually just removing something rather than adding another fancy cream, supplement, or wellness trend involving quail eggs.

Weight: I encourage you to throw this metric out the window and let the body land at a new homeostasis regarding body mass without any expectations. Sure, many quit drinking in hopes of losing weight, but others find themselves gaining weight now that they aren't consuming so many "empty" calories (while others experience the opposite—unintentional weight loss from cutting out hundreds of nightly calories). The body is an incredibly intelligent machine, and it will spring back to a more elastic state that's in line with your genetic makeup and lifestyle. Trust the process.

Mental Healing

First Week:

- Brain fog begins lifting by the end of the week. It's like someone finally cleaned the windshield you didn't even know was dirty.
- Suppressed emotions arrive on the scene, and this is a good thing—embrace them all.
- The ability to focus improves slightly. You can now string a couple of full sentences together without your brain wandering off like a toddler in a toy store.

- Mood swings may be intense, but begin to level out by the end of the week. Your emotional state swings between "I'm a supernatural being of light and power," and "I am literally the saddest human who has ever existed," approximately every 23 minutes.

- Memory recall starts improving.

- Anxiety levels begin decreasing (after possible initial spike).

- Depressive symptoms begin to lift. At the end of the first week, the dark cloud following you around upgrades from "apocalyptic thunderstorm" to "light drizzle with rare breaks of sunshine."

- How you view yourself begins to shift in a positive direction. Shame softens, and guilt begins to fade.

- New morale enters the system, knowing a nosedive has been averted. Your internal cheerleading squad cautiously shows up for practice again.

First Month:

- Clearer thinking and improved concentration as the prefrontal cortex begins to call the shots again. Although the mind is racing, you're not as tied to the thoughts as you previously were. The seed of awareness has sprouted.

- The dopamine system begins to produce dopamine not cued by alcohol—your brain rediscovers that sunsets, puppy videos, and compliments can feel good too, not just happy hour specials.

- More stable mood patterns. Emotional state graduates from a "wildly unpredictable weather system" to a "moderately unpredictable" one.

- The amygdala, the almond-shaped part of the brain located in the medial temporal lobe, which is primarily associated with emotional responses (particularly fear and anxiety), begins to settle into a more relaxed life without alcohol.

- Better stress management capabilities. By this time, you've inevitably made it through some stressful situations, and you're teaching yourself that life is possible without alcohol.

- Improved mental stamina. You can now read an entire chapter of a book or watch a full movie without checking your phone 17 times.

- There may be one to two moments where you realize it's the little things in life that suffice for happiness.

- You start making better decisions, your future self won't want to travel back in time to prevent.

First Six Months:

- Vastly improved emotional regulation. Category 5 emotional hurricanes are downgraded to uncomfortable life experiences.

- Awareness continues to build as you recognize the thoughts in your head as something different than you. "Oh, that's not ME thinking I'm a failure, that's just a THOUGHT about being a failure. Huge difference!"

- You begin recognizing triggers and start collecting data points as to why you drank in the first place. Turns out "day ending in Y" wasn't actually the trigger.

- The dopamine system is now creating new neural circuitry around activities not involving alcohol, such as reading a good book or walking in a park with a friend.

- Oxytocin has arrived on the scene, causing you to prefer a snuggle with a puppy over a pint.

- Melatonin production, responsible for sleep, has returned to its normal state. Your body finally remembers that night is for sleeping, and the nighttime routine becomes something enjoyable.

- Emotional states are entering High Definition territory with so many more pixels.

- Better long-term memory formation and recall. Your memory no longer includes alcohol-induced gaps.
- Serotonin production in the gut and brain is no longer tied to alcohol. Your happiness chemicals are now free-range and organic, not synthetic and booze-dependent.

First Year:

- Significant brain tissue repair and volume recovery. Your brain cells, which had been operating like a skeleton crew on a sinking ship, are now fully staffed and renovating the place.
- Forgiveness becomes less of a concept and more of a lived experience—including forgiving yourself, finally.
- Restored natural dopamine, serotonin, oxytocin, and endorphin function. Your brain's chemistry set is finally being used according to the manufacturer's instructions.
- A significant reduction in shame and guilt knowing you are doing what's best for your body, mind, soul, spirit, your family, friends, pets, future generations, and the planet.
- The ability to be alone with your thoughts without needing to reach for your smartphone or turn on the TV. Your mind becomes less like a haunted house and more like a quirky but ultimately comfortable apartment.
- Increased mental clarity and cognitive function result in the childlike feeling that you can do anything you put your mind to.
- Anxiety symptoms should be mostly gone, but remember, life comes with a healthy amount of anxiety. There is no getting around that. In addition, excitement is mixed in with anxiety, giving it a different texture.
- Depression and bouts of sadness do arrive, but they leave on their own within a few days and don't require medical intervention.

- Improved problem-solving abilities and the ability to handle complex tasks—you could definitely assemble IKEA furniture without crying.

- Return of confidence and self-esteem, knowing you are no longer on a pathway of destruction.

- Emotions are now viewed as messengers and guides, leaving you with a more authentic connection with emotions.

Spiritual Healing

Note: This segment has nothing to do with religion. In addition, spiritual growth definitely isn't linear; it's more like a cosmic game of Chutes and Ladders. Some days you're having profound revelations about the nature of consciousness, and other days you're wondering if eating an entire pizza counts as a spiritual practice. However, it seems that when we remove alcohol, we are eventually invited to cohabitate with an invisible dimension that we can't perceive with the five senses, but somehow we intuitively know is there. Much of the work done by 20th-century Swiss psychologist Carl Jung tries to explain this spiritual realm, and he said that "synchronicity is an ever-present reality for those who have the eyes to see." With alcohol in our lives, we don't have the eyes to see it—we can't see it. We don't have the awareness to realize we need hot to know cold, tall to know short, sound to know silence, and the world of form to know the world of the spirit.

For myself, I could barely spell the word spirituality and was very much an atheist well into my first year of sobriety. In fact, if I had read this book when I was quitting drinking, I think I would have stopped reading or skipped this section…I encourage you to keep reading and to remain open.

First Week:

- Probably nothing—although there may have been a moment before your last drink when time seemed to stop, you were pulled into the present moment, and without judgment, could clearly see where things were headed if you didn't quit drinking.

First Month:

- Your intuition may peek out from behind the couch, wondering if it's safe to come out now.
- Perhaps there is a pull to spend more time in nature, or rest against the trunk of a tree.
- You may experience 1 to 2 moments of intense gratitude that aren't tied to materialistic things.
- A bird landing on a nearby tree may hold your gaze for longer than expected, and you may wonder what type of bird it is and what its call sounds like.

First Six Months:

- Life synchronicities that seem so astronomically rare begin to take place.
- Self-centeredness begins to soften, and you begin to feel the pain and joy of other humans, animals, and perhaps even the planet.
- You begin to accurately decipher the signals your intuition picks up on.
- A genuine connection to something other than yourself that doesn't come in a bottle with a fancy label may emerge.
- Development of authentic wisdom that occasionally makes you sound like a fortune cookie, but in a good way.
- The universe's sense of humor becomes apparent—turns out the cosmic joke wasn't on you, you're in on it.

First Year:

- You find yourself noticing the gaps or spaces in life between the happenings of life.

- You realize your journey is less about becoming a new person, but more about returning to the self.
- Spiritual texts like the *Tao*, *The Power of Now*, or *A Course in Miracles* come across your horizon by happenstance. You may wonder about Buddhism, Hinduism, Christianity, Judaism, and Confucianism.
- Instead of killing the spider in your kitchen, you may trap it and release it outside, recognizing your connection to that living being.
- A realization occurs where you understand we aren't much different from the water buffalo in Africa, a barn owl, or even your dog. You begin wondering if they have souls, or if you're even still above them in terms of an imagined hierarchy.
- You may find yourself making big life decisions based on intuition as opposed to logic.
- You care less about driving a fancy car, a big house, or other materialistic pursuits.
- You begin to place more emphasis on this moment rather than what's coming tomorrow.
- You'll find yourself in a state of awe when viewing a waterfall, a deep canyon gorge, or the expansiveness of a desert.
- A desire to learn from our ancestors of all races emerges.
- A connection to the universe that no longer feels like a desperate drunk dial at 2:00 AM, but a continuous, loving conversation.
- A call to explore meditation—or to know the deeper self.
- You find yourself in activities like journaling or gardening where the passage of time accelerates; this would be called a flow state. You are flowing with the universe.

Beyond

- You begin walking others home and assisting them in their healing. You develop the ability to help others without trying to fix them in the process.

- You find yourself placing equal emphasis on the silence in life as well as the sounds.

- You learn that listening is more powerful than speaking.

- You realize there is no "us versus them" and we are all brothers and sisters.

- Gratitude, or a stance of appreciation toward what life has already provided you, as opposed to what is missing in life, is the desired state of being.

- Creativity returns through music, poetry, writing, painting, and dancing. You may find yourself spontaneously breaking out into song while cooking dinner or while driving. Note: this may return years after the last drink, and books like *The Artist's Way* by Julia Cameron can help unblock creative channels.

- Purpose and meaning start appearing in your life like unexpected but welcome house guests.

- The enmeshment of the dream world and the physical world occurs. You may see an owl in a dream, and the next day see an owl on your drive home from work.

- You're still aging, but the inner kiddo seems to be getting younger, and your overall demeanor returns to a childlike state. On occasion, you seem to wear life like a loose-fitting garment.

- You become less wave and more ocean. You begin to identify with the deeper part of you that is not affected by the happenings of life.

- You apply fewer labels of "good" and "bad" to what happens in life, knowing that it all fits with some master-orchestrated plan.

- A deeper understanding and acceptance of the nature of reality becomes omnipresent in your life.

- The idea that everything is perfect just the way it is seems to have permanently landed in the unconscious…well, most of the time.
- The realization that what you've been looking for all along has been inside you the entire time, and this process is happening for us, not to us.

Sleep

According to Stanford neuroscientist and renowned podcast host, Andrew Huberman, all health, longevity, your daily moods, and your overall state of being are tied to the quality of your sleep. When you drink alcohol or go to bed with any amount of alcohol in your system, the quality of your sleep drastically decreases, leaving you in a diminished state the following day.

Every species scientists have currently studied seems to sleep, even earthworms. As sleep research pioneer Allan Rechtschaffen said, "If sleep doesn't serve an absolute vital function, it's the biggest mistake that evolution has ever made." Whatever the core function of sleep is, it's an absolute non-negotiable life-supporting mechanism. The quality of our sleep, simply stated, determines the quality of our lives.

When we are not getting sufficient sleep—and this is just after one night of poor sleep—hormonal systems no longer function properly. For example, a male who sleeps around 4 to 5 hours per night and doesn't hit deep sleep cycles has testosterone levels of someone who is 10 years older than them. With females, it's a similar thing—there is a drop in estrogen, follicle-stimulating hormones, and luteinizing hormone, which plays a crucial role in regulating the menstrual cycle and ovulation. In the metabolic system, with insulin, which monitors blood sugar levels, just four nights of poor sleep causes your level of blood sugar impairment to be so severe that your doctor would classify you as pre-diabetic. With immune system function, just one night of restless sleep under four hours lowers the number of natural, critical cancer-fighting immune cells by 70%. Studies show that if someone gets less than six hours of sleep on average, they're almost three times as likely to develop the common cold. We're not done yet. The circulatory system begins to malfunction after losing just one hour of good sleep per night. When you sleep with alcohol in your system, you'll experience all of the aforementioned negative effects

The biggest wrench alcohol throws into your sleep is that your body doesn't drop into the deep restorative REM cycle. This sleep cycle is when the bulk of the restoration and healing takes place within the body and is also when we dream. When you go into REM sleep, the brain paralyzes the body, putting you into a state of "atonia," meaning your muscles are completely relaxed and are not tightened or tense. This is a huge one because it compounds over time. When we enter REM sleep, the muscles holding the tension in your neck from your 9-to-5 job fully release, and the body experiences a temporary state of harmony. Without REM sleep, the muscles never fully relinquish their grip, and you'll soon look like Quasimodo, the hunchback of Notre Dame. REM sleep also promotes the genesis of new neurons in the brain. Studies show a surge of electrical energy enters the brain right before we drop into REM sleep, and certain parts of the brain are 30% more active in REM sleep than during the day.

Another way alcohol impacts your sleep is by suppressing melatonin secretion from the pineal gland, and moderate alcohol consumption can decrease production by over 20%. Alcohol also disrupts the natural rhythm of cortisol, which works in tandem with melatonin like a tag team—each needed at the right time to regulate the sleep–wake cycle. As alcohol metabolizes during the night, your body often experiences a surge in adrenaline that counteracts melatonin's calming effect, leading to you being awake at 3:00 AM. Sound familiar?

When we remove alcohol and begin entering restorative dreamy sleep cycles again, all of the negative consequences of poor sleep I just mentioned vanish—and some of them vanish overnight. Now, keep in mind, at first, when you put the bottle down, sleep will seem a bit like hunting for a whisper in a windstorm, but with time, your sleep function will return to normal and healthy levels. I do not recommend taking sleep supplements or medications to get back on a sleep cycle[*], but instead,

---

[*] I'm not a doctor

begin by placing the body in a comfortable sleeping position, in a dark, quiet room, without your smartphone, at the same time every night. Reading a book before sleeping is a great way to cue the brain for sleep time.

The effects of alcohol and sleep are so extensive that perhaps I've got it all wrong in this book regarding healing. The key to healing might not be tied to quitting drinking, but instead is anchored to getting good sleep. However, proper sleep cannot be achieved with alcohol in our bloodstream when we hit the pillow. The occasional one or two-night break from alcohol, although beneficial, won't cut it in the long run if you are to fully capitalize on this non-negotiable for keeping you healthy: good sleep.

Your Bank Account Wellness Revolution

Let's face it, living in the capitalist world requires money—lots of it. When you quit drinking, your bank account experiences its own spiritual awakening. Your wallet—once thin and traumatized—develops a curious condition called "chronic expansion syndrome." Where alcohol once created financial black holes dense enough to make physicists nervous, you now witness money that actually stays put.

That $15 cocktail you're not drinking? It's reincarnating as tomorrow's lunch. The $40 saved since you're driving yourself home now? That's transforming into a massage that actually removes stress instead of temporarily numbing it. The hundreds spent on "just one more round"? They're gathering like giddy schoolchildren in your savings account, ready for summer break. Your credit score rises like your actual physical vibration. And the best part? Your finances, just like your body, mind, and soul, finally get a chance to heal.

Let's calculate what five daily drinks actually cost, including the missed potential to let that money grow.

At-home drinking:

Assuming moderately priced alcohol ($1–2 per beer or $15–20 for a bottle of wine that provides 4–5 glasses)

Approximately **$7–15 per day**
$210–450 per month
$2,520–5,400 per year

Bar/restaurant drinking:
Assuming $7–12 per drink, depending on location
Approximately **$35–60 per day**
$1,050–1,800 per month
$12,600–21,600 per year

Drinks at home and out:
A realistic middle ground
Approximately **$20–30 per day**
$600–900 per month
$7,200–10,800 per year

And keep in mind this doesn't include:

- Extra tacos ordered while drinking
- Rideshare/taxi costs
- Potential missed work days
- Lost productivity while hungover on the couch
- Higher health care costs
- Golf clubs thrown into the pond
- Potentially wrecked vehicle
- DUI costs (potentially tens of thousands)

Potential Savings
Let's take a conservative estimate of $600/month ($7,200/year) saved and see what happens:

After 5 years:
Principal amount saved: $36,000
With 7% average annual return: $43,000
That's $7,000 in growth just for not drinking

After 10 years:
Principal amount saved: $72,000
With 7% average annual return: $100,000
Your decision to quit has now generated nearly $30,000 in additional wealth

After 20 years:
Principal amount saved: $144,000
With 7% average annual return: $295,000
More than double what you put in

After 30 years:
Principal amount saved: $216,000
With 7% average annual return: $720,000
Your drinking money has now turned into a substantial retirement fund

You're doing more than just saving money—you're completely transforming your financial future. The $20 you don't spend on drinks tonight might be worth $100 in your retirement account. The choice to stay sober isn't simply a daily health decision; it's potentially a six-figure financial pivot that changes the trajectory of your life.

What could you do with an extra $300,000 to $700,000? Buy a vacation home outright? Fund your child's education? Make a significant donation to your favorite non-profit? Quit your job and start a business? Travel the world? The financial freedom that comes from sobriety makes life easier and opens doors you might never have imagined possible.

The Eternal Ripples of Your Sobriety

When you aim for the highest good for yourself, you're doing more than crossing a personal finish line—you're sending out a healing wave that touches everyone around you. The moment you choose clarity over chaos, you become a lighthouse instead of a storm. Those closest to you, who have perhaps been holding their breath for decades, let out a deep exhalation.

Your partner finally sleeps through the night without listening for crashes from the kitchen. Your kids no longer wonder what "dad" is coming home after work. Your friends receive the gift of real conversations instead of the greatest hits of your drunk stories on repeat. Your coworkers get to collaborate with your full brilliance rather than your hungover half-measures.

The barista who dreaded your grumpy morning orders now receives genuine smiles. The neighbor's dog stops hiding when you walk by. Even the delivery person notices something different about you—a presence that wasn't there before.

These immediate healings aren't small miracles; they're the first ripples of something much bigger. Each authentic connection, each moment of true presence, each promise kept—these all add up to one thing: a better life, or the Dolce Vita.

It's said that just one smile has the potential to prompt smiles in others for days, weeks, months, years, and even for decades. These are the pebbles dropping into the cosmic pond of your existence.

And those ripples? They're just getting started...

When you put down the bottle, you're doing more than changing your Friday night plans—you're bending the arc of your family tree. Think of it as cosmic graffiti: "Sobriety Was Here" tagged across the universe of your bloodline!

Your decision to quit drinking creates a whirlwind of positivity that rolls through time. The kids in your life (yours or others') get to observe an adult who solves problems without liquid courage. Twenty years later, when facing their own demons, they'll hear your laughter—not your bottle opening—in their memories. We've probably all heard the phrase "monkey see, monkey do," and those around you have the opportunity to witness an adult who meets the challenges of life without a Budweiser in hand.

Your DNA does a happy dance! The science of epigenetics suggests our choices affect how genes express themselves. Your cells are throwing a wellness party that your unnamed great-grandkids get invited to before they're even born.

You become the plot twist in your family story. Generations from now, someone will say, "Everything changed when Grandpa Pete put down the bottle in 2025." You're authoring a new chapter for people who haven't even been conceived yet!

Your authentic energy creates a spiritual trust fund. While others leave money or property, you leave something far more valuable—authentic connection and emotional presence that compounds interest through generations.

The Universe keeps a cosmic ledger of healing. Every painful cycle you break sends a pulse of wholeness through the fabric of existence. The Divine accountant is definitely tracking this! In the grand soul tapestry, your sobriety is as strong as a golden silk orb-weaver's thread that doesn't weaken with time—it becomes stronger as it extends outward, creating a pathway of wellness your descendants will walk with gratitude for eternity.

When we quit drinking, we develop a set of tools that we can almost copy and paste when facing other problems in our lives—and there will be more challenges. When we depart from an alcohol addiction, we leave a metaphysical footprint in the consciousness of humanity that other humans can pull from to assist them on their own journey to wholeness.

Your decision to quit drinking represents one of the first and most critical steps in your own river crossing of consciousness that the Buddha speaks of when he says all of humanity must make this crossing. Rare flowers have already made this river crossing in the history of our species, and you are now part of the first wave of significant numbers embarking upon this journey.

The stigma is wrong, as stigmas are often incorrectly placed on individuals or groups that go on to radically transform the trajectory of humanity. You're not broken or weak—you're evolving, and the process is well underway. As Gandhi famously said, you are becoming the change that you want to see in this world. It's the only way it can happen. True transformation can never come from the outside; it always comes from within.

Your healing represents the initial bloom of spring flowers on a mountainside. You may want to retract your vibrant colors because it seems you're the only one there, but your explosion of true color invites the rest of us to follow. Your courage creates a path for others who are still suffering in silence. When the conditions are right—and we are not far off—there will be the most beautiful flowering of our species, and you quitting drinking was a necessary part of it. Your journey isn't just about freeing yourself; it's about showing others what freedom looks like.

Chapter 20
The Journey Begins

To the Other Side

In this section of the book, I'll share how "I" quit drinking, but that's not an accurate statement because I had so much help along the way. Once I was ready to quit drinking, ready to ask for help, and then accept that help, it seems as if I was guided or led every step of the way, and I'm not sure if I can take credit for much or any of it at all. But once I had relinquished the idea that alcohol could be in my life in any capacity at all, a flood of energy arrived along with support from family, friends, those in recovery who walked this path before me, my dog, musical vibrations, books, the stars, waterfalls, streams, rivers, pine forests, nourishing food, and more. I think once we are truly ready to quit drinking—and the readiness is a big one—any pathway will work, but this is the path I took.

I Called the Fight

The strategies of "work harder,' 'double down," "wake up earlier," and "lift more weights" worked with every other challenge in my life, until I met the most formidable foe I've yet to encounter: alcohol. I kept getting back into the ring even though the ass whoopings only intensified. I think the roundhouses from alcohol were making me less intelligent. In fact, I know they were. "Never give up" was my motto, and my sports background reinforced this. Today, my mantra, at least when it comes to alcohol, is "never quit quitting"—how's that for a life twist? For me to quit drinking, I had to exit the ring, give up completely, raise my white wine flag, and admit total and undeniable defeat. I declared my bar tab permanently closed. I told my box of wine that we needed to see other beverages. I returned my drinking crown to the palace of hell. I officially retired my drinking jersey and put my shot glasses and beer goggles in storage. In the summer of 2014, I called the fight—you win, alcohol. I was done. Surprisingly, when I admitted unequivocal defeat, I felt liberated, and I no longer felt I was sinking in life, because I wasn't.

Now, I didn't hit the showers and then catapult into sobriety the moment I called the fight, but something shifted. Once my conscious and subconscious threw in the towel, I remember experiencing the pain of hangovers and withdrawals differently. One particularly bad one comes to mind shortly before I quit drinking. I remember walking down the sidewalk one morning after a particularly intense binge, sweat dripping down my temples, and I kept telling myself, "Remember this pain, don't forget it." Later that night at 3:00 AM, when I was lying awake in sweat-soaked bed sheets, I remember taking breaths and with each exhale, I'd let the cells in my body fall deeper into the scream for alcohol—"Remember this pain, Paul, do not forget." Pain is an incredibly effective catalyst to spark change. I welcomed it and embraced it.

A Shift in Priorities

I knew I had to make sobriety my absolute #1 priority in my life. I'd heard this recommendation before I quit drinking and laughed at the idea of placing sobriety above family, friends, travel, and my fantasy football team. Does this really have to be the MOST important thing in my life? Well, it makes perfect logical sense. Alcohol was pulling me into total destruction. Happiness, a family, marriage, a job, children—these were only a possibility in a life without alcohol. Therefore, the daily goal that sits on top of everything else has to be an alcohol-free life. Period. A full non-negotiable.

There are zero wins in my life if I'm drinking—none. Everything in my life crumbles like a stale cookie if I'm drinking alcohol. It's that simple. Once I removed the intoxicant and wrapped my head around this reality, life became simpler. It took some time for my subconscious to fully accept this, but once it did, I began planning my days around my non-negotiable recovery obligations like meetings, recovery work, time spent in nature with my dog, and time to rest.

In addition, I ditched the idea that this was my #1 priority for the rest of my life and began focusing on the goal for only the next 24 hours. I know "one day at a time" can make some roll their eyes, but this is perhaps one of the most profound teachings in recovery and all of life. All we have is this moment, or the current day we find ourselves in. The thought of not doing anything for a lifetime makes anyone tense up, but breaking it into daily bite-sized chunks makes the goal seem attainable. And sometimes, at least at first, the goal of 24 hours was broken down into smaller time blocks. "My number one goal for the next hour is to stay sober," I'd tell myself. There were a few days in early sobriety when I had to break it down to minutes, where I had to protect the #1 goal in life, sobriety, like a newborn child, for the next 10 minutes, and one day, I think it was day five, it was a minute-by-minute thing.

Playing the Tape Backward Then Forward

It's impossible to think yourself out of a drinking problem. It can't be done. If it could, you wouldn't be reading this, I wouldn't be writing it, and recovery programs like AA wouldn't be necessary. However, there is one effective mental strategy I used daily in the early days of my sobriety, which is called playing the tape backward or forward.

Playing the tape backward means remembering how things usually unfolded when I drank—how one drink always led to more, and where it typically ended. Playing the tape forward is about imagining what would likely happen if I chose to drink today, based on past patterns and experience.

Of course, I wanted to drink after putting the bottle down. Every time the thought came to mind, it was accompanied by the convincing Bruno Voice telling me it would be "just one." I fell for it hundreds of times in the past, but this time was different.

When the thought to drink came, and at first they came often, I would "play the tape backward" and mentally explore what happened the last 10 times I drank. I was only interested in the facts about what actually happened. Did I ever stop drinking after one or two? How about the last 50 to 100 times I drank? Was I ever able to shut it down after a couple of drinks? The past data shows that I haven't stopped after one drink in probably the last 10 years, and I never stopped after the second or third drink either. When I play the tape backward, it clearly shows that one drink always leads to at least 10 more, and has the potential to hit the 50 to 60-drink mark if I slide into a multi-day binge. While the tape is playing backward, the soundtrack is a series of sad trombone sound effects followed by the Britney Spears song, "Oops I Did It Again."

When I played the tape backward, the data wasn't just clear—it was a high-definition, surround-sound wake-up call that I'd been hitting snooze on for years. I kept telling myself "just one drink," like I was some magical unicorn who could suddenly develop moderation superpowers despite all evidence to the contrary. When the tape played backward, it brought images of me drinking my own piss one evening while doing a puzzle alone, shit-faced in my parents' basement while listening to Coldplay's "Fix You" on repeat (I really didn't want to include that line in this book).

Like Shakira's hips don't lie, my drinking data didn't either. It was pure wreckage in the past, and when playing the tape forward, that's all it would be again in the future. Despite wishful thinking that I'd have just one drink, when I played the tape forward, I could predict with 99.9% accuracy that the first drink would lead to a chasm of pain and turmoil. I then had a clear image of looming pain to combat the brain synapses firing for a drink.

Given how far my drinking had progressed, playing the tape forward now included the very real possibility of death or suicide. The theme song of that mixtape? "Boulevard of Broken Dreams" by Green Day—right before the ribbon unraveled and the whole cassette blew apart.

I do want to mention again that relying on your thinking to depart from a drinking problem is never a sound strategy, mostly because you've tasked the same person who got you into this pickle to get you out of it. But with nearly 100% accuracy, we can use the thinking mind to give us an idea of what will happen when we take that first drink.

Chapter 21
The Crossing

I took my last drink of alcohol on September 6th, 2014, and haven't had a drink since. Was it easy? I like to phrase it this way: The only thing harder than quitting drinking would have been to not quit drinking and continue down the path of absolute destruction until death.

I finally accepted I couldn't beat alcohol, meaning there was no way I could ever moderately drink or control my drinking. After enough field research and connecting the data points, I knew unequivocally that if I wanted to live anything that resembled a happy and productive life, alcohol could not be part of the equation. So I threw in the towel, I gave up, surrendered, called the fight, and took the path of least resistance, which was a life without alcohol. I believe it is the only reason I am still here today.

Quitting drinking fixed things that I didn't even know were broken. Alcohol had sunk its teeth into every aspect of my life, and with each passing day without alcohol, life became lighter, more enjoyable, more spontaneous, colors more vibrant, music made my feet tap, my eyelids preferred being open rather than closed, and I felt like living again. It seemed like the Holy Grail to wholeness consisted of just two things: the passage of time and not drinking alcohol.

My body physically began to heal with better sleep, I ate three meals per day, and my nervous system said hallelujah since its baseline state was no longer anchored to chaos and unpredictability. Mentally, it felt like I was the living version of the Jimmy Cliff song, "I Can See Clearly Now."

At first, quitting drinking did nothing to change the state of the world, but small glimmers of brilliance began to appear in my outside world as I began the process of cleaning up my inner world. I noticed things that seemed to be invisible before, like animal shapes in cumulus clouds or sandhill cranes bellowing in the distance. My dog's perpetual good mood no longer annoyed me, and I accepted his invitations to join him outside with vigor. People at the supermarket or bank were no longer enemies; they were on the same human journey as me. I was squaring my shoulders toward life, and I began to embrace life as it is.

As I mentioned earlier, alcohol destroys us first spiritually, mentally, then physically—the healing happens in reverse order. Within 30 days of my last drink, the bloating in my face and body was gone, the knot of anxiety in my solar plexus nearly fully disappeared, and I was filled with an intense, seemingly limitless energy. Within six months, mental clarity returned, self-confidence soared, and I shed layers of shame I didn't even know I was carrying. Spiritually, around the two-year mark, I felt a pull to learn the constellations, I craved to know where the moon was at all times, I began learning the names of the trees in my nearby forest, and I swear if I sat next to a Douglas Fir long enough, it would begin whispering to me.

When I quit drinking in September 2014, the recovery landscape looked much different. The explosion of quit lit books, sobriety podcasts, and AF beverages had not yet arrived. There were no online meetings or recovery groups, and it was basically just AA—so that's what I did. I went to well over 90 meetings in 90 days, read the Big Book, got a sponsor, and started working the steps. I'm incredibly thankful to my sponsor, who met with me every Wednesday at noon on his lunch break for over a year to walk me through the 12 Steps. Although AA is not my primary recovery path today, I still attend meetings, and I look at it as a way to build community with others who don't drink. I know AA isn't everyone's cup of tea, but it's undeniable that the founders created an amazing program that has helped millions quit drinking and return to normal functioning. Going through the 12 steps is something that would benefit all of humanity, as much of it is centered around honesty, forgiveness, making amends when we have done wrong, becoming aware of our own bullshit, accepting the true nature of life, and then passing along what we have learned to other humans. I do want to mention that although five of the 12 steps have a direct reference to God, AA is not a religious program, but indeed a highly spiritual one.

In my first 30 days, I knew I had to kill the idle time, so I drove 40 minutes to a trailhead in the Spanish Creek wilderness southwest of Bozeman, Montana, where I did a 7-mile round-trip hike to a waterfall almost every afternoon. When I made it to the waterfall, I'd sit at the top of the falls and turn my gaze inward. My mind was in a perpetual state of rumination or thinking, with the content mostly unpleasant. However, something had ever so slightly shifted, which I couldn't grasp at the time—it seemed I had mentally taken a step away from the thoughts in my mind, which created a newfound "space" of sorts in the brain. It was as if there was more distance between me and my thoughts; it seemed I was no longer coupling "me" or "I" with the thought.

Now let's pause for a second…this subtle shift in the mind is everything, and I mean ***everything***. I was still bombarded with thoughts, but the difference was that the thoughts didn't seem quite as juicy or believable, and I was able to let them go. "I" was no longer the thoughts, or at least I wasn't fully identified with the thoughts like I was just a few weeks prior—this is the miracle an addiction can gift us. During the physical and mental warfare of the previous months in my life, I had somehow changed my internal seat of where the "I" was housed.

"I" was no longer the voice inside the head that said I was done drinking. "I" was no longer the voice inside the head that said it's time for tequila shots.

"I" had relocated the seat of my soul to an area in the arena where I could witness the thoughts taking place without being pulled into the incessant loop of thinking. This is the focal theme in Michael Singer's book *The Untethered Soul,* where he says we aren't the voices in our heads, but the one who witnesses them. The firefight of my addiction apparently had booted me from the center of my thinking mind to a box seat where I could look down from above and observe the cascade of thoughts—I had become aware, for perhaps the first time in my life, of the incessant cycle of thinking.

Now this was painful at first, extremely painful. As the Red Hot Chili Peppers frontman Anthony Kiedis said when he talked about his addiction struggles, if you steal from Peter, you'll eventually have to pay Paul. As I sat next to the waterfall, I wasn't levitating in a state of blissful meditation—I was paying Paul. My dopamine system was recalibrating, horse flies and ants bit me, the sun burned my skin, serotonin production hadn't seemed to come online yet, and the oxytocin valves were still in the off position. I felt lonely, disconnected, fearful, and of course, I had cravings, but the quality of these sensations felt different—they were no longer me. Just something uncomfortable pulsing through the body that I inhabited. Thoughts of drinking and self-annihilation did arise, but with this newfound distance, I let them go. Until they showed up again, then I let those thoughts go, again and again.

The quality of our healing is tied to the state of our nervous system. I had been in a state of fight or flight the past several months with my sympathetic nervous system activated while navigating the Fire Swamp, and perhaps the intelligence in my body knew it was essential for me to cue my parasympathetic nervous system, which brings us into a calmer state.

There's a concept in Japan called Shinrin-Yoku, which translates to forest bathing. It was introduced in 1982 as a response to urbanization and a growing disconnect between humans and nature. They found this practice lowers healthcare costs in Japan since spending time in nature lowers blood pressure, stress levels, improves immune system function, and basically does wonders to enhance the overall health of the human body. At the time, I didn't know the concept of forest bathing, but that's exactly what I was doing in my first month away from alcohol while spending so much time in nature. When I returned to my vehicle after my hike to the waterfall, I'd lie on my back on a picnic table and wait until the first star emerged before I began driving home. My dog Ben accompanied me on every hike to the waterfall, and he watched over me as we were deep in grizzly bear country. I was watched, supported, and protected.

I threw the kitchen sink at sobriety–I had to if I wanted to live–and something worked, as I'm still here today. There's a concept, which is probably a universal law in sobriety, that says you have to put at least as much time and effort into your recovery as you put into your drinking. That's what I did and more.

Let's Throw Tools at the Wall & See What Sticks

Here's a list of things that I have tried in my recovery efforts over the last decade. Some were done only once, others repeated, and many I still incorporate today. All of them played a role in my healing path.

Read quit lit books
Listening to sobriety podcasts (only three were in existence in 2014)
Journaling
Meditation
Mindfulness practices
Clarity Breathwork
Exercise (running, hiking, walking, etc.)
Alcoholics Anonymous
Read the Big Book of Alcoholics Anonymous
Working the 12 Steps with a sponsor
Getting a service position with my local AA group
Café RE and Café RE Chats
Recovery Dharma
SMART Recovery
Starting a podcast to keep myself accountable
Burning the ships
Float tank therapy
Talk therapy
Psychotherapy
Music as therapy (ukulele, singing, playing with others)
Psilocybin
Ayahuasca
San Pedro

Aromatherapy
Brainspotting
Crystal healing
Reiki sessions
Sound baths
Improving routines
Core values workshops
Daily gratitude practices
Drumming circles
Labyrinth walking
Vitamins and supplements
Prayer
Drinking more water
Blood analysis
Bilateral sound therapy
Screaming into the void while in a dark closet therapy :)
EFT tapping therapy
Somatic experiencing
Tuning forks
Ecstatic dance
Positive affirmations
Ice cream therapy
Ice bath plunges
Sleep training
Hypnotherapy
Vision boards
Volunteering
Manifestation mind maps
Antidepressants
ADHD medication
Sauna therapy
Forest bathing (Shinrin-yoku)
Yoga
Hot yoga

Goat yoga
Snake yoga (not kidding)
Acupuncture
Astrology readings
Chinese medicine and herbal remedies
Connecting with other sober people
Chairing recovery meetings & chats
Recovery retreats
Men's retreats
Tarot card readings
$1 into the Zoltar game (from the movie Big)
Energy healing sessions
Sweat lodges
Cacao ceremonies

While reading that list, if you said to yourself, "My goodness, do I have to do all of that if I want to quit drinking and stay quit?" Take a breath, and remember that's just what *my* journey looked like. In addition, my career is now in the addiction field, so I wanted real-life experience with as many healing modalities as possible, but if I had to give you the big hitters from this list, it's talk therapy, recovery meetings, and connection with others who no longer drink. There are also pharmacological interventions, which I have not tried, such as Naltrexone or Antabuse, which help many. Naltrexone, also known as the Sinclair method, is a pill or shot that acts as an opiate receptor antagonist that blocks the euphoric effects of alcohol. Or Antabuse, which will cause you to hurl your lunch if you ingest alcohol while taking the medication. If you feel particularly stuck, plant medicines such as ayahuasca, psilocybin, or mescaline may be an option, but always under the guidance of an experienced practitioner or shaman. I believe psychedelics have a place in recovery—they're even woven into the origin story of Alcoholics Anonymous itself.

Chapter 22
Burning The Ships: The Most Critical Step

In 1519, Spanish conquistador Hernán Cortés sailed from Cuba to Veracruz, Mexico, hoping to conquer the Aztecs—a goal others had failed to achieve for over 500 years. His first order to his troops once they landed: burn the ships. The message was clear—there would be no turning back. The only way home was victory. The rest is history.

When I announced the true depths of my drinking to my parents at 7:00 AM on the houseboat trip that previous summer in 2014, then to my brother, and then my seven best friends at my Fantasy Football Draft in August, I had burned the ships and made declarations I could never walk back. If I had to pick the most important thing I did to give me the best chances of quitting drinking, **it would be burning the ships.**

When we burn the ships with people who care about us, it then creates accountability, and this felt sense of connection with another human then leads to deeper communal ties. When we hear the opposite of addiction is connection, in my opinion, burning the ships is the absolute most effective and fastest way to get there. Human beings are social creatures wired for connection, and when we are vulnerable and share our challenges with others, it cues a chemical reaction in the other person, causing them to open up about something they are struggling with. With each person I burned the ships with, I heard reciprocal stories of their challenges—one person told me they had struggled with severe depression, another told me of their addiction to pornography, and another opened up to me about how alcohol had nearly destroyed their entire family. With each ship set ablaze, a genuine connection formed— and for the first time in a long time, I felt like I belonged to something again. Like I belonged to the human race.

An addiction wants you alone, in a dark room, far from other human beings, and when we burn the ships, we begin to exit the darkness. The accountability I had created through burning the ships in the summer of 2014 doused the flame of my addiction, but there were still smoldering embers. In early November 2014, with just over two months away from my last drink, I found myself hiding behind a pine tree outside of an AA meeting. Hiding because I didn't want anyone driving by to see me, and I was contemplating not going to the meeting because the Bruno Voice was convincing me I didn't need to go. It said, "Paul, we just went two months sober; alcoholics can't do this." And then the three most dangerous words someone with a drinking problem can say entered my mind—"I Got This."

This moment behind the pine tree was a critical juncture in my life. I remember thinking how I had a full day ahead of me, and I didn't have time for the meeting, and with 60+ days away from alcohol, I was cured, right? Maybe the Blue Spruce tree I was hiding behind found a way to cut through my highly irrational thinking, but I remember time stopped, and I knew if I didn't go into that meeting, I'd be done for. At the same time, the idea of creating a podcast for accountability entered my consciousness. I stood there pondering the idea of podcasting to give myself accountability and possibly help others along the way. In addition, if I could do something to chip away at the stigma, which had me ridiculously hiding behind a tree, then that's a bonus. I said to myself, "This is bullshit that so many people struggle with alcohol, yet there is so much shame around it." I stepped out from behind the tree, took a deep breath, attended the AA meeting, and the idea of the podcast seemed to gain momentum in my mind.

It was fun to mentally explore the idea of a podcast, but absolutely terrifying when I began writing the first episode. "Wait a second, am I really going to upload my deepest darkest secret (that I'm a raging alcoholic, and I used to drink beer and wine for breakfast) to iTunes, in MP3 format for the world to hear?" Oh shit…not a chance. But something deeper inside me kept pushing. It's something I knew I had to do. On February 25th, 2015, the first episode of the *Recovery Elevator* podcast was released. I remember the date well since I had trouble sleeping that night. A part of me was saying "Delete, delete, delete," but another part knew this was the path.

I was relieved after checking download numbers from the first three episodes; it appeared it was just me and my mom listening to the podcast. Thank goodness, no one was tuning in. When I checked the download statistics after the 4th episode, my chest tightened as I saw it had 15 downloads from multiple states and a different country. When the podcast made the "New and Noteworthy" section in Apple Podcasts, I said an audible "Oh shit," and I really started to panic when I saw the *Recovery Elevator* podcast was the 9th-rated podcast in the Health and Fitness section, which contained hundreds and hundreds of podcasts. 100 people were listening to the episodes, then 200, then 300, then 1,000.

When I received my first email from a listener, I was too afraid to open it for three weeks—again, thank you stigma. When I finally opened it, it was a short message about how the podcast had helped a listener quit drinking, and they looked forward to the new episodes each Monday.

At first, it was a challenge finding people who wanted to share their story into and out of an alcohol addiction in such a public format, but after about the 10th episode, I began getting emails from listeners who wanted to share their story for the sole purpose of helping others, and I now receive emails daily from people who want to share their story.

The *Recovery Elevator* podcast hit 5,000 downloads. Then 10,000, then 25,000, then 50,000, then 100,000. Holy buckets, I hit a million downloads, and my oh my, we are now at over 10 million downloads. My decision to selfishly create a podcast for accountability and release an episode for over 550 consecutive weeks was the best decision I ever made. With pen and paper in hand, I learned so much from the guests I interviewed. For the first 50 interviews, I was convinced I'd hear at least a couple of successful stories of moderation—nope. None at 100 interviews, either, and none at 500 interviews. Not a single person was able to successfully control or moderate their drinking. Not one person was able to control an uncontrollable thing.

Everyone's stories were, of course, different, but also remarkably similar. We formed a fruitful relationship with alcohol until the alcohol stopped reciprocating and began harming our lives. We then attempted to cut back or drink only on the weekends. Once we realized this strategy wasn't working, energies began shifting towards a life without alcohol. Everyone tries to quit drinking alone at first, but after getting punched in the groin enough times, we surrender, accept the current circumstances, ask for help, and begin a much healthier chapter of life. Pain is the common driver of change, suffering is the ticket punched, and it is also the glue that makes sober connections so tight.

The decision to burn the ships with myself, family, friends, and in a podcast changed the outcome of my life, and I know it saved my life. Call it pride, or ego, there was no way I was going to announce on the podcast that I drank again, and the only way to ensure that was to not drink. It worked.

Chapter 23
When I Learned to Party in the Right Rooms

I was afraid life wouldn't be any fun without alcohol. When I thought about quitting drinking, I'd always romanticize about the glory days when I was a normal drinker and didn't think about the last ten years of torture. For at least the last 100 to 200 times I drank, it wasn't fun at all. It was just pain, misery, and large gaps in my memory, which I assume was just more pain and misery.

I incorrectly thought my social life was going to end, and I'd never have fun again without alcohol. Sure, there was some rearranging in my friend circles, and friendships built over drinks slowly faded away, which I didn't really notice, but most remained. Thankfully, I found my friends didn't really care if I was drinking or not; they just wanted me to be happy, and if that meant no more alcohol, then they supported me.

A few months after quitting drinking, I started to emerge from my sobriety cocoon—still a little wobbly, but held up by the accountability I'd built. Everyone in my friend group knew I wasn't drinking, though, which gave me just enough confidence to start socializing again. I went to restaurants, street fairs, concerts, rodeos, camping trips, and even to my Fantasy Football draft in Las Vegas.

At times, the highs in sobriety didn't match the highs from drinking, but the next morning, I wasn't fighting a hangover or explosive shits. Overall, I can undoubtedly say that I was having more fun in sobriety than I was when drinking. I remembered conversations, made deeper connections with friends, and was more present in every social event I attended since my goal wasn't to get shit-faced. I got into mountain biking, found myself on numerous mountain peaks, surfed waves in the

Pacific Ocean, learned to play the ukulele, and created a life that no longer required alcohol.

In my first two years away from alcohol, I was totally fine being in bars or establishments that served alcohol. For me, it was a sense of accomplishment that I could still be on the dance floor sober at last call. But as I continued the recovery work and got to know myself better through journaling, meditation, therapy, and self-discovery, I felt a shift in who I was. I thought I was 100% an extrovert, but the further I got away from my last drink, the more I heard the introvert inside of me calling out for attention.

Artist Yung Pueblo has a poem that says:

Maturity is knowing that endings are a part of life. Jobs change. Who you hang out with changes. Your idea of what is good evolves. An ending is a sign that you are opening a new chapter.

As I matured in sobriety, I found myself seeking the company of pine trees and a good audiobook over hanging out in bars. I still enjoyed myself in those places, but it became apparent I was in the wrong room as I was no longer resonating with those types of venues or people who gathered there.

At this point, I was still DJing in bars and nightclubs. One night after the bar had just closed around 2:00 AM, I was packing up my DJ equipment when I heard a fight break out in the entryway to the bar. I ran in to break up the fight, and this guy was so drunk that he forgot who he was fighting, and he turned his fists of fury towards me. I was like, "Oh shit, I just got punched in the head, and this guy is huge." I later came to find out he was about 6'2", 225 pounds, and practiced mixed martial arts, a.k.a. UFC fighting. I found myself bent over, in a headlock, taking knees to the face, faster than I could say F-U-C-K. I knew I had one option, and I went for it. I grabbed his nuts, twisted, and this giant man fell to the floor with a squeal. The bar bouncers then arrived to apprehend him before the cops took the guy to jail. That night was the last time I ever DJed in a bar. Turns out, getting choked out by a drunk UFC fighter is a pretty solid career exit strategy.

My body never fails to communicate to me if I'm in the right room or not. I'm a sensitive being with a newly wired nervous system, and if I'm in a place or around a group of people that aren't a vibrational match, I'll get the signals in the language of emotions. The soul communicates with the body, and then the body and mind produce a concoction of chemicals, giving me real-time feedback. When I'm in nature or with good friends, I feel good. On the rare occasion when I find myself in a dive bar, my body sends me an SOS signal telling me to get out. Not because I'm triggered, but because my body no longer resonates with that type of environment.

I still attend recovery meetings weekly. I consistently attend because I enjoy them and feel a sense of belonging. It doesn't matter if it's an in-person meeting or an online chat; my body responds with the warm chemicals of connection when I'm there. It's a place where you can show up as yourself, in a denim vest or suit, and have authentic conversations without judgment. Yes, the discussion topics are usually alcohol-related, but we all speak about the shared frustrations of the human condition, which is mostly tied to the thinking mind or the Bruno Voice—after all, alcohol is but a symptom.

I once attended a retreat that wasn't in the recovery space, and was surprised to find that everyone profoundly struggles with the human condition. For some reason, I incorrectly think normal drinkers have it all figured out, and their lives are perfect, but of course, that isn't correct. What I heard multiple times from others at the retreat is that they all felt alone, and they didn't have people in their lives to share life's burdens with. I'm so thankful I have rooms or Café RE chats where we can come together and support each other in this magical and incredibly difficult adventure called life.

In these rooms, there is laughter, there is love, there is acceptance, and there is a knowing that everything is going to be okay if we stick together. I had been on a lifelong mission to find my tribe, to find my people, to find the right room. Who would have thought an alcohol addiction was responsible for bringing me to my tribe? A great line I heard in a chat once was "sobriety gave me the keys to my dream car, I just hate the color at times."

Today I enjoy life, not 100% of the time, of course, but I'm able to find peace daily. Much of my recovery work, and this is a non-negotiable, is to have fun, laugh, and enjoy life.

Recovery Plan: Play Ukulele at 3:00 PM and learn Somewhere Over the Rainbow.

Paul: "Oh, come on, are you serious? I guess if I have to."

This is great news; the antidote for this disease, or whatever you want to call it, is to laugh, have fun, and genuinely enjoy life. For us to do that, we have to be in the right room. Although I still hang out with normies often, I've found that the deepest, most altruistic connections I've made in the last ten years have been with other people walking the alcohol-free journey. The camaraderie of sobriety is the most intense glue I've ever witnessed within a group of people. We all punched a ticket of intense emotional and physical pain. We all know what it's like to tell ourselves we're done forever yet continue to drink for several more years. With normies, you'd have to explain a drinking problem until the sun comes up, but with someone in recovery, no explanations are needed. We get it, we get each other.

When I'm in these rooms, surrounded by people who fully embrace the Paul that shows up, then fun, lightness, laughter, and authenticity are the byproducts. And after all, I didn't quit drinking to not have fun in this human journey. Hallelujah.

Stick With the Pack

A Lakota Indian Chief once said the answers to all our problems can be found by looking to nature. When American bison encounter a blizzard, they don't seek shelter or run in the opposite direction. The herd comes together, shoulder to shoulder, and they walk towards the storm.

When we come together, we are stronger. This seems obvious, but when we're dealing with a disease that tells us we don't have a disease—in our own familiar voice—this can be difficult to comprehend. Add stigma to this, and there's no mystery why only 10% of people who struggle with drinking seek help.

In the late 1700s, a Seneca man named Handsome Lake found that when he brought his tribesmen together around a fire to talk about alcohol addiction, many of his people healed. Bill W. and Dr. Bob took this to the next level with Alcoholics Anonymous in the 1930s and beyond.

I tried quitting drinking alone. After some initial success fueled by a temporary pink cloud and then willpower, I drank again. What followed was EXTENSIVE field research, aka I continued down the deep, dark rabbit hole of addiction (remember the Fire Swamp?). I like the phrase field research better than relapse, because of the lessons that can be learned during field research. My alcohol-free journey didn't stand a chance until I burned the ships and started walking this path with others.

When I first began attending recovery meetings, I'd hear someone share who had 20+ years away from alcohol, and I would say two things to myself: 1) Why does this person still go to meetings? And 2) I hope I don't have to attend these meetings for the rest of my life.

I now understand why people attend recovery meetings for years, even decades after their last drink. They have made it a non-negotiable to stick with the pack. They know the group consciousness is potent armor against the Bruno Voice, which will inevitably say, "It's been 15 years since our last drink, why the hell are we still here?" When someone does go back to drinking after years of abstinence, the story is always the same—they slowly begin drifting away from the pack, and the spirit of alcohol begins to prey on them just like a lion on the Serengeti would select prey that had separated from the herd.

I still attend 12-step recovery meetings and Café RE chats years after my last drink—to stick with the pack and move closer to the fire. Weekly, I try to host one to two chats in Café RE, attend a couple more, and then attend in-person AA meetings on occasion. Yes, the subject matter is usually alcohol-related, but in reality, I'm there to satisfy my biological requirement to connect with other human beings on an authentic and altruistic level.

At first, the meetings were a sentence, an obligation. Today, I love these meetings. I don't *have* to go to meetings; I *get* to go to meetings. I hear something at every meeting that nourishes the soul, and usually it's the newcomer who drops the biggest value bombs.

All 8 billion human beings walking the planet are broken, but people in recovery meetings are the broken lot who dare to uncover the stones in their lives and become less broken. There's also a constituency of saints who attend meetings with the sole purpose of showing others it can be done or to help walk each other home. These are the modern-day bodhisattvas. These are the people I want to surround myself with.

Recovery meetings have given me a chance to be part of a group or fellowship because this doesn't happen organically for me. I feel like I am missing some essential circuitry when it comes to building close friendships. I know this stems from childhood when I was ostracized for being non-Mormon, and also the conditional acceptance from my older brother, who only gave me attention when I let him beat on me or bully me.

I am deeply skilled, chameleon-like, at fitting in and making friends, but very few of them make it to the level of good friends. It's like there's a subconscious operating system in me that doesn't allow my guard or walls to fully come down. I'm on the fringes of many friend groups, and I don't know how to move closer. I pull out my phone to text friends to hang out, delete what I write, then type again, then delete again—it's a challenge for me.

I crave deep connection, and in today's world, it rarely happens organically. Sometimes, while driving to the store to purchase groceries, I think of times when men would go on hunting parties for days, and I yearn for the connections that would develop. But I guess I have to be okay with the parking lot conversations after meetings and the seemingly rushed conversations I have with other humans in our busy lives. This is why I still attend meetings—to stick with the pack and keep the Bruno Voice in check, at least for today.

Another tool that still keeps me grounded is playing the tape forward and backward—running through how drinking always ends versus how sobriety keeps opening up more life. It worked in the early days, and it works just as much now.

I highly recommend attending recovery meetings or our Café RE chats for the sole purpose of community—to feel that you are part of a group, and that you are not alone in your struggles. The importance of this cannot be understated, as humans at the fundamental level are pack animals that <u>require</u> connection for optimal functioning.

Chapter 24
The Messy Middle: Downgrading Addictions & The Bad Days

When we remove alcohol, something has to fill the void or go in contra to the drinking. For many, myself included, this can look like addiction whack-a-mole, which is where you push one addiction or behavior down only to find it pop up in another area of your life, but hopefully with less damaging consequences. In her recovery memoir *Blackout*, Sarah Hepola has a great line where she says her recovery was a series of downgrading addictions, and my journey followed a similar trajectory. I definitely experienced addiction whack-a-mole in the early days away from alcohol, and well, I'm still downgrading to this day.

At first, I had intense sugar cravings, and I went hard in the paint with Reese's Pieces and ice cream, especially in my first thirty days. I gave myself a hard pass on these sugar binges, knowing there would be a time and a place to deal with it, but as long as I wasn't drinking alcohol, I chalked it up to a major win. Many people don't realize that a significant component of alcohol cravings are tied to sugar, and I definitely allowed myself to scratch the itch. On one occasion, I ate so much salted caramel ice cream that I was so sick to my stomach I had to pull over and force myself to throw up, which definitely could present itself as an eating disorder, but I reminded myself that ice cream wasn't ruining my life at the moment.

Around month two away from alcohol, I found myself pulling out my eyebrows to the point where there were visible gaps. There's a medical term for this called trichotillomania, which can be a serious mental health condition characterized by the irresistible urge to pull out one's hair…shit. But as long as I wasn't drinking, I was okay with it, and eventually I learned how to resist the urge to pull. When I found myself about to pull, I would close my eyes, take a deep breath, exhale, and find where I was holding tension in my body; many times, I was clenching my teeth without even realizing it.

I found my coffee consumption ramped up, and I had difficulties stopping after two cups of coffee. Many times, despite telling myself I'd only have two cups of coffee, I'd find myself drinking my 4th and 5th cups of coffee, knowing I'd have trouble falling asleep at night. Some days, I had to play the caffeine tape forward to walk myself away from the coffee maker after 12:00 PM. Even on the days when I did blast my adrenals with excess caffeine, I gave myself a pass as long as I wasn't drinking.

My alcohol addiction transferred itself to my businesses, but that's okay since working more hours and longer days wasn't a looming threat to my life, and I found myself with expanding work opportunities and more money. There's a word for this—it's called workaholic—but as long as I wasn't drinking, I was totally fine with it.

I made sure to give myself a hard pass with these new imbalances in my life, knowing there would be a time and place to deal with them. I think if I didn't allow these behaviors to unfold, it would have been too big a shock for my nervous system, and I probably would have returned to the bottle. So I let them be. I brought acceptance to these behaviors, I became aware of them, I befriended them, and while working late hours, with gaps in my eyebrows, I ate a shit ton of Reese's Pieces and loved every single one.

Around year three, I began to question if I truly had ADHD, or it was the alcohol that was wrecking my focus. I had been clinically diagnosed with ADHD on more than one occasion, which I was treating with medication. Now I do believe ADHD is a real thing, but I don't think it's a genetic neurological disorder, but rather a multitude of acutely painful linked present moments that force us to turn our attention elsewhere. I also came to learn the primary class of medications used to treat ADHD (think Adderall) was simply a pharmaceutical grade of methamphetamine that one can find on the street, so I began to taper off my ADHD medications, which was extremely difficult, but to my surprise, after initial discomfort, my focus improved—so much so that I wrote my first book a year after stopping the meds. I also learned that the ADHD meds were fueling the coffee consumption and eyebrow pulling.

Sometimes in sobriety, and in the game of life, it's two steps forward and one step back. I never used nicotine prior to quitting drinking, yet I found myself experimenting with smokeless chewing tobacco and the slightly healthier nicotine pouches called Zyn. I was able to apply the same tools toward these less destructive addictions that I used to quit drinking. I started communicating with others about my desire to quit the nicotine products. I created accountability by finding a couple of guys who also wanted to quit chewing tobacco, and when I played the tape forward, I realized I'd always want more, more, more, and more. Quitting nicotine wasn't easy, but I'm thankful for the experience.

At year four, I began wondering if my antidepressant medication was still necessary since I hadn't had a major bout with depression for roughly four years—go figure. I was still occasionally visited by the black dog, depression, which I covered in episode 118 of the *Recovery Elevator* podcast, but without alcohol, they weren't existential crises, and they'd always pass within a day or two, and sometimes within the same day. So with medical supervision, I began tapering off my daily 30 mg Paxil tablet, which was a butt-kicking, but I now had tools, and I knew the discomfort wouldn't kill me. It turns out, like anxiety, alcohol was driving 90% of my depressive states and I was fine without the medication—as long as I didn't drink.

I never considered myself having a problem with food, but for most of my adult life, I had to have a comfort meal before going to bed. With each passing year away from alcohol, I found this urge soften until one day I realized it had been months since I binged on food before going to bed.

In October 2018, I went to my doctor to have a small bump on my right testicle examined and was told it was nothing to be concerned about, but after three back-to-back colds during the summer months, I knew something was off. When I got a second opinion, I was informed

I had testicular cancer, which bloodwork and imaging later confirmed. I remember receiving the diagnosis at 4:48 PM via phone call. I was sitting alone in the cancer center waiting room, just 12 minutes before the clinic closed. I was the only person there. The news sank in slowly as a janitor methodically vacuumed the carpet on the other side of the waiting room. Outside the window, the first snowflurries of winter began to fall from the darkening sky.

Questions swirled in my mind. Am I going to survive this? Can I ever have kids? I was jolted back to reality when a hospital staff member said, "Sir, we are closing in a few minutes." I felt so alone, yet somehow I found the strength to make it to my car in the parking lot. All I knew was that I was scheduled for surgery two days later.

Post-surgery, I found myself with a bottle full of opiates. After taking three to four tablets, I took a drive and emptied the bottle on the side of the road, opting for edibles instead. (Side note: I went back the next day to where I'd dumped the pills. With an ice pack on my groin, I crawled on the ground trying to find them, but thankfully they had dissolved in the melting snow from the late October sun.)

My parents drove up from Colorado to help with my recovery. One night, after my parents had gone to bed, while under the effects of a 10 mg edible, I opened my refrigerator to see a bottle of white wine staring at me. I've always heard that marijuana is the gateway drug, but an interesting thing happened that night while in a standoff with a bottle of Pinot Grigio. At first, there was an "oh shit" moment—knowing that my guard was perhaps down while in an altered state of mind—but I looked at that bottle of wine and saw it for what it truly was: not comfort, not celebration, but a cancer-causing substance. I had just had a cancerous tumor removed from my body. Why would I voluntarily pour another carcinogen into my system? "Not today," I whispered to the bottle, which seemed to gaze back at me with a forked tongue. I closed the refrigerator door, knowing that my resolve to not drink appeared to be stronger than ever. After recovery from surgery, I shelved the edibles and was thankful for the role they played.

In ten years without alcohol, I have been able to cut out substances or pharmaceuticals that were never needed in the first place. I learned alcohol was the primary driver of the discomfort in my life. I still mentally explore cutting ties with caffeine but I love coffee, and a 3rd cup before noon has yet to land me in jail.

What I've come to understand is that this downgrading process is not just normal—it's necessary. Our brains are hardwired for pleasure and reward, and when we remove the main source, they'll hunt for substitutes. The key isn't perfection or complete abstinence from everything enjoyable; it's about making increasingly better choices that align with the life we actually want. Recovery isn't about becoming a saint—it's about becoming yourself again, messy parts and all. And sometimes, that journey involves a few detours through the candy aisle and heaps of maple donuts.

Disclaimer: I quit drinking and discontinued the use of some medications—this was my experience. You may quit drinking and go on medications, and that would be your experience. I'll share how I ended up going back on some of the meds I initially stopped. Again, it's just my path. Always consult with a medical professional before stopping the use of medications. If you're struggling with disordered eating or notice food-related behaviors becoming distressing, please seek guidance from a qualified healthcare or mental-health professional.

The Bad Days

Although removing alcohol from my life did wonders for my overall health and happiness, it wasn't a panacea. The storms of life still arrived with gale-force winds, sometimes seemingly for no reason at all. Some days would start off peachy, then a single thought would nudge me towards a ledge, and boom—my mind would push me right off a cliff. There was no breathing exercise, at least none that I discovered, that could pull me back from the mental abyss.

Before quitting drinking, I wondered how in the hell I was supposed to make it through bad days, and then the really bad days, without alcohol. My circuitry is that of an artist; I'm sensitive, I feel deeply; my highs are sublimely high, and the lows are excruciatingly painful. I used alcohol to stabilize the expansive palette of emotions that I felt, and it worked damn well—until it didn't. What if someone dies? What if my dog has an accident? What do I do on the days the Bruno Voice convinces me I have nothing to offer this world and nobody loves me?

I used alcohol as a way to circumvent these days, and the thought of raw-dogging the dip days, or life in general, gave me a lump of anxiety the size of Jupiter in my stomach.

But when my uncle died of cancer and I was holding his hand as he took his last breath, I didn't drink. When my dog was hit by a car, I was able to drive him to the vet and assist him in his recovery without taking a drink. When I learned of my mom's stage 4 cancer diagnosis, I didn't drink—and as I write this line, while at my parents' house, with my mom on 24/7 oxygen, knowing the end is approaching, the plan is to be present for all of it, and of course, not drink.

When days loaded to the brim with shit arrived, I found most of my tools went out the window. It was raw and messy. I would go to the forest to yell, cry, and scream obscenities at the Douglas Firs in hopes of feeling better. On one particularly bad day, when the physical and emotional pain was so intense that I was 100% convinced I was dying, I googled how much it would cost to hire Third Eye Blind to play at my funeral, and I even started working on the set list I wanted them to play. I didn't die, but parts of the old personality were very much indeed dying. On another occasion, while unpacking 15 boxes of stuffed animals for the crane games in the new arcade I decided to invest in (more on that later), I found myself having shouting matches with stuffed teddy bears and dinosaurs.

But as long as I didn't drink, the passage of time seemed to remedy all. With every challenging day surpassed without taking a drink, my confidence grew, and I realized it's the challenging days that present us with the richest opportunities to build new, healthier habits and circuitry that no longer involve alcohol. Of course, it's easier to stay sober on the good days, but it's the bad days that force us to collect all parts of the personality, hunker down, and face the storm–ideally not alone.

When I first entered recovery, I incorrectly thought a bad day meant I was doing something wrong, that my recovery was broken, and I definitely wasn't fit to be behind the mic podcasting or writing books on wholeness. For some reason, and I still struggle with this, I forget that bad days are a totally normal and expected part of the human experience. In fact, the shit days are equally important because in this world of duality, you need a bad day to define a good day.

I do my best to embody the concept that there is no such thing as a bad day. If we can find a way to channel the energy, shit days bring hidden gems and expansive opportunities for growth. One morning, around six years away from alcohol, I could sense a mental implosion knocking at the door and knew I was in trouble. It wasn't even 9:00 AM yet, and the Bruno Voice was destroying me. I grabbed my ukulele, went to the basement, and started playing. Without a doubt, I wanted to run away from the pain, but I kept furiously strumming. Then the words "I am Here" came to my mind, and I started singing that line over and over—reinforcing that I'm no longer leaving my inner kiddo on shit days, and that I AM HERE. And then the words "I am Whole" came to my consciousness. For the next 45 minutes, I sang out loud, "I am Here, I am Whole." With each passing of the lyrics, I let myself fall deeper into the pain while I kept reinforcing that I AM HERE, that I'm not going anywhere, ever. "I am WHOLE" represents that I'm perfect just the way I am, and nothing has to change for me to be content with myself. I imagined I was singing directly to the Bruno Voice, who seemed to deflate with each repetition of the 6-word song.

"I am Here, I am Whole" later became the flagship song at Recovery Elevator retreats. It's currently my podcast intro music, my favorite song to play on the ukulele, and it even became the inspiration for a tattoo. At a retreat in August 2024, I had everyone give a round of applause to the Douglas Fir trees surrounding the stage that have been supporting us at the camp for the last seven years, and then shared fun facts about the trees. For example, the Douglas Fir is the tallest tree in the world. They grow taller than redwoods and sequoias, but the 460+ft monsters have all been harvested for wood. A couple of weeks later, I got an email from a retreat attendee with a picture of her new tattoo on her forearm, which had a towering Douglas Fir—on top of scars from cutting—with the lyrics "I am Here, I am Whole" on each side of the trunk.

I still find myself, with regularity, revolting against life, and I still have bad days. I wish I could tell you that removing alcohol also eliminated bad days, but that's not the case. What's changed is that I no longer need to escape the pain—I can sit with it, honor it, and let it teach me. These days aren't interruptions to my recovery; they're integral parts of it.

As Buddhist teacher Pema Chödrön reminds us, "We think that the point is to pass the test or overcome the problem, but the truth is that things don't really get solved. They come together and they fall apart. Then they come together again and fall apart again… The healing comes from letting there be room for all of this to happen: room for grief, for relief, for misery, for joy."

So when the storm clouds gather and that familiar darkness looms, I remember what sobriety has taught me: I don't need to outrun the storm anymore. I can stand in the rain, feel every drop, and trust that, like all weather, this too shall pass—leaving me stronger, more resilient, and more whole than before. Because in sobriety, we don't just survive the bad days, we alchemize them into something beautiful, one present moment at a time.

Chapter 25
New Pathways

My first two years away from alcohol were challenging; however, my life seemed to take off at the same time. Remember the Pink Cloud that sometimes arrives in early sobriety? This is when we stop ingesting poison, and every cell in our body rejoices. Not everyone experiences the Pink Cloud, but I did, and I felt invincible. It can show up soon after the last drink and shine brilliance in your life for months, years, or forever. I think it's the soul that summons this Pink Cloud when we put the bottle down, and I felt good for the first time in a long time.

Looking back, I realize this outer expansion wasn't just coincidence—it mirrored what was happening inside my brain. New neural pathways were forming, rewiring me for curiosity, connection, and creativity instead of survival and escape.

I never thought I was a morning person, but it turns out I just didn't like to be awake during the crescendos of a hangover. My circadian rhythm, no longer on liquor store hours, attached itself to the sun, and I found myself waking up earlier. I read the book *The Miracle Morning* by Hal Elrod, and I began waking up at 5:00 AM each morning to meditate, exercise, read a self-help book, journal, and then do something creative—all in ten-minute blocks. I'll be honest, it was grueling at first to make this habit stick, but after a week of nourishing my mind, soul, and body before the sun came up, I felt incredible and kept this morning routine going for almost two years. My nighttime routine consisted of Reese's Pieces, salted caramel ice cream, and reruns of *Forensic Files*.

I never enjoyed running until I quit drinking. I would rarely run over two miles, but shortly after ditching the booze, I began to find myself in flow states where I was consistently running four to five miles and well below my 10-minute mile average before. It's assuring when we get real-time data on our progress—I have a running app on my phone which summarizes my runs over the past three years, and when I quit drinking, all of my stats dramatically improved seemingly overnight. I dropped about 15 pounds in the first 5 months, which I attribute to cutting out empty calories (alcohol), not eating gas station hot dogs, eating consistent healthy meals, and running.

Before quitting drinking, I avoided mirrors. I used to wait until the steam from the shower covered the entire mirror before getting out. Without even realizing it, this behavior of self-loathing went away, and the first thing I'd do after drying myself is I'd take my hand and wipe off the steam on the mirror so I could see myself. I realized I no longer hated the guy I saw in the mirror; I could hold the gaze now that I was no longer trashing my body and mind, and I liked what I saw. In addition, since I had improved my diet and had been running so much, I began to see abdominals.

At seven months, I returned as a chaperone to Peru, where, surprisingly, my best friend from high school, Brady, didn't fire me after I showed up drunk the previous year. Where I had been wheezy and weak a year earlier on the Inca Trail, this time I felt unstoppable. I'd make it to camp first, then walk back a couple of miles to grab the packs of others. I couldn't believe all that I had missed the previous year while hiking the Inca Trail in survival mode. The glaciers on the 18,000-foot Andean Peaks pulled me into a state of awe, and how had I missed the thousands of blooming flowers welcoming me on the trail.

I aimed for a redo from last year's debacle in the Fire Swamp, and after the Peru trip, I went to Brazil, where I visited my roommate from Spain during the Dolce Vita days named Marcos. I then went to Buenos Aires, Argentina, to visit another friend. I carried my microphone and mixer with me in my backpack and continued releasing weekly podcast episodes throughout my trip. I once recorded an episode in an airport where I had to edit out the airport announcements. With Skype, I was able to interview guests for the podcast even while in the Southern Hemisphere. This accountability was massive, and it kept sobriety at the front of my mind at all times.

After the one-year mark, I started dating again, and I quickly found that not drinking was a wonderful filter. If sobriety was an issue for someone, which it rarely was, we'd learn it wasn't the best fit on the first date and not the tenth. In addition, my sobriety was something that women saw as an asset or a superpower since women seeking a stable relationship are generally looking for someone trustworthy, reliable, healthy, and someone who could potentially be a good father—all of which sobriety enhances. I even found that once I put "sober" on my profile on the dating apps, I got more dates since most women have been burned by alcohol in previous relationships.

The aperture of life was opening, and I began to see opportunities that I had missed when I was in survival mode while drinking. In the spring of 2015, while walking in my local mall, I saw a small empty storefront, and I approached the mall's general manager, asking if I could put some arcade games in the space. She said she liked the idea and offered me an even bigger storefront. Previously, I had only a handful of arcade games in a couple of locations, but with new eyes, at least triple the energy, and a nervous system that wasn't totally wrecked, I could evaluate the potential opportunity, and I went for it. I took out a business loan and invested in an arcade.

I remember one morning, the mall's general manager called me into her office, where she showed me the newspaper that had just done a story on the *Recovery Elevator* podcast and my sobriety. I felt my pulse quicken as she slid the newspaper article in front of me, but then she told me she had almost lost her own daughter to alcohol addiction, and she became one of my biggest advocates.

That arcade turned into two, two into three, and I soon had arcades across the state of Montana. I bought an office warehouse where semi trucks could deliver arcade games, and I created a podcasting studio upstairs, which worked perfectly until freight trains rolled past—but that's okay, I love trains.

For the first two years sober, I took the extra time and energy on my hands and grew my small businesses. In 2016, I had a record year across the board. My Mobile DJ business did over 150 weddings that summer.

My adult sports league, Overtime Sports, which is still in operation today, offering kickball, dodgeball, cornhole, and more, was exploding. I kept adding new arcade locations, and there were buckets of quarters in my apartment that I couldn't seem to deposit fast enough.

Recovery Elevator produced zero income for the first year, which was fine since that wasn't the goal. The idea was to create accountability to stay sober, and that was working—priceless. However, it took about 20+ hours per week to run the podcast and the growing Recovery Elevator accountability group on Facebook. With the growth of my other businesses, I was struggling to keep up with it all.

After about 70 weeks of podcasting, I found myself at a crossroads with *Recovery Elevator* and the Facebook accountability group, which was growing in size daily. In addition, I was losing money each month since I had expenses such as podcast hosting fees, website fees, and more.

On April 16th, 2015, I launched the online alcohol-free community Café RE with a monthly membership of $12 per month. The transition from the free group to the paid group was a major challenge, and it almost didn't work. Most people understood why I could no longer afford to volunteer so many weekly hours, but a few kept trolling me, saying that AA was free and I was a horrible person for trying to monetize recovery. Okay, AA is free if you don't put money in the basket, and I needed to at least cover my expenses. This was Drama with a capital D, and a few individuals almost tore the whole thing down.

Café RE is a bit like a mental hospital run by the mental patients, but somehow we are still here, and we just turned nine years old this past April. The first two members are still in Café RE, myself and my podcast editor, Ty, and we have several members who have been in the community for 5+ years. When I first launched Café RE, everyone was new to sobriety, and there wasn't much alcohol-free time in the community, but with each lap around the sun, that problem solved itself, and now we have hundreds of years combined sobriety time.

Running Café RE has been the most rewarding yet hardest position I've ever held. Some days, the pressure of maintaining my own sobriety while operating Café RE is a palpable weight I don't think I can carry another step. When there were issues, and there were many, I felt like I let the whole community down, and many of the problems were my fault. I placed pressure on my shoulders that I had to fix everyone, which, of course, wasn't possible. When a Café RE member dies from alcoholism, and this unfortunately happens a couple of times a year, I always blame myself.

My sleep was suffering due to stress and anxiety. I'd wake up at around 2:30 AM and be unable to fall back asleep. I lost weight to the point where friends asked if I was okay. In February 2020, absolutely wiped, I pulled the plug on Recovery Elevator and the Café RE community, informing them it would be closing in a couple of months—then COVID happened. With lockdowns in place and members falling off the wagon, I knew it wasn't the right thing to do. I hired a community manager, a new member coordinator, a yoga teacher, put a committee in place, and started building a team to help me shoulder the challenges. I'm actually quite thankful for COVID and the turn of events that kept Café RE alive. I needed the community. I still do. I attend two to three chats (meetings) per week and host another two more. There is so much love, acceptance, empathy, and willingness within the community. The members truly are legends. I'm forever thankful to all the Café RE members who have been part of my alcohol-free journey.

In August 2017, Recovery Elevator held its first alcohol-free retreat in Bozeman, Montana, with nearly 30 in attendance. Since then, we've hosted more than 20 retreats and events—including trips to Thailand, Cambodia, Peru, Vietnam, and three separate retreats in Costa Rica. I have near panic attacks before each event because I take myself way too seriously, but I also care deeply about this work, and when people are flying across the globe to attend an event, we have to have our shit together—which we do most of the time. We did unintentionally find ourselves on a legit booze cruise once in Costa Rica, but we circled up the lounge chairs on the roof of the boat, had our own AF dance party, and everyone made it through sober.

Pathways continued to open for me the longer I stayed sober. As long as I kept going to in-person AA meetings, kept attending Café RE chats, kept hosting chats, and held sobriety as my #1 priority, my life kept expanding.

In February 2021, while traveling in Colombia, I connected with a gal on an online dating app where we agreed to meet at Crêpes and Waffles. I was so struck by her beauty that I panicked when the waiter arrived and I ordered a salad. Who orders a salad at Crêpes and Waffles? My soon-to-be wife kept making fun of me while she ate her delicious waffle with fresh strawberries and whipped cream.

In the spring of 2022, after saving over $95,000 from quitting drinking (according to the Recovery Elevator sobriety tracker app) and after selling my DJ business, sports league, and arcade, I bought a 25-acre farm in Guanacaste, a region in northwestern Costa Rica. Though it makes up just 0.03% of the Earth's landmass—roughly the size of West Virginia—this small country holds 5% of all living flora and fauna on the planet. I was ready to get my Shinrin-Yoku on and start forest bathing in the planet's fifth official Blue Zone, which are geographic regions where people outlive other human beings. On the first morning in Costa Rica, I asked my girlfriend from Colombia to marry me. Thankfully, she said yes because I hired a mariachi band and they were hiding in the jungle awaiting my cue—it was a good day.

In June 2024, at the age of 42, almost 10 years from my last drink, I had my first child, a baby boy we named Rio, who has been an incredible blessing. For a long time in my life, about the same amount of time that alcohol was present, I didn't think a wife, a family, or a child was a possibility. In fact, it would have been a horrible idea.

When an alcohol addiction takes hold, it's always a matter of life or death. Sure, some ride alcohol to the bitter end, but I'm mostly referring to the fact that life isn't being lived when we are in active addiction. Today, life is being lived—I'm physically, mentally, and spiritually healthy enough to embrace new pathways when they emerge in life. Today, I'm excited for the future, and I have the clarity, peace, energy, and presence to embark upon whatever the universe has in store for me.

Chapter 26
Whisky a No-Go:
Rediscovering My Creative Spark

In August 2003, at the age of 22, I was standing backstage with my bandmates in the green room at the iconic Whisky a Go Go concert venue. Autographed framed pictures of legendary bands such as Led Zeppelin, The Doors, and Guns N' Roses, who had previously played at the venue lined the walls, and I couldn't help but feel like I was in the presence of giants. After the opening act, we took the stage, and when the curtain rose, revealing hundreds of fans in the audience, many of whom were singing the lyrics to our opening song, I knew without a doubt this was why I was on planet earth: to be a rockstar and to play music.

But the dream didn't last long as alcohol had different plans for me. The band soon broke up, and alcohol began nudging creativity and music out of my life, but I kept trying to make it work. One evening, after auditioning for a new rock band and downing several beers, I thought I had loaded up my custom-made electric guitar until I heard a sickening thud as I reversed over it with my truck. The sound of splintering wood and twanging strings might as well have been the sound of my dreams shattering. The music dream died that summer, and it died hard—I didn't even have a guitar to play.

When I quit drinking eleven years later, I thought my love for playing music would return, but it didn't. I picked up another guitar, but every time I sat down to play it, nothing came out. It was as if the dream of being a musician had shriveled up like a houseplant your neighbor forgets to water when you're out of town.

At the end of year two, I thought to myself, "Maybe the guitar has run its course and I need to try a different instrument," so I bought myself a keyboard, which sat in the box for another 10 months. When I pulled it out of the box, it was like I had claw hands and a level-ten creative block. When I pressed the keys, no matter how much I tried to force it, there was no inner spark, and the keyboard started collecting dust.

In August 2017, Recovery Elevator had its first-ever retreat, and there was an open mic on the last night. An extremely talented guest named David L. played an acoustic song on guitar while we sat around the campfire. I remember a firework show of dopamine in my brain went off as David played an incredibly fast and technical bluegrass tune. Although I didn't know where to start, I knew I had to make music a part of my life again.

A couple of years later, when I noticed myself humming and singing in the car and shower, I signed up for four voice lessons, as maybe vocals were the entry point back into music. I hated the first lesson, felt remarkably silly the second and third lessons, but on the fourth lesson, while singing Elvis Presley's "Can't Help Falling in Love," I felt a warm buzzing sensation in the heart area, which is difficult to describe, but it was the message of "Paul, if you keep watering this seed, good things will come."

I was unable to sign up for additional voice lessons since the music store was shut down for COVID, but later that year, while walking the touristy streets of Lahaina in Maui, Hawaii, a ukulele on the wall seemed to be calling my name like in the movie Three Amigos when the Singing Bush tries to get Chevy Chase and Steve Martin's attention. "Look at me, Paul, look over here." I bought the ukulele from the small shop, which I later learned burned down in the 2023 Maui fires.

From Maui, I flew to Colombia, where, during the layovers, I watched YouTube videos on how to play basic chords and a couple of days later found myself improvising a song on the ukulele to my soon-to-be wife in hopes of a kiss.

In early 2021, in the middle of another COVID lockdown, I was jamming hard on the ukulele when a jolt of electricity pulsed through me, which forced me to stop, and I said to myself, "Oh shit, this dream might not be dead after all." I had no idea what my future with music was going to look like, but I knew this was where I had to go. When I play music, and it's always been this way, there's a knowing that I have to share this gift with the world. So I had the idea to offer an alcohol-free ukulele class. When I created the course content and finalized the landing page on the Recovery Elevator website, I thought it was going to be me and maybe four to eight other sober ukulele players. But when over 100 people signed up for the course, I hired three more sober ukulele instructors who had ironically just shown up in my life, and I reached out to Kala Brand Ukulele to see if they wanted to sponsor the course.

When I was in my late teens, I was certain I'd become a rock star with multiple world tours under my belt. None of that happened—but by the age of 42, I had taught over 300 students the ukulele, was sponsored by Kala Brand Ukuleles, and at Recovery Elevator retreats, many arrive with ukuleles, where we play songs I wrote for the ukulele classes. I may not have platinum records hanging on my walls, but sharing the stage at our retreats with fellow sober ukulele players is just as good.

Perhaps the universe was looking out for me, because I know with 100% certainty that if I were a global touring rockstar, I would have fallen into the abyss with alcohol and probably would have been another one of those sad stories in the music industry—artists who left us too soon.

Behind the scenes in the early 2020s, I recorded my first album in over 20 years under the artist name Pablo Church, which is available on Spotify and iTunes. You betcha I play the ukulele on a couple of tracks. I also learned the Native American flute, which I play over electronic music. This album is so incredibly special to me, knowing all the detours and deep crevasses life took me through before I was able to write music again. Searching for my own music on Spotify, where other musical legends such as Third Eye Blind, Coldplay, and Metallica house their repertoire of art, is a miracle in its own right—and only sobriety made it possible.

Maybe the dream isn't dead; I just had to learn some valuable life lessons first and clear the system of the poison alcohol. And what if the dream has evolved from playing sold-out stadiums in Europe to playing private ukulele concerts to pine trees and aspens in the forest? I think I'm already living the dream.

Music can be a profound tool on our alcohol-free journeys. Every single cell in the human body (trillions of them) has something called a primary cilium, which is basically an antenna-like structure that is exquisitely wired for vibration. We are drawn to frequencies that resonate with us, and tones, songs, and musical vibrations have the ability to raise our vibrations or change our emotional states, making us feel better.

I've gone through three pairs of Bose noise-cancelling headphones, and for me, this is a must-have piece of recovery equipment. There are certain songs—the theme song from the Last of the Mohicans soundtrack is one of them—that always give me the strength to move forward in this human life, which can be a shit burger at times, as we all know. There's an instrumental version of Elton John's "Can You Feel the Love Tonight" by Floritatura that never fails to flush out sadness and grief through my tear ducts when I hear it. At times, when excess frustration builds up in the system, I blast a heavy metal playlist through my headphones and scream along to the tracks.

Without a doubt, I am a better musician sober. Music is all timing, with beats and rhythms lining up on musical mathematical grids, and once the prefrontal cortex is gummed up with alcohol, it's hard to play in time or in beat.

I falsely thought alcohol made me a better musician or took concerts to the next level, but none of that is true. I've been to over 100 concerts sober—I've seen the Foo Fighters, Lil Jon, DJ Steve Aoki, O.A.R, Journey, Dirtwire, and my favorite concert was when I saw Ludacris with my good sober buddy Dusty. If music is to be part of my life, alcohol cannot be involved—it's that simple. Alcohol nearly killed my musical aspirations, and with each passing day without alcohol, a wind fans the musical spark in my life.

Currently, Coldplay has over 92 million monthly listeners on Spotify. Pablo Church has roughly 19, which I'm so incredibly proud of because I remember the trenches I had to crawl through to get here. What direction will music take my life moving forward? I have no idea, but as long as alcohol is sidelined, it should take me somewhere fun.

The Relentless Inner Flame

I began regularly meeting with therapists in my mid-twenties, and after lying to them (or to myself) about my alcohol consumption, within the first session, they would always conclude that I'm too hard on myself, or that I expect too much of myself. I have a big energy, meaning a significant amount of energy moves through my system daily, and this has been both a blessing and a curse. A blessing because I've learned that I can make things happen, I can get shit done, and taking action isn't something I struggle with. It's been a curse because it feels like every day is the gosh darn Super Bowl, and I take on oversized burdens because I ambitiously and perhaps foolishly think I can make a difference. For example, my goal with Recovery Elevator, the podcast, Café RE, my previous book, this book, and all my efforts in this space is to cure addiction. That's a tall order, one where the most brilliant of medical minds have yet to find a solution, yet there's a part of me deep within that fully believes I can make this happen. It's this incessant drive within that I wish would let me take a nap at times.

It's similar to my Bruno Voice, but also different, as it has more of a loving, tough love quality to it. It's an incessant inner drive that seems to be so deeply ingrained in the operating system of my subconscious.

It's like a sort of Self-Bullying Disorder that has driven me to do some pretty amazing things, but in a way that would make even the meanest middle school bully think, "Dude...too far." It has been a thorn in my side my entire life, which alcohol provided relief from, until it didn't, and I still don't know how to handle it.

Take this book, for example. About two years ago, an inner coach, with a clipboard and a whistle, whom I'm still deciding if I like or not, started saying, "Yo, it's time to start writing." After my first book, I planned to wait at least a decade or four before writing another one. However, this coach acts like I've missed a deadline I wasn't aware of, and he starts grilling me about how long it's taken to write this book, as I'm going on nine months of writing, with another 12 months of notes, research, sticky notes, and mind maps before that.

I'll get seriously down on myself, and I completely miss the fact that writing a book is an incredibly difficult process. Maya Angelou had such severe writer's block that she would rent hotel rooms, strip them bare of all decorations, and lie on the bed with only a Bible, a thesaurus, and yellow legal pads. She'd write lying down, often struggling for hours to produce just a few pages. Stephen King once got so stuck on *The Stand* that he literally put the 500-page manuscript in a drawer and didn't touch it for years. Charles Dickens would rearrange furniture compulsively, walk 20 to 30 miles through London at night when stuck, and touch certain objects a specific number of times before he could write. Writing a book is a grind for all authors, yet I think I should be effortlessly cranking out a flawless manuscript that I then gleefully hand over to my editor. The hardest part of college and grad school was the onslaught of papers I had to write, and this is like taking my longest paper in college and then continuing for another 250 pages. I've had beautiful writing sessions where my fingers can't keep up with the mind, but I've also sat down intending to write the holy grail of recovery, then cried at my desk for the next 10 minutes.

I also incorrectly think I write in a vacuum and always reject my recent life experiences as a valid reason why this book has taken longer than the Panama Canal to finish. For the entire duration of the writing process, I've had an infant and now a toddler in my house who has refused from the start to sleep in a crib or his own bed, and no chance of him sleeping in his own bedroom. I'll get four hours of heavily interrupted sleep, and wonder why my fingers feel like weighted sausages on the keyboard.

I can't seem to nail down a writing routine either. On some mornings, harsh language gets me out of bed and in front of the computer at 5:30 AM, and other mornings I'll hit snooze over 25 times and roll out of bed around 8:00 AM. If you're reading this book, well, we hit the finish line, but it wasn't easy.

I've battled with the last 850 words for three days now. I've tried writing in different areas of the house, and I furiously rode my bike around my neighborhood in hopes of finding the right words. I even dumped out my coffee, thinking I'm too caffeinated, and switched to chamomile tea. And I'm now writing next to a large San Pedro cactus on my kitchen table, asking it to provide me with the clarity needed to finish this book and help others quit drinking.

I think I'll always be too hard on myself, but maybe that's the point. Perhaps this relentless inner critic or coach, annoying as it is, might actually be part of what drives me to keep going. Maybe it's the same voice that got me to put down the bottle—and sometimes our harshest inner voices are also our most honest ones. There's something darkly funny about a self-bullying disorder that somehow bullied me into writing a book to help people.

I wish I could report that I've healed or at least made progress in this area of my life. I wish I gave myself the same amount of grace I give others, but I can't. I wish I were kinder and softer to myself.

I expect way too much out of myself, and I don't think this will ever change. Perhaps this circuitry isn't actually faulty, but rather put there by design. As I just mentioned, my goal is to cure addiction, or to help as many people as possible quit drinking, and if I am to come anywhere close to achieving this, then I'm going to need a never-ending inner flame that keeps me moving. I am learning to trust that this part of my personality exists for a reason and that one day it will all make sense. I've also learned this inner air horn is in line with the timing of the universe, and it seems to know the precise time something needs to get done.

Chapter 27
The Slow Spiral Upward: From "You Fucking Idiot' to 'I Fucking Love You"

My healing after putting down the bottle continues, and as long as I don't take that first drink, I don't anticipate this changing. In some regards, the healing happens at ludicrous speed. In other areas, the growth matches the pace of pine trees and cannot be measured in days, months, or sometimes even years.

I think the biggest win over the past decade, which has taken years to move the needle, is how I speak to myself. For the majority of my life, I spoke to myself in a way that I would never speak to a stranger, a friend, or even someone I didn't like.

In the first couple years away from alcohol, the inner narrative "you fucking idiot" seemed to be on repeat. It had always been there, but without alcohol to drown the voice out, it seemed as if the Bruno Voice had now acquired a megaphone. That line was so deeply ingrained into my subconscious that I imagine I had been saying that for years, probably since I was a teenager, and the worst part was I believed it. I've yet to meet anyone who has been successful in recovery who hasn't addressed self-loathing, or the inner critic, so that's where I went to work.

Upon awakening, with the most presence and consciousness I could put forth, I'd shower myself with love and positive affirmations, only to hear "you fucking idiot" a couple minutes later while tying my shoes. I did meditations on loving the self, which seemed to only work for the duration of the meditation. There was still a deeply rooted dissatisfaction with the self that I began to think I'd never get to the source of. Then one day, 4+ years after my last drink, I made a mistake, and a softer voice with a less pejorative tone chimed in with, "Paul, you goofball." I remember I immediately stopped what I was doing and said to myself,

"Did I really just hear that?" Yes, somehow and somewhere, a new set of neurons had just fired together that wasn't a full-on diatribe toward the self. I didn't know how bad the previous verbiage stung until this kinder, more playful voice arrived. "You goofball..." I repeated to myself, "I'll take it."

"You goofball," I said again. I like it.

It took over 1,500 days to nudge the Bruno Voice into a more loving tone, or more accurately said, I think the Bruno Voice was silenced while a deeper circuitry fired. I wish I could report exactly how I accomplished this. It may have been the buckshot of positive morning affirmations, thousands of forced smiles, and countless journal entries on self-love, or it organically happened since the destructive act of poisoning myself with alcohol was no longer taking place. Whatever it was, I was so thankful for the micro, yet monumental shift in the kinder tone of how I spoke to myself. It was like Enya was on tour in my brain, and there was no more room for self-destructive talk. I'm now a goofball instead of a fucking idiot.

Around day 3,000, another milestone occurred. Sometime during year eight, while reading a book about pregnancy as I was soon to be a father and I could feel my blood pressure rising with each passing day, I heard a voice inside that said, "I fucking love you, Paul." It was sweeping, all-encompassing, and I could tell the voice meant business. It wasn't an "I fucking love you, Paul" if everything went well and I got my shit done, but a statement of unconditional love regardless of what unfolded. The wonderful news I am so pleased to share with you is that my subconscious fires this line dozens of times daily. "I fucking love you, Paul." This new narrative has a different quality or tone than the Bruno Voice, as it comes from deeper within my core and not from the swirling thoughts in my head. The five words, "I fucking love you, Paul," contain so much. They remind me there is no manual for life, which can be so incredibly messy at times. When I'm at a crossroads, the "I fucking love you, Paul" means: Paul, go left, go right, eat some ice cream—it doesn't matter. I got your back, and I FUCKING LOVE YOU regardless of what you do.

My oh my, has this progress been slow...but I didn't walk into the woods in a day, and another question comes to mind: where am I actually going? Yes, there's all that fun recovery jazz about becoming your most authentic self and creating a life that no longer requires alcohol, but are those actual destinations? Will there be a harp sound letting me know I have arrived? Or is the point that there is no "arriving" at all—only the journey, looping back on itself, again and again...

Walking the Sacred Loop

Perhaps the slowest of transformations in my life without alcohol, which is still very much under construction, is swapping the emphasis from the destination to the journey itself. I didn't have this one on my bingo recovery card, but it may be the greatest gift a life without alcohol provides—orienting my energy not toward some finish line, but into the only moment that matters: this one right here. What if this path isn't leading to some mythical finish line where I collect my "Fixed Human" medal? Maybe the whole journey—the stumbles, the blackouts, the small victories, and the maddeningly slow changes—is the journey of life itself.

What if I don't walk out of the woods and choose to build a home nestled below a deeply rooted Douglas Fir? If I were to finally "walk out" of the woods, I'd probably stop, turn around and say to myself, "Welp, let's head back in," because I'm learning everything in life has cycles that resemble a circle.

Most cultures, prior to the ones currently setting the planet ablaze, recognized that life is a continuous circle—unlike our modern linear view that commences with birth, finalizes with death, and hopefully includes paying off a mortgage in between.

This circular life journey is represented everywhere in nature for us to not only follow, but to embrace as how life actually is.

Winter's dormancy gives way to budding aspen leaves, which grow into summer's fullness, then the leaves turn golden before falling to the ground, providing nutrients to the animals and plants below, then followed by frost and winter's rest. This cycle never truly begins or ends—it simply continues.

Another circle would be the journey we are currently on as our delicate floating spaceship without a roof circles around the sun for 365 days before it starts again. The earth even has a cyclical companion as it takes 27 days for the Moon to make a full circle around the earth.

Water evaporates from oceans, forms clouds, falls as rain, flows through rivers back to the ocean, and rises again as vapor. This endless circulation of water connects sky, land, and sea in a continuous loop of transformation.

The salmon's life journey embodies the sacred circle perfectly. Born in freshwater streams, they journey to the ocean to grow and mature, then return to their exact place of birth to spawn the next generation before dying. Their bodies decompose, nourishing the very streams where their offspring will hatch, completing a perfect circle of life, death, and renewal.

Trees grow in circular rings, each one telling the story of a year passed. Seeds fall from trees, take root, grow into new trees, which drop new seeds—a continuous circle of regeneration spanning generations.

In many Indigenous perspectives, birth and death aren't seen as absolute beginnings and endings but as transitions within the greater circle. The materials of our bodies come from the galaxies and return to them, nourishing new life.

Let's talk about the circle of life in your house. Once you've finally caught up with the mountain of dirty clothes in the hamper, you've now earned the privilege of starting all over again in just a couple of days.

Quitting drinking, along with heaps of meditation, breathwork, and charred Palo Santo sticks, has allowed me to see the "I'll be happy when" trap as the cosmic joke. There's a very good chance there is no destination, there is no top of the mountain, and this is a beautiful thing.

If you think about it, our obsession with destinations is exhausting. It's like being on vacation but spending the entire time taking photos for social media instead of actually experiencing the place. "I'm at the Grand Canyon! Hold on, let me upload this to six social media platforms while missing the actual canyon!"

Although I declined the first several thousand invitations, a life without alcohol has invited me to put down the camera and just be present for the view.

As I continue to embody the journey as what's most important, I notice more: flowers, birds, even a small river in the distance that I can only hear a few hours a day when the pitch of the air pressure is just right. I'm realizing the universe's primary goal is for me to witness its beauty and to fall in love with it.

The further I go without a drink, as my body and cells release the memory of alcohol, which creates more space within, the more I'm able to observe and notice. And the more I notice, the more in awe I am of this spectacular show we are all a part of, and slowly, so very slowly, I have found gratitude creeps in to nudge everything else out to become the baseline state. Even in challenging moments, and on the super shit days, the first words I mutter within are: thank you for the struggle, as I know it's here to help me grow.

Today, I have peace in my life, which wasn't the case 10 years ago. Not 24/7 peace, as I have a toddler in my home and my inner sails still catch the winds of wildly unpredictable mood swings required for an artist to create art, but every day, I find it, or better said, I place my body and mind in a position for peace and stillness to find me. The peace curve has been trending in the right direction since I put down the bottle, but it has taken a long time (much longer than I had expected) for the chemicals of stress to leave the system and even longer for the subconscious to embody the new circuitry.

There's a mantra that says you can be right, or you can have peace. Now, just a couple of weeks ago, I had to remind someone they had cut in front of me in line at Ross, even though there was an inner voice whispering, "Paul, don't do it, let it go." Just yesterday, I almost got my ass kicked at a gas station when I told a guy I thought the Confederate flag on his oversized diesel truck was fucking lame.

But over the years, there has been a snail's pace internal reorganization of what I value most, and peace continues to climb the list. I still find myself wanting to be "right," but it's less frequent, and I even find myself sending warm, heartfelt energies and peace to people who piss me off.

An Audible Pop

With all these internal shifts, I found my posture was next on the chopping block. On July 4th, 2018, while on a walk, my body suddenly stopped, my pelvis arched forward, my gaze lifted, and my shoulders pulled back. The way I carried myself was no longer congruent with my inner state, and my body no longer allowed me to slouch in chairs or work hunched over with slouched shoulders. With this new posture, my breathing expanded, which gave the cells in my body, and most importantly, my brain, extra oxygen.

With a straighter spine and diaphragm and lungs finally hitting their stride after years of constriction due to poor posture, came cathartic pops and cracks in the back that one would only hope to achieve while visiting a chiropractor. First, it started in the lower neck and upper back, and with each passing month or two, the release of pressure seemed to travel down the spinal column until one day I felt an audible pop at the base of the spine, followed by the body letting out a deep exhale.

For more than a decade, I battled chronic lower back pain—a struggle I know is all too common. At times, the pain sidelined me from the active lifestyle I loved, and the mental toll was just as heavy as the physical. Several doctors told me I had structural issues like herniated discs, and one even diagnosed me with degenerative disc disease—yikes.

With meditation and expanded self-awareness, I realized the back pain didn't fire at all times and was triggered by stress or certain situations—similar events and circumstances that prompted me to drink. If the reason for my lower back pain was structural and there were bulging discs, then why could I lift heavy items one day and be unable to tie my shoes the next? I came across two instrumental books that helped me view my lower back pain as accumulated stress or energetic blockages: the first book was *Healing Back Pain: The Mind-Body Connection* by John E. Sarno, MD, and the other was *The Way Out: The Revolutionary, Scientifically Proven Protocol to Stop Chronic Pain* by Alan Gordon. With this shift in thinking, when I did experience back pain, I began to curiously investigate my surroundings, my current emotional state, and would even thank the back pain for the messages it was trying to tell me. When my back hurt, I would place my energy and awareness into the area of discomfort, and I'd always notice the muscles were fully tensed like I was about to storm Normandy beach. I'd take several breaths and audibly tell myself to relax, and with repetition and countless breaths, the muscle fibers would return to an elastic state. The true marker of progress was when I woke up one morning and realized the muscles in my lower back weren't like closed fists upon awakening. The first thing I did in the morning, for probably two-plus years, was relax the muscles in my lower back before getting out of bed. The day my lower back stayed relaxed without me even thinking about it, I knew I'd hit a milestone I'd been working toward for years.

I'm so glad I opted out of back surgery, despite the recommendation of a couple of orthopedic surgeons, because today I am free of back pain and can carry 75 lb hay bales no problem. If I hadn't quit drinking, well, I would probably be dead, but if not, I'd still be hobbling around with shit posture and crippling back pain.

I was dead wrong when I assumed my healing from an alcohol addiction would flatline within the first year or two. Different themes of healing commenced on their own schedule as if they were following an astral clock. Around year six, or right when COVID happened, I found my body placing itself in strange positions that I later learned had names like boat pose, pigeon pose, or triangle pose. Although I was physically in challenging poses, I'd consider this a spiritual chapter of healing, as the yogic practice of connecting the body and breath is a highly spiritual one.

We hold short-term stress in our shoulders and long-term stress in our hips. My body knew it had to release these stagnant pockets of energy, and I dedicated time to these stretches, which always amplified when done on grass or in nature with a good soundtrack and my Bose headphones.

I placed a wooden pole on my shoulders, like I was about to do squats, and I'd straighten up tall and take deep conscious breaths into the shoulder sockets. Oh, how much love and attention my shoulders needed, as I have dislocated my shoulders a total of 14 times. On some stretching occasions, a bundle of muscle fibers would release or "let go" that had been contracted for years, probably decades.

Then one day, perhaps when Saturn was in retrograde with Texas Roadhouse, I found myself stretching my hips, especially the right hip of overdoing. It took me three years before I could do a yogi squat, and now I don't have to sit in a chair or at the edge of my bed to get dressed each morning. The yogi squat, also known as the Malasana in yoga, is a natural resting position that humans are designed to spend a lot of time in. Our hip, knee, and ankle joints are all perfectly constructed to allow for deep squatting, and it's the mobility and flexibility in the hips, knees, and ankles that many modern people have lost due to sitting in chairs. Research suggests that regular squatting helps maintain joint health, improves digestion, and even contributes to better pelvic floor function, resulting in healthier bowel movements. The loss of this movement in Western cultures is connected to several musculoskeletal and digestive issues.

As my body, psyche, and soul kept being pulled into new themes of healing, well after my last drink, I came to realize that without a drinking problem, there's a good chance none of this healing would have taken place. With this realization comes the discovery that perhaps I was never lost in the woods in the first place. Maybe I was never on the wrong path, but on a dark section of the circle of life that would soon bring me into the light.

Recognizing that life is a circle, I also understand the peace I experience today is temporary, and as more gray hairs make an unwelcome appearance in my beard, I know eventually all this expansive healing will reach a stage of contraction. So I guess all there is to do is count my blessings and be thankful for what I have today, and do my best to share what I have learned with others.

After drinking ayahuasca in 2018, there was a two-to-three-year reprieve from the anxieties of death, but today, I find myself thinking about this inevitable future life experience more than I'd like to admit. I'm a seeker, always have been, and probably always will be. At times, I desperately want to know what happens after I die; after we all die. The number one selling book of all time paints a picture of eternal sunshine and happiness, but if life follows a circle, I'm not so sure. I guess I'll have to wait to find out. But in the meantime, as long as I don't drink, I'm sure I'll enter a new preparatory chapter in life, preparing me for eternal bliss or perhaps another cycle of reincarnation on planet earth or somewhere else in the galaxy.

Chapter 28
The River Crossing:
A Journey Back to the Self

Recovery is full of cheesy slogans, and one of them I mocked is "you're giving up one thing for everything." The last ten years of life without alcohol have been just that—EVERYTHING. Sure, I have been metaphorically punched in the goat blocks and actually punched in the face, but so much quality life has been lived post-drink. New experiences, new adventures, road trips, new people, new career, new house, marriage, child, more pets, goats, more bank accounts, more nighttime nature walks, more waves surfed, more books read, more hugs, and I'm at an all-time high-water mark with love for the self.

In my youth, I loved to ride bikes in the woods, catch snakes, work on my model train set, play music, and hang out with friends. Today, things have come full circle, and this is again what my life looks like. I ride my mountain bike to the trails near my house. I put on a headlamp at night and go looking for creatures. I have 85 feet of track and four tunnels cut into the walls of my house as my Lionel O-scale train goes from my office, through the crawl space, into the basement, and back in a loop that takes about 55 seconds. At sunset, I play ukulele to my 14-month-old son, my dog Ben, and four Nigerian Dwarf goats, while my wife claps to the beat.

Sobriety has allowed me to see through the egoic façades of Western culture. It's like the fishing parable, where a wealthy businessman from America, while visiting a small Mexican fishing village, takes a walk to a nearby dock where he sees a poor fisherman return with three fish in his small boat. He learns it took the fisherman just two hours to catch the fish, and he then asks him what he's going to do with the rest of the day after he sells the fish at the market. The poor fisherman replied, "Well,

I'll go home, lie in my hammock, play guitar, and hang out with my wife and family." The rich businessman, with a serious tone, then says, "Okay, okay, listen closely. You need to go out fishing for 12 hours straight, and in six months, you'll have enough money for a second boat. When you have two boats out for 12 hours a day, then it will take three months to get a third boat. Keep doing this till you have 20 boats. Then you can build your own fish cannery and cut out the middleman. Once you have done this for 10 to 15 years, you can build a central cannery in Mexico City where you can then ship your product worldwide. Within another ten years, you'll be a publicly traded company and you'll have millions of dollars in your pocket." "How does that sound?" he asked the poor fisherman. "Well, I think that sounds great," he replied. Then the rich businessman asked the poor fisherman, "With all that money, you'll be able to do whatever you'd like. What do you think you'll do?" The fisherman reflected for a moment, then said, "Well, I'd go home, lie in my hammock, play guitar, and hang out with my wife and family."

Sometimes I wonder what I would do if I had a million dollars. Apart from two chicks at the same time (kidding, that 's an *Office Space* line), I think I know exactly what I would do. I'd stand barefoot in my yard playing the ukulele while watching the sun set. Next to me, my son is learning to kick a soccer ball, my goats are trying to ignore my dog, who keeps nudging them to play, and my wife is clapping along to the song I'm singing to our son.

There is no top of the mountain, and there is no destination. Sure, I've got worldly goals, but I've landed more at the knowing that I've already arrived, and there is nowhere else to go. In his book *The Wayfinders*, anthropologist Wade Davis describes languages in the Amazon and elsewhere that have no word for time. To me, that's still baffling and hard to even imagine. But the lessons addiction and recovery have taught me align far more with the timeless than with the world of time. This moment, the one we both find ourselves in, is more important than anything that has ever happened in the past or will ever happen in the future. When my mind wanders, and it still does often, I have trained myself, using the breath as the vehicle, to return to this moment where infinite riches and wealth reside.

I'm a fan of money and would prefer to have more of it than less of it. However, I'm starting to realize why the Waoroni people, one of the last uncontacted tribes of the Ecuadorian Amazon jungle, called money Tokoré, meaning worthless paper. Everything was free to them in the jungle, and once this paper money arrived, crime, murder, drunkenness, and the concept of poverty came thereafter. Yes, I still have a retirement plan, but wealth, money, fancy cars, and job titles have lost most of their allure.

Today I live a life that is more harmonious with nature and results in less waste; in fact, I drink mostly tap water. There was a time when my trash was filled with glass bottles, aluminum cans, and fast food bags. Late-night drunken food binges of hot dogs, Jack in the Box hamburgers, and shawarmas have been replaced with cleaner foods and salads, where fewer animals have to die for an unhealthy way of living. I'm not a vegetarian and still love a juicy hamburger, but my red meat consumption has probably declined by 90%. It wasn't intentional—it just happened. Apparently, it takes 1,000 gallons of water to make roughly 1 lb of beef, so now that my body craves less red meat, I guess my decision to quit drinking has also resulted in thousands of gallons of water saved and fewer animals slaughtered.

It feels good knowing I'm no longer participating in industries that require massive amounts of water, energy, and resources to produce substances that ultimately harm both people and the planet.

Every thought, emotion, and intention I carry creates energetic vibrations that extend far beyond my physical body. I was constantly broadcasting frequencies of shame, guilt, regret, and self-loathing into the quantum field—that invisible web of energy that connects all consciousness.

Now, instead of polluting this field with the heavy, dense vibrations of addiction and self-hatred, I'm contributing lighter frequencies: gratitude, clarity, authenticity, and "Somewhere Over the Rainbow" on the ukulele. I've stopped being an energetic drain on the collective consciousness and now contribute creative and healing energy—most of the time.

I had no idea that my addiction would be responsible for bringing me back full circle to the Dolce Vita, or the good life. I had labeled that dark period of my life as a tragic misstep and was convinced I had successfully imploded my life. Little did I know, I was on a journey of intense self-discovery where I would need to collect all parts of myself to move forward and heal. It's the addiction I have to thank for obliterating me into the person I am today. Not everybody who grapples with an addiction makes it to the other side, and the statistics show that I'm incredibly lucky. Each day is a gift, and although the Bruno Voice still tries to hone in on what's wrong with me and the world, a bigger part of me can't stop rejoicing. There will always be "recovery work" to do, or areas of my life where I can improve, but I feel I've crossed over to the other side. However, what does that even really mean since it sounds like the "other side" is a destination? Doesn't the addiction try to teach us destinations are a trap? I think the best way to describe it is what Jesus told his disciples in his infamous Sermon on the Mount, which is "Heaven is right here in the midst of you." That's a big line, and one that most of Christianity has difficulty reconciling because that teaching throws most of the Bible out the window.

In the English language, when you ask someone to point to heaven, almost everyone points straight up to the sky. In Spanish, they use the word Cielo, or sky, to describe heaven, which has a different overall meaning since the sky is all around us, even below us at times if we find ourselves in a plane, in a tree, or even standing up. In the Spanish language, and hundreds of other languages, we are much closer to heaven than we think, and perhaps even there already.

The river crossing of consciousness the Buddha spoke about 2,500 years ago is the realization that heaven, the good life, or the Dolce Vita is right here, among us in this moment, and we have ALREADY arrived. When this is embraced and embodied in our circuitry, water in lakes and streams turns clear, the air is purer, there is more fruit on the trees, more birds soar the sky, and the world is a more peaceful and harmonious place.

I am not the first or last to cross the river. Millions meet daily online or in the rooms of 12 steps to build the foundation for a stronger humanity. Those who have already crossed the river of consciousness are numerous and are dotted across the earth. You've most likely already interacted with them. The voices and the expressions on their faces are different: more confident, stronger, radiant. There's something different about their eyes; there is always more light. They begin where the rest of humanity leaves off, and many of them are unrecognizable unless you know what to look for. They do not feel called to draw attention to themselves. You think you are being kind to them, when really, they are being kind to you. They seem to find a way to build you up every time you have an encounter with them. It appears they are working with additional hours in the day, as they rarely seem stressed or in a hurry. At first, you may think these people are above you, but they always seem to place themselves below. They are humble people, and someone super famous once said that it's the meek or the humble who will inherit the world.

If you're reading this, wondering if you have already crossed the river of consciousness or are still in the parking lot blowing up your water wings, then let me tell you this. You've already departed. You're already in motion. You're much further across than you think. In fact, you may already be "there." Wherever "there" is. Your journey or crossing started years ago, perhaps decades ago. It began with dysfunction, and through the process of recognizing who you are not, the true self emerges. And who are you not? Well, you're not the Bruno Voice, you're not the voice inside the head, and this realization is the start of the river crossing.

Have I crossed the river? You bet your ass I have. I'm kidding. It's not a one-and-done thing, and the river has to be crossed at all hours of the day, every minute of the day, and every second. In the spiritual text, *A Course in Miracles,* it says that we must choose between the crucifixion and the resurrection each moment we find ourselves in. We may find ourselves on the "other side" only to have the Bruno Voice yank us right back. The key to the river crossing, and this is a practice, is embodying this new circuitry where the baseline state of being is much less responsive to the Bruno Voice and more connected to the heart. It's not ignoring the Bruno Voice, but being aware this voice will never bring us lasting happiness.

To be honest, I'm not sure if I've crossed over to the other side. Of course, I'd like to think I have, but I need to be careful I don't give myself a new identity of an enlightened being who has crossed over. There are days, weeks, and even months where life feels effortless and things happen with ease. There are other times when I wonder if I should even be writing this book in the first place because I'm a wreck. If God made man in his image, sometimes I wonder if God is as messed up as me.

One wrench with the whole River Crossing thing is that you can't use the thinking mind to gauge progress. The mind will create a destination, an idea, and a vision of how grand it's supposed to be on the other side, but the point is separating from these false fantasies created by the mind in the first place.

Most utopian visions end in disappointment, and the extreme examples are well documented in history books—think Hitler. This river crossing, initiated by an addiction that smacked you across the temple with an oar, is the slow and painful realization that nothing external has to happen for you to be okay or happy. You don't need to go anywhere to find wholeness because it's already here, inside of you.

Geographical cures present themselves as a sound logical strategy to quit drinking, but we almost always forget to leave the drinking problem behind. Sure, some environments are more conducive than others when it comes to sobriety, but the metamorphosis, or the river crossing, can happen anywhere, at any place, in any room, on any sidewalk, with any particular cloud pattern in the sky, at any time of day or night.

I'm writing this chapter in the drunkest county in the United States of America. Gallatin County, located in Southwest Montana, according to a recent Centers for Disease Control (CDC) study, reported 26.8% of its residents drink excessively—the highest rate in the nation.

To me, it's almost comically coincidental that most of this book, which is anchored in the sobriety and quit drinking space, was written in the drunkest place in the country. I find it ironic that out of the 3,144 counties in America, the *Recovery Elevator* podcast, which has been downloaded over 10 million times, is broadcast to the world from the most inebriated county in America.

I include this to plant the seed that whether you're reading this from the drunkest county in America, a penthouse in Manhattan, or what feels like your own personal prison cell of addiction, the river crossing doesn't require a change of address. The key to your prison isn't hidden somewhere else—it's been in your pocket this whole time, and it was the addiction, accompanied by heaps of pain and suffering, that brought your search for wholeness back full circle to the self and made it clear that you were never actually trapped in the first place.

Chapter 29
Trust: Leaning Into the Universe

Writing a book about sobriety, healing, and stepping away from one of the most addictive drugs on the planet without covering the higher power or GOD component would be like writing a book about bicycles and never mentioning the rider. Alcohol dulls or completely severs our electrical connection with the universe. If we put the drink down and ride the alcohol-free life long enough, eventually we'll be graciously invited into exploring a world of spirituality, God, the Universe, or a Great Universal Spirit, as the Native Americans called it—none of which has anything to do with religion. Apparently, the higher power thing, which can be a major obstacle for some at first, is so important in AA that seven out of the 12 steps have a direct or indirect reference to God.

Almost all physicians and healers see the value of pulling strength from something outside of yourself, ideally something more powerful than you. The primary reason for this is what Einstein said: you can't use the same level of thinking that got you into a mess to get you out of the mess. Einstein also said at the end of his career, as his work with quantum calculations brought him closer to the spirit of the universe, "I want to know the mind of God; everything else is just details."

Once the body has rid itself of the toxin alcohol and we have mentally stabilized, then the organism starts presenting the big hitter questions, such as "Why am I here?" "What's the point of all this?" "What's my purpose?" These questions, coupled with a gaze into a moonless night sky, can spark a dormant fire within, and we begin to open up, listen, and even start to let go. We begin to consciously ponder, and we even begin to consciously listen—we start seeking the truth and perhaps ask for guidance and direction. Here's the thing—the truth is also seeking you. What 13th-century Sufi mystic Rumi intuitively knew, quantum science has now proven with math equations: what you seek is seeking you as well. After the body and mind have found a significantly healthier homeostasis without alcohol, a gust of wind in the pine trees or a ray of sunlight at dawn reflecting off a snow-capped peak will reignite the search for truth.

Now I do not have the answers to life's biggest questions—nobody does. Even if I did have the answers, to think I could accurately describe the miracle of the universe with 26 alphabet characters, limited vowels, and a handful of consonants would be presumptuous at best. In ancient Hebrew texts, one was not permitted to even attempt to spell GOD—they had to use a dash G-D. Once words, thoughts, and mental constructs begin to define the Universal Spirit, a creator, we have actually just diminished GOD. The main reason for this is that the Universe/God lives in the timeless/eternal, and everything in this world follows the properties of time—this includes thoughts, words, and concepts about GOD. In addition, once you have "thought" about connecting with the Universe or a higher power, you have just "missed the mark" since thoughts are rooted in time, and a thought about connecting with GOD is a future action when the only time we can connect with Spirit is now.

The same principle applies to presence. Once we have a thought about becoming present, although the recognition of "not being present" is a major win, each thought about becoming present places that desired state in the future, when the only time for pure consciousness and deep presence is now. Said another way, thinking blocks any possibility of connection with a power greater than yourself. You're either with God in the moment or you're not; and if you're thinking, you're not.

Last fall, I attended a community event where spiritual and motivational speaker John Ortberg discussed ways of connecting deeper with the Universe or God. During his talk, he gave numerous shoutouts to those in AA and people in recovery. So many that when I approached him after his talk, I thought for sure I'd learn he was in recovery, but he wasn't. He was simply in awe, perhaps envious, of how people who struggle with and surrender to addictions are forced to connect to God, and they are some of the most spiritually connected people he has ever met.

He told a story of a man who was new to town and was touring a Church. After the priest showed him the impressive architecture, ample spaces of worship, and pointed out the stained glass windows, he said in jest at the end of the tour, "You know, if you really want to meet God, come back Wednesday nights at 7:00 PM, enter the back door, and take the stairs that lead to the basement for an AA meeting."

Ortberg simplified the first three steps of Alcoholics Anonymous, and remember, the only step you have to master is step one, because it's all about becoming ultra self-aware and honest with yourself.

1. We admitted we were powerless over alcohol—that our lives had become unmanageable.
2. Came to believe that a Power greater than ourselves could restore us to sanity.
3. Made a decision to turn our will and our lives over to the care of God as we understood Him.

This is how John Ortberg took the 47 words of the first three steps and summarized them into 6.

Step 1: I Can't
Step 2: You Can
Step 3: Take It

I Can't — You Can — Take It. The addiction forces us to start seeking guidance outside ourselves—then opens an aperture of "willingness" that something apart from ourselves can assist in our healing—then we let go, over and over and over.

Now, it's not my place or goal to convince you of your religious or spiritual direction, but like I said earlier, to write a book about sobriety, healing, stepping into wholeness, and recovering our authentic selves without mentioning GOD would be an oversight. It was the early twentieth-century psychologist Carl Jung who suggested that a spiritual remedy was necessary to overcome an addiction. I'm also a huge fan of science and knowledge in general, but I do want to mention that many physicists, quantum theorists, and astronomers, if they stay in their field long enough, eventually become believers in something. Even my favorite astronomer, Neil deGrasse Tyson, denies being an atheist.

Again, I am in no position to tell you the truth regarding the mechanics of how GOD and the universe work. I don't know, and I don't want to know. But I can unequivocally tell you, based on my experiences in recovery, that something magical is taking place behind the scenes. Carl Jung, who penned letters back and forth with Bill Wilson, giving him advice on starting Alcoholics Anonymous, spent much of his career exploring the synchronicities of life. He says, "synchronicity is a meaningful coincidence of events where something other than the probability of chance is involved." He goes further to say that the synchronicities are the "bread crumbs of life," and they symbolize a healthy tether with the universe, and that we are on the right track. Through his work in this area, he concluded that "there is no such thing as coincidences."

Now, to be honest, I did experience these seemingly bizarre life synchronicities when alcohol was part of my life, but they occurred every couple of years at most, and only when I wasn't hungover or had alcohol in my system. Now, with over a decade since my last drink, these beautiful life synchronicities that replenish the soul happen weekly, if not daily. Since I cannot adequately explain this concept with words, the remainder of this chapter is journal entries of mine where I've written about these baffling, magical synchronicities that have occurred in my life since removing alcohol. At least for me, it's enough "proof" that something benevolent is walking this life alongside me. I hope these experiences can potentially crack open a window ever so slightly to the universe, letting in just enough breeze to make you wonder what else might be out there.

A Mountain of Stars

September 17th, 2021 - The most incredible thing happened today at the lake. As the pages of this journal reflect, I have been wondering if I should invite Nimia to come visit for Christmas. In fact, I've asked the universe for guidance with this question several times in the past months. I was standing waist-deep in water, at the lake's edge, thinking about this very question, knowing that if I invite her to visit, it's most likely for her to stay and to move from Colombia to Montana. As I visualized the pro and con sheets I had made over the months, something pulled me out of my thinking mind. Am I hearing what I think I'm hearing? In the distance, about 40 yards out, a small watercraft, operated by a lone fisherman, passed by while playing the song "Un Montón de Estrellas" by Polo Montañez. When Nimia and I met in February earlier this year, it was clear that it was our song; we had danced to it on the boardwalk, in a salsa nightclub, and we heard it at the restaurant on our first date because I remember asking if she knew who sang the song. At first, when I heard the song from a small rowboat in a remote lake in the Montana wilderness, I turned my head left and right to make sure it was coming from the boat. I then listened intently to make sure it was the song, and it was. For final confirmation, I yelled out, "Hey, is that Un Montón de Estrellas by Polo Montañez?" The boat driver didn't hear me since he was now 100-150 yards away from me, but I already knew it was the song.

The first thing I did when I got back into cell phone service was send Nimia a WhatsApp message inviting her to visit for Christmas, and she said yes. I knew it was a sign from the Universe; in fact, I'd have to be a total idiot not to see it. Montana's musical landscape is dominated by country music, not rare salsa tracks from a dead Cuban musician whom most people couldn't name.

The Green Bucket

November 17th, 2023 - This morning, after providing hay and fresh water for the goats, I sat inside their small barn before returning to the house to get my day started. I began to place my attention on the green water bucket, and I realized the goats, who are always roughhousing, have yet to knock over their water bucket, which is especially impressive in wintertime since the snow shrinks the available real estate where they can play. I said to myself, "It's crazy they haven't pushed one of their goat brothers or sisters into the..." And before I could finish the sentence, Oreo blasted Elliot with a surprise headbutt to his hindquarters, sending him flying into the green bucket, spilling the water onto the frozen ground. I sat there in awe, knowing my thoughts, my consciousness, were playing an active role in the unfolding of the universe. To grasp just how wildly improbable this moment was—me sitting there thinking about the green bucket precisely as it toppled over—I consulted my math-wizard friend Sam. He calculated the odds at a slim 1/691,200 chance (that's 0.00014%) that the bucket tipped over while I was there to witness it—statistically incredibly low chances.

As of November, 2025, the green bucket has yet to be tipped over a second time.

The Jaguar Spirit

Saturday, March 1st, 2025 - Earlier this year, I read a fascinating book about the Waorani indigenous tribe in Ecuador's jungles (*We Will Be Jaguars*), who were an "uncontacted tribe" up until about 40 years ago. They believe their ancestors return as jaguars after death, and the Waorani constantly pray to these jaguar spirits for everything—guidance, abundant hunting trips, and support during life's struggles. The book mentioned Christian missionaries living among them, spreading the gospel, yet interestingly, they were curious why the Bible says nothing about jaguar spirits. About a week ago, I found myself doing something unexpected—praying to these jaguar spirits, to my own ancestors, seeking direction as life has felt particularly challenging lately. I'd been feeling rudderless and lost these past few months. While my son Rio joining our family nine months ago has been an incredible blessing, I now lie awake at night with new worries: Am I a good father? How will I keep him safe? What will the planet look like when he grows up?

Last night, after unwinding with some stretching on my patio, I put on my headlamp and ventured into my backyard on a personal safari to spot nocturnal critters in Costa Rica. About 35 yards in, as I approached a massive tree, the night erupted with a heart-stopping sequence: a heavy thud, a guttural exhalation of thick, heavy breath, then thunderous footsteps—thankfully pounding away from me, not toward me. My body reacted before my mind could catch up—dropping into a wrestler's stance, blood surging to my extremities, heart drumming against my ribs. My instincts knew what my conscious brain was still processing: something with serious teeth and claws had just launched itself from the tree barely ten feet away. My headlamp caught a fleeting glimpse of a substantial, muscular form slipping between trees before the creature vanished from sight, leaving only sound trails to track its retreat into the jungle. It's amazing what your ears can tell you when your eyes can't see in the darkness—only something weighing well over 100 pounds could snap those thick branches I heard cracking for some 200 yards until the mystery animal disappeared into the mangrove swamp behind my house.

"Holy shit! What the hell was that?" I gasped, simultaneously thanking the universe for the incredible wildlife encounter. I knew the robust animal could have ambushed me from above rather than seeking refuge in the mangrove. While not 100% certain what enormous mammal had leaped to the ground so close to me, I knew it was either a puma or the jungle's absolute apex predator—the jaguar.

Before going to bed that night, I asked the universe for a sign to identify what had jumped from the tree. Upon awakening, I completely forgot about this request and went about my busy day of work, errands, an oil change, and normal family duties. Later, during my nightly reflection, when I give thanks to people who helped me that day, my mind wandered to the mechanic's shop. I thanked the attendant who directed me where to park, the mechanic who changed my oil and cleaned my air filter, and then the guy who picked up my dropped keys...

That's when it hit me. "No way...how did I miss that!" While waiting in line to pay, I dropped my keys, and the man behind me, who picked them up, wore a shirt with a giant jaguar face in vibrant mosaic colors. The jaguar's face couldn't have been any larger, and the bright colors held my gaze—I'd nearly complimented him on it. A warm, soft embrace filled me as I realized the universe had answered my question. A jaguar—and the jaguar spirit—had indeed visited me in my backyard.

As if one sign wasn't enough, before going to bed, my wife handed me a framed photo she had purchased earlier in the day while shopping. Keep in mind, I hadn't told her about the wildlife encounter so close to our house—she'd never step foot in the backyard again if she knew. The photo contained a jaguar resting on a tree, which eerily resembled the shape of the tree in my backyard. "Wow, I love it, thank you so much," I said. "What do you mean?" she replied. "That's just the stock photo that comes with the frame." I didn't remove the stock photo.

Bleached Driftwood

Sunday, March 2nd, 2025 - A couple of days ago, I had the idea of attaching a tree trunk and its branches as a piece of wall art inside my house in Costa Rica. After surfing today, while walking back to where my vehicle was parked, a large piece of sun-bleached driftwood caught my attention as it lay enmeshed among the hundreds of logs and sticks piled up at the high tide mark. I walked about 100 yards back to where my truck was parked, put my surfboard on the rack, and began walking back toward where I had seen the log. As I walked back, in the distance, I saw a local standing near the tree I had identified. As I got closer, I saw his hand was on the exact tree trunk I was returning to pick up. I first wondered where this guy had come from since I thought I was the only one on that section of the beach, and then quickly began pondering: out of the vast expanse of intertwined logs on the beach, how is this guy holding the exact tree trunk I'm returning for?

When I arrived at the log, I said to the guy, "This tree caught your eye, too?" I told him I was planning on taking the tree trunk home and turning it into an art piece to adorn a wall, but first, I asked him if he wanted the tree since the large trunk was currently in his hand. He said, "Nope, it's yours, I was just admiring it." As I took a couple of steps with the large water-soaked tree, he offered to help, which I gladly accepted. We walked the 100 yards back to my vehicle, parts of the tree cradled in each of our hands, where he helped me load the 150+ pound tree trunk and branches into my truck.

I find it peculiar that once I had spotted the tree, someone else, just moments later, who seemingly arrived out of nowhere, picked up the same log out of the hundreds of logs on the beach. Or perhaps it works the other way—the consciousness of the tree, even though the tree is dead or no longer possesses life, was calling me, or wanted to be found, which was why the other guy was pulled to the same tree I was. I don't think I'll ever know, but I'm excited to wash, sand, stain, and hang up the tree on the wall, as I think the shape of branches emerging from a trunk is among the most beautiful ones in nature.

Everything Is Perfect Just the Way It Is

Sunday, March 9th, 2025 - This morning, while cruising down the dirt road to an AA meeting in Playa Negra, Costa Rica, I kept whispering to myself, "Everything is perfect just the way it is." But let's be real—I felt completely off-kilter, with knots of fear having set up camp in my solar plexus. The last few days? Pure anxiety soup as I fumble through this new father gig—and life in general. How much sunscreen do I apply to my son? Is that mosquito bite swelling too much? Where will he go to school? When will our house finally have a working refrigerator instead of an oversized paperweight? As I drove, teetering on the edge of a full-blown spiral, a gentle voice cut through the mental chaos: "Everything is perfect just the way it is." I said this on repeat until I reached the meeting.

At the AA meeting, I asked my buddy Dan if he'd checked out that Radiohead song I sent him days ago. He shook his head—nope, missed it—but what was the song called? "I don't remember," I smiled, while fishing for my phone. I pulled up the message, and there it was, the universe winking at me through a song title: "Everything in Its Right Place."

Chapter 30
Will We Ever Beat This Thing?

Here's what I've come to believe after watching thousands of people transform their relationship with alcohol: we're not supposed to beat this thing. We're supposed to have it.

I know that sounds backwards. I know you picked up this book because you want to be free from addiction, not make peace with it. But hear me out.

What if your addiction isn't the problem—what if it's the answer? What if it's your soul's way of saying, "Hey, you're living unconsciously, and I'm going to make this so uncomfortable that you have no choice but to wake up"?

Who are the people doing the deepest spiritual work? Who are the ones in therapy, reading books like this, questioning everything, committed to growth? It's us. The alcoholics, the addicts, the person with Alcohol Use Disorder (AUD), the one with the "disease" of addiction. The people who hit bottom so hard we had to claw our way back to the light, and then we reflect this light back to all.

This isn't new wisdom. Jesus kept pointing toward the narrow path, telling anyone who'd listen that the kingdom of heaven was right here, right now, if we could just wake up enough to see it. The Buddha sat under a tree until he understood that our suffering comes from our desperate attempts to avoid reality instead of embracing it. Nietzsche wrote about the eternal return—the idea that we should live as if we'd have to repeat this exact life forever, which means we'd better make it worth repeating.

The Italians have a phrase for it: La Dolce Vita—the sweet life. But here's what we got wrong about that concept. We thought the sweet life was something we had to achieve, something waiting for us tomorrow after we got our shit together, lost the weight, made the money, found the person.

Alcohol promised to deliver us to that sweet life—just one more drink and we'd finally feel the magic, that effortless joy, that sense of being fully alive. But it was the ultimate bait and switch. Every sip took us further away from the very presence that makes life sweet.

When we quit drinking, we don't just get sober—we step into the true Dolce Vita. Not the fantasy version where we tightrope the perfect buzz, but the actual sweet life that's been waiting for us in this moment all along. The sweet life that's found in really tasting your morning coffee, in feeling the sun on your face, in being present enough to receive your child's hug instead of mentally planning your next escape.

This entire book has been about that journey—from the illusion of the Dolce Vita that alcohol promised to the real Dolce Vita that sobriety delivers. Not tomorrow, not when everything is perfect, but right here, right now, in this messy, beautiful, fully-felt, lifey moment.

From Rumi to Jung, they were all saying the same thing in different languages: the way through is the way in. The American Bison, or the Buffalo, were showing us the same thing. The path to freedom runs directly through the center of our pain, not around it. The sweet life isn't a destination—it's a way of being awake to what's already here.

Meanwhile, the "normal" people—the ones who can have one glass of wine and stop—they're often sleepwalking through life. They're not asking the big questions because they've never been forced to. They're not excavating their childhood trauma because wine never made them black out and then clench the bedsheets at 3:00 AM.

Your addiction was your spiritual emergency. It cracked you open so the light could enter.

And now? Now you get to carry this tender awareness for the rest of your life. You get to be the one who stays grounded when everyone else is spinning out. You get to choose love over being right, peace over proving a point. You get to see through the collective bullshit because you've spent years sorting through your own.

This thing—this sensitivity, this awareness, this inability to numb out—it's your superpower now. It's what keeps you real when the world embraces fake. It's what makes you choose connection when the culture pushes isolation. It's what helps you see the sacred in the ordinary when everyone else is chasing the next high.

But here's where it gets really beautiful: your quiet revolution doesn't stay quiet. It ripples out in ways you can't even imagine.

When you stop drinking, your kids notice you're actually present for bedtime stories instead of half-checked out. Your partner feels safe enough to be vulnerable because you're reciprocating and not numbing your emotions anymore. Your friends start questioning their own relationship with alcohol because you're proof that there's another way to live.

You don't need to preach or point fingers or post manifestos on social media. You don't need to shame anyone or make them feel bad about their choices. You just need to keep showing up as your authentic, sober, awake self.

Your nervous system starts to regulate, and suddenly everyone around you feels a little calmer. Your kids learn emotional regulation by watching you actually feel your feelings instead of drowning them. Your workplace becomes a little more peaceful because you're not bringing hungover anxiety into every meeting.

This is how we heal the world—one nervous system at a time. One authentic conversation at a time. One person choosing love over fear, presence over numbing, truth over comfortable lies.

We don't heal the world by talking shit about people who aren't awake yet, or talking shit in general. We heal it by doing our own work so completely, so authentically, that our very presence becomes the invitation for others to do their work.

When you walk into a room now, people feel something different. They can't quite put their finger on it, but there's a groundedness to you, a realness that's rare in a world full of people performing their lives instead of living them.

You become living proof that it's possible to feel everything and not die from it. That it's possible to face reality without chemical armor. That it's possible to be physically, mentally, and spiritually strong without being superior, conscious without being condescending.

We're not trying to beat addiction. We're learning to dance with it. To let it be our teacher instead of our master. To transform our greatest wound into our greatest gift to the world.

The universe needs us conscious. It needs us awake. It needs us to be the ones who feel everything so deeply that we can't help but respond with love instead of fear.

So no, you'll probably never "beat" this thing completely. Thank God. Because the day you think you've got it all figured out is the day you stop growing. The day you forget how fragile and precious sobriety is is the day you might lose it.

Keep the awareness. Keep the tenderness. Keep the willingness to do the work that most people never even attempt. This is how we all heal.

Chapter 31
Curing Addiction

My goal in life is to cure addiction. But I need to be honest with you about something: I don't think there actually is a cure for addiction.

Sure, there are effective treatments, therapies, programs, and powerful plant medicines that radically help people heal. But in reality, addiction isn't something you cure—it's something that doesn't happen in the first place when the proper conditions for human flourishing exist.

There's also no cure because addiction is the messenger that painfully alerts us when things are out of balance.

In fact, the real goal shouldn't be curing your own addiction—it should be to create an environment you don't need to escape from in the first place. Maybe you grew up in a challenging family, and while most of that is likely behind you now, the real work is about coming closer to the campfire with other human beings and building tighter bonds within our communities. It's about embracing different cultures, languages, skin colors, beliefs, and creeds.

Oh, and side note: you want to solve racism? Love yourself. And a good way to start doing that is to stop poisoning your insides with alcohol.

The cure to addiction begins with us cleaning up our own inner pollution. When we stop numbing ourselves, we can finally see clearly. When we can see clearly, we start making different choices. When we make different choices, we create ripples that extend far beyond our own lives.

And then it comes back full circle—we start walking each other home. Walking others home with their struggles with alcohol, with how to be a better person, and helping others reach their goals in life. We become the village that raises the child instead of leaving everyone to figure it out alone.

This is a long play, however. If enough of us follow this path, we should see addiction leveling off within our lifetime. It may be Dolce Vita Lite for a generation or two, then Dolce Vita on training wheels for another couple of generations, but then I believe we'll step into the full Dolce Vita in perhaps 100 to 200 years. I know some of you may find this contradictory, that the Dolce Vita or the Good Life has to happen NOW, but the truth is, we live within the constraints of time, and it's going to take time for enough humans to embody this new circuitry.

We can't cure addiction, but we can listen to its message and make changes with the wellness of future generations in mind. Yes, when you quit drinking, you'll see big changes in your own life. But the full effect of your transformation may not fully manifest until your great-grandchild graduates from college 75 years from now.

When we address the prisons within ourselves and remove our inner boundaries and borders, we'll most likely see fewer borders in the outside world. There will sure as hell be fewer walls constructed to keep people out.

What I'm saying is that your sobriety isn't just about you. It's about the great-great-grandchildren you'll never meet but whose lives will be fundamentally different because you chose to wake up. Because you chose to feel everything instead of numbing it all away. Because you chose to build bridges instead of walls, both inside yourself and in the world around you.

This is how we cure addiction: not by fixing the people who have it, but by creating a world where it's no longer necessary as a messenger. A world where people feel so connected, so purposeful, so held by their community that the idea of escaping from life seems absurd.

Until then, we do the work. One day at a time. One person at a time. One healed liver at a time. One generation at a time. Walking each other home.

Chapter 32
Where Do We Go From Here?

So, where do we go from here? If you're in the middle of your quest for sobriety, you have to meet yourself where you are in this moment. If you're in the throes of it, you can't think yourself out of an addiction, but I want you to start visualizing your alcohol-free life in your mind.

Find a quiet place, put on a good song that raises your energy, and start role-playing in your mind. How does that version of you look? How do you decline a drink? Where is the sun in the sky? Who are you with? What do you smell? Are you playing pickleball? The moment your mind goes back to the addiction or your old life, or starts wondering when you'll take the next drink, pull your mental energy back to the other side of the river. This is a Herculean effort at first, but stick with it.

Start asking, start demanding, and refine this practice. To whom? Well, that's for you to decide, but there's a line in the book that has sold the most copies of all time that simplifies things: Ask and you shall receive.

Don't forget that healing from addiction is all about words that begin with RE. Begin the REturn to the self with a few more conscious breaths per day. Start REconnecting with planet earth and find ways for your hands to mix with the soil in your yard. REbuild the trust with yourself and loved ones inside your home. REconcile with your past and give it to the wind. REhabilitate the mind, body, and soul with clean water and healthy food. REtrieve and REcover the person you were always meant to be.

And when the Bruno Voice pops up, remember to play the tape forward and backward. Run through h ow drinking really ends, and then picture how sobriety keeps opening up more life. That simple practice carried me in the early days, and it still does today.

Don't forget to move your body in your pursuit of an alcohol-free life. The body was meant to move, and you'll be rewarded with feel-good chemicals like dopamine and endorphins that naturally block pain. Run, jog, walk, hike, stretch, lift weights—whatever calls to you. Ideally this is done outside where mother earth can work her magic on your nervous system. The key is moving your body 2-3 times per week for at least 20 minutes in a way that raises your heart rate, and ideally makes you sweat. Make this a non-negotiable in your REcovery.

Place your bare feet on the planet—and do it often. This is called grounding, and it connects your body to a limitless flow of electrons. The moment your skin touches the earth, electrons flow to the positive charges in your body, neutralizing the acid and inflammation. Here's the simple science: inflammation and disease carry a positive charge, while health and wholeness carry a negative charge. The rubber on our feet cut us off from this natural energy exchange, forcing us to rely on our own limited electron generation instead of tapping into an energy source that spans 25,000 miles in circumference.

You absolutely have to enter closer to community—ideally an alcohol-free community like Café RE or AA. YOU CANNOT DO THIS ALONE. You were never meant to. It doesn't even matter if you're still drinking. Don't flatter yourself and think you'd be the first person to show up to an AA meeting drunk, or the first person to unmute themselves and say something inaudible while intoxicated on an online Café RE chat. When you've decided to come closer to the campfire with other human beings, this means you've already gotten honest with yourself—you're done listening to the Bruno Voice, and you're ready for the crossing.

We're at an incredible time in history when it comes to healing from addiction. Non-patentable plant medicines such as ayahuasca, ibogaine, psilocybin, mescaline, MDMA, and more are REemerging to assist humans in their healing. The 12 Steps of Alcoholics Anonymous were influenced by Bill W.'s spiritual awakening in December 1934, which occurred while he was undergoing an experimental treatment with the psychedelic belladonna at Towns Hospital in New York. During this experience, he cried out for help, then reported seeing an "indescribable white light" and feeling profound ecstasy, leading to his permanent sobriety and later creation of the 12 Steps in 1938.

As I've said earlier in this book, burning the ships is the most important thing you can do on your alcohol-free journey, and the ships must first be burned with the self. Once this has been done with yourself, then set them ablaze with other human beings in recovery, and then with humans who are not in recovery. Once these three steps have been unequivocally completed, everything else will fall into place—it's just a matter of time and you not taking a drink. If you don't know where to start, I want you to join our AF community Café RE and be part of the change you want to see within yourself.

Café RE opened its doors in April 2016 and just received nonprofit status—and we're pioneering some incredible pathways in the recovery world. We've got over 25 weekly meetings/chats on the calendar, including Men's and Women's groups, Smart Recovery, Recovery Dharma book club, movie club, and even our own in-house AA meetings, which serve as a great entry point into the 12 Step world. Another service we provide is pairing members with Accountability Partners, as many times as you'd like. If you're looking for a community of sober people who are saying YES to life, we've got you covered. There are in-person meetups across the country where authentic connections are built that aren't anchored to alcohol. At Café RE, we fully embrace that there's no right or wrong way to ditch the booze, and we come together as a community around the campfire (or Zoom squares in today's world) to share how we quit drinking. The most potent armor against alcohol that we provide? You're no longer alone.

Recovery has "looked" a certain way for quite some time, but *Recovery Elevator* and Café RE are hoping to change that. Our version of recovery has taken the form of playing skeeball (inside bars, no less), kicking kickballs, battling it out in laser tag, strumming ukuleles, ziplining through jungles, hiking the Inca Trail, singing Coolio's "Gangsta's Paradise," surfing in Costa Rica, dancing at a silent disco that had to be shut down by hotel staff, and doing the electric slide together on a booze cruise—true story. Things are shifting, and I want you to be part of this exciting change. I'd also like to ask for a donation to help our cause, which can be made at www.cafe-re.org.

Life Today

Today, life is good. Not perfect, of course, but I'm living the Dolce Vita. I've logged nineteen sunsets so far this summer, and I'm still five days away from the solstice. I'm learning to play the drums with just my left hand so I can play a synthesizer with my right hand, and the neighbors haven't told me to shut up yet. I'm currently drawing up plans to build a half-pipe with a chicken coop attached. I'm showing my son how to properly hold drumsticks, and I'm still hanging out with my goats while playing the ukulele barefoot in the grass.

Do I have it all figured out? Absolutely not. And I hope I never do. I am still a student of the game of life. I'm still in the middle of my life curriculum. There is something I feel I need to mention in this book: I use cannabis. My first four years sober, I was just that—sober. I didn't use pot, and I experienced a new baseline without any mind-altering substances, but I've found cannabis to be a tool in my recovery journey. Now I **DO NOT** recommend removing alcohol, then adding THC to your diet. It's crucial to let your mind and body reset without alcohol for at least the first six to 12 months, or the healing can become convoluted if you're swapping out one chemical for the other. However, with pot and alcohol, it's not apples to apples—not even close. And if in some fictitious world, cannabis and alcohol were discovered at the same time, pot would be legalized and alcohol would be sent to the laboratory basement with an industrial-grade lid and steel padlock.

The world likes labels, and I guess I'd be classified as California Sober. I've been called much worse, and I'm accepting of where I am on my journey. Currently, cannabis is giving more than it's taking, but I would like to phase it out in the future, mostly because my spoon seems like a magnet to ice cream and I wake up the next day with a sugar hangover. But today, I have lines in the sand regarding my cannabis use that seem to be holding. Every word in this book was written sober—

no THC involved. I don't use it in the morning or the afternoon. I can stop when I want to, and there are no secrets with my family and work team.

I do my best to bring awareness to how I'm using the plant. I don't use cannabis on the bad days to escape because, well, it would make a bad day even worse. Where alcohol would dull the pain and numb the life experience, cannabis allows me to connect deeper with the present moment and myself. When I drank alcohol, I'd black out and find mystery dents in my car. When I use cannabis, I find myself meditating in trees and seeing how many birds I can identify from sound alone.

I do sometimes question my relationship with cannabis, and I can see the potential paradox of someone writing a book on sobriety while using a medicine that alters the mind. But when I zoom out, my life has never been better. If I do recognize an unhealthy relationship with cannabis, then I will use the same tools I applied to quitting drinking to quit cannabis. I'll implement the same strategies and tools I recommend in this book—I believe in them all. Your path might look different, and that's okay. What matters is staying honest with yourself, paying attention to what's helping or hurting, and being willing to make changes when something no longer serves you.

Do You Want a Happy Ending Or a Real One?

In the Disney movie *Encanto*, the characters overcome the Bruno Voice (the ego), and the family's magical house is REbuilt and REstored after it crumbles. All becomes perfect in Disney's world. Yes, I fully believe in the title of this book—that when we quit drinking, become aware of the ego, and surrender to life as it is, we step into the good life: the Dolce Vita.

But the Dolce Vita doesn't necessarily mean life becomes easier. More often than I'd like to admit, I still find myself revolting against life's terms. I've punched walls, slammed doors, spit on ink printer cartridges—all with the intention of expressing the feeling that I have been severely duped by life.

I cry, and often. I cry because I'm no longer disconnected from my emotions and feelings. I cry watching movies, for my fellow brothers and sisters still struggling with addiction, for the animals who are leaving the planet at alarming rates, and I cry for Earth herself. Sometimes it seems I cry for no apparent reason other than to clear out my tear ducts.

Since quitting drinking, the masthead of my anxiety is gone, but there are still days when I want to find the deepest recesses of a cave and never emerge—I find this is a similar experience with artists.

During the writing process of this book, many mornings I'd find myself waking up around 3:00 to 3:30 AM, unable to return to sleep due to a knot of anxiety that seemed to increase with every snooze cycle. Occasionally, the pressure of maintaining my own sobriety while being the executive director of Café RE, a nonprofit geared toward helping others quit drinking, feels like an impossible weight. But sign me up again tomorrow. I'm honored to be in this position. My solar plexus still experiences random volcanic bursts of anxiety that make simple tasks extremely uncomfortable. Sometimes I lose all hope—in myself, in humanity.

But I'm learning to trust the process. To trust that the universe will take care of me, like it already has. That everything moves in cycles, returns full circle, only to begin again—each rotation a little different, a little deeper, a little more beautiful than the last.

I used to DJ in Spanish nightclubs until the sun came up, lost in strobe lights and thundering beats. Now I herd Nigerian Dwarf goats at sunset, watching the sky paint itself in colors that no club lighting could ever match.

Before I was here, it was the Native Americans, listening to these same crickets, watching these same sunsets. Before them, woolly mammoths wandered this land. Sixty-five million years ago, dinosaurs ruled. One hundred and fourteen million years ago, the first red flower bloomed—can you imagine?

Before that, mass collected into spherical shapes we call planets, finding their comfortable, predictable dance around a burning ball of hydrogen we call the sun. And fourteen billion years ago, one magnificent implosion then explosion—the Big Bang—set all of this in motion.

Everything that ever was, everything that is, everything that will be— it's all connected in this endless, sacred spiral. I'm just one small note in this cosmic symphony, but what a privilege it is to be here, with you, finally awake enough to hear the music.

I write these final words at dusk near the foothills south of Bozeman, Montana. Venus, the brightest light in the sky, is making her entrance in the moonless night. The cricket chorus grows stronger as more voices are invited to join the song—the same song that's been playing for millions of years, long before humans were here to listen.

I'm writing in the same place where I heard wolves howl just a couple of weeks ago. The REwilding is already taking place. Aspen leaves whisper together in the cool evening breeze.

As I write, I pause and take conscious breaths, knowing this thin slice of time when both birds and bats share the sky will pass in moments. The sacred in-between. This threshold where day becomes night, where one breath becomes the next.

Time stops.

I'm writing this passage alone, but with each breath, I know I'm not alone. In the near distance, vast pine forests with towering Douglas firs stretch toward mountains where wolves and grizzly bears are making their comeback—ancient spirits REturning to REclaim their home.

There was a time when alcohol was steadily hollowing me out, when I almost became the very emptiness I was trying to escape. But tonight, I am here, and I am whole. The jaguar spirit is walking with us, thousands of miles from any jungle. My ancestors' voices carry in the mountain wind—whispers that echo from that June day in 1944 when a German soldier swiveled the tank barrel toward my seventeen-year-old French grandmother's balcony, finger on the trigger, before the officer gave the order not to fire. Howler monkeys call across dimensions of time and space, celebrating the impossible chain of moments that led to this one.

My dog Ben breathes softly beside me. My family is settling into bed in the room next to me—the sounds of life being lived.

So much had to happen for us all to be here, and none of it is separate. When you really think about it, it's the greatest miracle of all time. One that we are already a part of and get to experience in each moment.

As I type, I look out the window and see more stars have arrived on the scene. I see a dark shape moving through a field in the distance—it's most likely a deer. I begin to wonder what's next. Where will this life take me?

I'm not sure, but I have a feeling the next chapter has already begun.

And yours has too.

Right here.

Right now.

In this breath.

This very moment.

This miracle of being awake.

The universe has been waiting 14 billion years for us to arrive at this exact moment, holding this book.

The beginning starts now.

Epilogue

Our species is at a crossroads right now. Most of us can feel it in our bones—the man-made problems we face today have us backed into a corner like never before. Nuclear war, climate change, artificial intelligence, rising rates of depression, inequality, addiction—the list goes on. Scientists, world leaders, and spiritual teachers are all saying the same thing: we're running out of time.

What's remarkable is that almost every ancient culture, from the Hopi to the Hindus to the Maya, prophesied about this exact moment in history. They all speak of our modern era as the time when humanity would face its greatest test—and its greatest opportunity for transformation. A time when we'd either evolve or perish. A time when, as Buzz Aldrin would say, a "giant leap for mankind" wouldn't just be recommended—it would be required for our very survival.

Native American wisdom, specifically the Anishinaabe (Ojibwe), speaks of The Prophecy of the Seventh Fire—and according to them, we have entered into this time. This ancient prophecy describes our current moment as the ultimate fork in the road for humanity. We can choose the path of endless technology and materialism, which leads to a scorched and lifeless earth. Or we can choose the path back to ancient wisdom and harmony with all living beings—a world where children can swim in clean rivers and inherit a planet that's thriving, not dying.

While the Mayan Calendar was widely misinterpreted as predicting the end of the world in 2012, Mayan scholars explain it differently: December 21, 2012, marked the end of a 5,126-year cycle. Rather than an apocalypse, it signified the transition to a new world age or consciousness. Many Mayan elders saw this as the beginning of a period of transformation and spiritual awakening, not the literal end of the world.

The Hopi tradition contains prophecies about what they call "Koyaanisqatsi," or "life out of balance." They speak of a time when the world would be crossed by "roads in the sky" (airplanes) and "cobwebs" (power lines on poles). Their prophecies mention a "gourd of ashes" that would be dropped from the sky, bringing destruction—interpreted by some as bombs and nuclear weapons. They describe a time when the land would be crisscrossed with rivers of stone (highways) and people would live in "square houses" withdrawn from nature.

In Hindu cosmology, we're said to be living in the Kali Yuga, the last of four ages in a cosmic cycle, characterized by spiritual darkness, materialism, and moral decay. Many Hindu teachers believe we've reached a transition point that must lead to spiritual renewal, or we perish.

Zoroastrian prophecies speak of a cosmic struggle between good and evil culminating in the 2000s—a final battle between the forces of light and darkness, a period of purification through which humanity must pass.

From the Bible to Tibetan Buddhists, from Nostradamus to Taoists, from Aborigines to Inuits to the Jehovah's Witnesses who knocked on my door last week, all speak of our modern era as a time when the battle between light and darkness reaches a crescendo.

Maybe there is something to these prophecies that come from different parts of the globe in a time without the telephone, yet all say we are currently living at a critical juncture for humanity. Who knows? Maybe the Mayans ran out of space on their calendar, or maybe the Hopi were just tripping balls on peyote, or maybe Jesus turned too much water into wine. But jokes aside, when prophecies from cultures that never communicated with each other, from all across the globe, point to our specific moment in history as a time of reckoning, and it appears the world is well on fire, it makes you wonder if maybe, just maybe, there's something to all this. The message is clear: we're at a turning point as a species, one that includes the possibility of either destruction or renewal depending on our collective choices—and you are here to help.

The current system is dying. It's decaying before our very eyes. In the 2024 presidential debate in the United States of America, we saw two old white men (one more orange than white) face off, both barely able to string together words to make coherent sentences. We're watching the old ways crumble in real time, and while it's scary, it's also creating space for something new to emerge. This isn't collapse—it's compost, breaking down so fresh life can grow. So the natural cycle can continue.

It's addiction that has already forced so many of us to step outside the boundaries of the ego, to confront the Bruno Voice, and forced us to shed, or let go of, what is no longer working. The addiction—the very thing that brought us to our knees—is also what's preparing us to stand up and help heal the world.

The Species That Knits Penguin Sweaters

Homo sapiens are an interesting lot. In order for us to survive, we have to come to a reckoning with our bellicose nature. We are an extremely violent species. When we left northeast Africa around 200,000 to 300,000 years ago, we shared the planet with over two dozen other species of humans such as Homo habilis, Homo erectus, and the Neanderthals, to name a few. These other humans, who had existed for millions of years, met their demise when Homo sapiens arrived on the scene. Anthropologists theorize Homo sapiens wiped out all other human species and also interbred with Neanderthals, which is why all humans on the planet have roughly 2 to 5% Neanderthal DNA inside of them.

Homo sapiens have disrupted cultures and ecosystems from the beginning. Forty-four thousand years ago, when Homo sapiens landed in Australia, within 1,000 years, 23 of the 24 largest animals on the continent went extinct—minus the kangaroo. A similar thing happened in the Americas after humans crossed the Bering Strait and ventured south. We not only wage war on flora and fauna wherever we go, but we also turn that aggression toward ourselves with almost predictable certainty. The supposedly "civilized" society that labeled Native Americans as savages would soon kill 100 million of its own brothers and sisters in the 20th century in theaters of war and destruction all across the globe.

We have a seemingly unquenchable appetite for more, more, more, and more. Unless we become brutally aware of our self-defeating traits,

I can tell you exactly how this ends: we self-destruct. The author Robin Wall Kimmerer, in her book *Braiding Sweetgrass*, says we're on track to need four planet Earths to fulfill our species' needs as we continue to industrialize. In 2025, a presidential executive order was signed for the immediate expansion of timber production to log over half of America's remaining natural forests (112 million acres), or an area roughly the size of California. Less habitat means more species become extinct, and eventually, we'll lose some tiny insect that we didn't know was holding so much together, and no amount of money from a federal printer or novel cryptocurrency can reverse the process.

On the other side of the coin, humans are soft, delicate, and have a tremendous capacity for love that shows up in the most beautifully ridiculous ways. We rescue animals with such dedication that a 110-year-old Australian man spent his final years knitting tiny sweaters for penguins injured in an oil spill. We welcome abandoned cats and dogs into our homes, turning them into spoiled family members who sleep in our beds and eat better than we do. We're the species that stops traffic to help a turtle cross the road, builds elaborate hospitals for wild animals, and cries at videos of soldiers reuniting with their dogs. We're capable of intense sacrifice for the well-being of others—one man in particular claimed to have died for the sins of all humanity in an excruciatingly painful way, which could be said to be the ultimate act of love. For thousands of human generations, we have embraced dance, movement, music, and art, creating beauty for no other reason than it makes our souls feel alive. We're the only species that puts decorative lights on trees, throws parties for no reason, and laughs until our stomachs hurt.

If you haven't noticed, I've referenced Native Americans several times in this book because they represent cultures that lived in harmony and balance with the earth, animals, plants, and stars—before 90 to 95% of them died from Old World diseases in the 16th and 17th centuries, making it one of the most catastrophic demographic events in human history. Much of their ancient wisdom was lost in this devastation, but there is still so much we can REvive and embrace again.

They have the parable of the Two Wolves, which is a powerful teaching story: An old Cherokee grandfather is teaching his grandson about life. He says, "A fight is going on inside me. It is a terrible fight between two wolves. One is evil—filled with anger, envy, sorrow, regret, greed, arrogance, self-pity, guilt, resentment, inferiority, lies, false pride, superiority, and ego."

He continued, "The other is good—filled with joy, peace, love, hope, serenity, humility, kindness, benevolence, empathy, generosity, truth, compassion, and faith."

"The same fight is going on inside you, and inside every other person, too."

The grandson thought about it for a minute and then asked his grandfather, "Which wolf will win?"

The old Cherokee simply replied, "The one you feed."

Another wrinkle to this parable is that you can't simply ignore the evil wolf, because eventually the wolf will force you to hear him. This tale is about living in balance, and the Native Americans had many teaching parables about perfecting balance, such as "take only what you need" and "never shoot the first deer." Western folklore is absent of tales teaching moderation or the perils of overconsumption.

As I covered earlier in this book, life isn't linear and more accurately follows the path of a circle, or what the natives called the sacred hoop. I still have much faith in humanity, and many of us are waking up to the fact that unchecked consumerism and economic growth at any cost are leading us to a mass grave. In short, we're burning this mother fucker down.

For me, it was the depths of my alcohol addiction that brought all of this to light, and I know many more are waking up to this truth as well. We are collectively traveling the dark depths of the sacred hoop, and we're recognizing we're at a crossroads—one wolf will lead us to a scorched, lifeless earth, and the other wolf will return us to clear rivers and old-growth forests.

Not long ago, an artist wrote a song about a world with no borders or religions, which eventually was the catalyst for someone to shoot him four times, taking his life. If you think about the concept of borders and how a privileged group can obtain a small packet of papers that allow them to enter certain areas of planet Earth, it's almost laughable. Sure, some animals have territories and stick to certain regions, but we are the only species that have built walls and defended them with spears, hot liquid tar, flesh-piercing bullets, and now nuclear arsenals.

One of these metaphorical wolves will lead us to a world where all humans can freely move about planet Earth. And speaking of wolves, they have already begun their return to part of their original habitat in the Rocky Mountains before they were nearly eradicated in the early 1900s. Shortly after wolves returned to Yellowstone National Park in the '90s, the elk behavior changed, reducing browsing pressure on willows and aspens along riverbanks. This allowed vegetation to recover along streams and rivers, which stabilized banks and reduced erosion. The restored vegetation slowed water flow, and shortly thereafter, there was an explosion of beavers who now had trees to make dams and dens. With these beaver dams, the fish, amphibian, and waterfowl populations exploded since they now had a suitable habitat. Turns out wolves are better stewards of the land than humans are.

There was a politician who once said that all things woke go to shit, and they are 100% correct. Once we take off the beer goggles and realize the unchecked, endless pursuit of paper money (tokoré—worthless paper) is destroying our children's future, then yes, for some, things will go to shit. But for most, this is when we come alive. This is when we REconnect and REturn to nature and our true selves.

You individually putting the bottle down is a major step in the collective healing of all, but something else I encourage you to do is to turn it off. Turn off the news, whose goal is to put you in a fearful state. Turn off your social media accounts whose goal is to sell your personal information to data brokers. Turn off the notifications that ping you every thirty seconds like a slot machine designed to hijack your attention. Turn off the streaming services that keep you binge-watching until 2:00 AM instead of getting restorative sleep. Turn off the talk radio that fills your commute with anger and outrage. Turn off the political podcasts that make your blood pressure spike before breakfast. Turn off the shopping apps that whisper "you need this" every time you're bored. Turn off the dating apps that turn human connection into an endless swipe-fest. Turn off the financial shows that make you feel like a failure for not having a seven-figure portfolio. Turn off anything that leaves you feeling more anxious, angry, or empty than when you started. Turn it all off, and walk over to your neighbor's house and introduce yourself.

Turn it off. Dump out the booze. Share this book with a friend. Invite an old acquaintance to a coffee shop. Open your home to an animal that needs a safe place to live. Learn a new language. Read a book about a culture you don't understand. Learn to use a paintbrush on a fence or a canvas, explore the fretboard on a ukulele. Investigate what types of soil a tomato plant prefers best. RElearn the notes of the song that make you happy. The universe is deeply calling for you to fall in love with her again. And, if you are looking for an authentic community that has begun the crossing, come join us in Café RE. We're here to walk each other home, step by step, toward our own version of the Dolce Vita. And as we walk, we remember — the path is not somewhere out there in the distance. It's right here, under our feet, in every choice we make to live fully awake.

Your Quiet Revolution

Before you close this book, I want to leave you with one last message. Something I'd say if we were sitting across from each other right now.

Maybe you're reading this right now curled up in your favorite chair, maybe stealing a few quiet minutes before the day demands everything from you again, and you're tired. Not just sleepy tired—but soul tired. The kind of tired that comes from trying to clean up your inner world while the outer world feels like it's run by toddlers having the world's most expensive tantrum.

You're doing the hard work. You're choosing not to drink today, or this week, or maybe you're still thinking about it. You're tending to your physical, mental, and spiritual garden, pulling weeds, planting seeds of hope. You're dog-earing pages about consciousness and listening to podcasts about healing trauma, and you're genuinely trying to become the person you know you're meant to be.

There they are—billionaire daddies, grown men with more money than small countries, acting like schoolyard bullies with chocolate stains around their mouths. Fighting over who gets the most attention. Throwing around their wealth like toddlers throwing toys, while the rest of us are over here trying to figure out how to heal our inner child, how to afford groceries and childcare. My hand went up on the last one.

It's exhausting, isn't it?

Watching powerful people act powerless over their own emotions while you're doing the daily work of not numbing yours with alcohol. They're having public meltdowns with their blue checkmarks and billion-dollar temper tantrums, and you're quietly in therapy working on your attachment issues.

And your heart—oh, your tender heart—breaks a little more each day. You see immigrant families being torn apart, the hot dog vendor whose cart gets overturned by a masked ICE agent having a bad day.

You feel it all because you're not numbing anymore. Every image of injustice, every video of cruelty, every moment of unnecessary suffering lands right in your core.

This is what happens when we start healing. We become more sensitive, not less. More aware, not more ignorant.

Put down the bottle? The world doesn't get easier to watch—we just get braver about watching it without looking away.

So here you are, trying to be a grownup in a world that seems determined to reward the biggest tantrums. You're choosing consciousness while others choose chaos. You're picking love while they're picking fights. You're building your spiritual muscles while they're flexing crypto wallets.

I see the contradiction you're living in. I see how hard it is to stay sober, raw, real, and authentic in a deeply fractured world that rewards pretentiousness. I see how you're trying to be the change while change feels impossible. I see you choosing healing in a culture that profits from your pain.

And I want you to know something: your quiet revolution matters. Your decision to face your demons instead of drowning them matters. Your choice to feel everything instead of nothing matters.

You're not just quitting drinking—you're quitting the lie that says we have to be drunk to survive this world. You're turning it all off. You're crossing over. You're well on the way.

You're proving that we can be awake, aware, and alive even when everything around us is still in a deep slumber.

You, my friend, are a total badass. Never forget that. You are doing the heaviest of lifting that a human can do. You're doing it for yourself, and more importantly, for others.

I once heard that the inner work we do when we quit drinking heals for seven generations before us and seven generations down the line. Now, my thinking mind has trouble grappling with the healing channel operating in reverse order, but if the laws of quantum science and time hold true, well, then it's possible.

There is no other group of people I'd rather be writing to. While most are floating along with whatever current feels easiest—numbing out, checking out, scrolling out—you're doing the hardest thing a human can do: you're staying awake. You're the ones who looked at a culture that says "drink to celebrate, drink to commiserate, drink to cope" and said, "Nah, I'm going to feel this." You're choosing the razor's edge of consciousness in a world that's designed to keep you unconscious. You're the rebels who figured out that the real revolution isn't in the streets—it's in your nervous system, in your daily choice to show up without armor, to love without anesthesia, to grieve without shortcuts. And every single day you don't drink, every moment you choose presence over numbness, you're not just saving yourself—you're showing the rest of us what's possible. You're living proof that we don't have to sleepwalk through this beautiful, heartbreaking, sacred mess of a life. That makes you the most courageous people I know. The most awake. The most alive. The most absolutely, completely, undeniably badass. Never forget—you're already living the Dolce Vita. Right here, right now, and you're showing others how to do the same. That's why you're here.

Acknowledgements

Thank you alcohol for forcing me to step into the true Dolce Vita. Thank you to my family, my wife, my son, and my dog Ben who sat with me for much of the writing process. I'd like to recognize my goats Elliot, Oreo, Mocha, Hot Dog, Nick and Sandy for the comedic relief when I took breaks writing. Thank you to the RE team, and Café RE community for all the support over the years. Thank you Dusty, my sober sidekick in Bozeman for always being there when I needed guidance. I want to thank my stellar editing team Danielle and Katya for helping me get this book to the finish line. Thank you Pacha Mama (Mother Earth) and the crickets for reminding me to place my mental energies in the present moment.

Reach out
https://www.recoveryelevator.com
info@recoveryelevator.com

THANK YOU FOR READING

Dolce Vita

If you've decided to remove alcohol from your life, be proud of this decision and let others know. Remember, burning the ships is the most impactful thing you can do.

If you've enjoyed this book, please leave a review on Amazon, share it with someone who might need it, and invite friends who still drink to read it too.

For more information about Recovery Elevator, the podcast, our courses, retreats, and sober travel trips, visit https://www.recoveryelevator.com.

Recovery Elevator on Instagram @recoveryelevator

If you'd like to join Café RE or make a donation, visit us at https://www.cafe-re.org.

Thoughts and comments? We'd love to hear from you. Email us at info@recoveryelevator.com.

Don't forget—the Dolce Vita is in every moment we find ourselves in.